Strategic Managerial Accounting: Hospitality, Tourism and Events Applications

Tracy Jones, Helen Atkinson, Angela Lorenz with Peter Harris

(G) Goodfellow Publishers Ltd

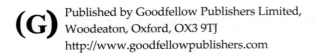

Published by Goodfellow Publishers Limited,
Woodeaton, Oxford, OX3 9TJ
http://www.goodfellowpublishers.com

British Library Cataloguing in Publication Data: a catalogue record for this title is available from the British Library.

Library of Congress Catalog Card Number: on file.

ISBN: 978-1-908999-01-6

 Design and typesetting by P.K. McBride, www.macbride.org.uk

Printed by Marston Book Services, www.marston.co.uk

Cover design by Cylinder, www.cylindermedia.com

Contents

Foreword by Professor Peter Harris

This book was first published in 1972 as the second of two volumes, entitled *Accounting & Financial Management in the Hotel and Catering Industry Vol.I* (accounting) *and Vol.II* (financial management). *Vol.I* was revised three times, to 1987 and *Vol.II* revised four times, to 1992.

During their period in publication the structure and content of the volumes underwent a transformation in line with the evolving role of professional hospitality managers and developments in the wider field of accounting; resulting in the volumes being developed latterly as independent titles. With the evolution of management accounting and the growing emphasis on managers understanding the financial implications of planning and business decisions *Vol.II* was revised and retitled *Managerial Accounting in the Hospitality Industry,* 5th edition, 1992.

Throughout the period of the Harris and Hazzard editions we researched, developed and applied emerging, state-of-the-art, generic accounting methods in order to give greater financial insights into hospitality products and services and improve the effectiveness of managers' decision-making. Peter Hazzard's contribution to this process was invaluable, enabling the adaptation and transfer of accounting techniques, traditionally used in production and manufacturing industry, to hospitality sectors of the service industry.

Now, alongside hospitality, the growth in tourism and recent emergence of the events sector makes it timely and relevant to encompass these additional, complementary, service sectors in a single integrated managerial accounting text. Who better to achieve such an undertaking, and take the work forward to a new generation of students and managers, than the three authors of this new landmark edition!

Tracy Jones, Helen Atkinson, and Angela Lorenz are three talented academics whose backgrounds combine professional accounting, service-sector management practice and extensive research and teaching experience. Their knowledge and understanding of hospitality, tourism and events management shines through the explanations, examples, and illustrations presented in the text. I congratulate their results and commend this title.

Peter Harris

Professor Emeritus of Accounting and Financial Management

Oxford School of Hospitality Management

Faculty of Business

Oxford Brookes University
8th August, 2012

Preface to the Sixth Edition

Previously published as *Managerial Accounting in the Hospitality Industry* by Harris and Hazzard, this book has a history of over 30 years. With new authors, this edition has been rewritten, expanded and updated to meet the needs of a modern audience.

There are a number of key changes since the last edition, with many new chapters to keep abreast of current accounting developments. The application of the text has also been expanded to cover various hospitality, tourism and event uses of management accounting, from a management perspective. Management accounting is a specific discipline within accounting, this text takes management accounting tools, but views them from the perspective of managers, hence the title of Managerial Accounting, not management accounting.

Structure of chapters

Each chapter of the book has a number of standard key features. All chapters start with a section 'Introduction and objectives'; which gives an overview of the purpose and learning objectives of the chapter. At the end of each chapter there is a 'Summary' of the key points from the chapter. Every chapter consciously considers the theoretical context of the subject under discussion. The summary section in chapters is followed by 'References' and advice for 'Further reading' to develop a deeper understanding in specialist aspects of the chapter. The 'Student self-check questions' section aids checking understand and knowledge of the chapter contents. If applicable, this section includes a numerical question where the student can check their own answers. A 'Further problems' section completes each chapter, the answers to these are available online as part of the book's online resource package.

Online additional resources

This textbook is supported by a number of online resources. For students, the answers to problem questions are available online. For registered tutors, lecture slides, further problems, and answers will aid the use of this book as a core text for many applied undergraduate and postgraduate classes.

Use of hospitality, tourism and events examples

A variety of illustrative examples are used throughout this book. There is a balance of examples covering: local, national and international organisations; commercial and non-commercial organisations; hospitality examples, including various hotel and restaurant illustrations; tourism examples, including transportation, tour operation and tourist facility management; and event sector examples, including music events, festivals, weddings, sporting events, and charitable events. Where specific management accounting techniques lend themselves more to a specific sector or environment this is stated. Generally, unless specifically mentioned, techniques discussed in the book can be equally applied across these service sector environments (hospitality, tourism and events), the use of a specific example is for illustration of concepts and methods more generally. The authors have experience of teaching students within all these industry sectors and this is reflected in the wide range of examples used within this text.

Specific notes

Each chapter covers a specific topic, some including many numerical calculations, and need much additional supporting explanation, whilst others are more discursive in nature. Given this, chapters do vary considerably in length. The authors have taken a positive decision not to combine some shorter topics into single chapters, or split some topics over two chapters to artificially manage chapter length.

This text focuses on managerial accounting, managers' use of accounting information within organisations. No discipline has a fixed boundary and management accounting does have strong links to aspects of operations management, marketing, financial accounting and financial management. Within this text these links are made to aid students and managers' in fully understanding aspects of management accounting. An example of this is the inclusion of a chapter concerning financing businesses. This chapter supports the users of this text in having a more holistic view of the implications of financing options in relation to managerial accounting implications and decision making.

As managerial accounting focuses on the internal use of accounting information to aid managers, generally it is not concerned with matters of external financial reporting. With this in mind, matters of taxation, including VAT, are excluded when discussing topics such as pricing calculations, as is common within other management accounting texts.

We would like to thank those that have allowed us to use their financial data and information to provide 'real life' examples within this text. Thanks also to HOSPA (formerly BAHA) for allowing the use of questions from their Strategic Management Accounting exam papers.

Tracy Jones, Helen Atkinson, and Angela Lorenz
July 2012

1 A Strategic Managerial Accounting Perspective to Hospitality, Tourism and Events Operations

1.1 Introduction and objectives

Accounting and finance are generally considered as three separate disciplines: financial accounting; management accounting; and financial management. This textbook focuses on management accounting, including contemporary strategic management accounting tools and techniques. The discussion of this subject discipline is related specifically to hospitality, tourism and events and viewed from a manager's perspective – hence the title: Strategic Managerial Accounting: Hospitality, Tourism and Events Applications.

After studying this chapter you should be able to:

■ Understand the difference between managerial and other forms of accounting

■ Explain the main characteristics and feature of the hospitality, tourism and events businesses and their implication for accounting

■ Reflect on the way managers can utilise strategic management accounting information to aid planning, control and decision making.

1.2 Defining accounting and finance

Before discussing strategic managerial accounting the standard three disciplines of: financial accounting, management accounting, and financial management will be defined and explained. Management accounting shares some common terminology with financial accounting and even though the basic data for both can be collected and collated within the same computer systems, financial and management accounting have many differences, as summarised in Table 1.1.

Table 1.1: The differences between financial and management accounting

	Financial accounting	Management accounting
Users	External to organisation, including shareholders, lenders, suppliers, regulatory authorities, government, employees, customers	Internal to organisation, including managers at all levels
Purpose	Reporting for accountability and corporate governance purposes. Historically focused, recording what has happened.	Decision support – information designed to be used by non- accountants to aid them in decision making. Forward focused, using financial information to aid the future of the operation.
Frequency	Annual – routine	Monthly, weekly, daily, either routine and non–routine reporting (ad hoc)
Level of reporting	Whole organisation, plus some limited reporting of different segments of business	Multiple levels – unit/venue level, product or service level, departmental level, by customer, geographic region or whole organisation as required
Type of data	Financial data and compliance data	Financial and non-financial data
Focus of reporting	Accurate and verifiable (audited)	Timely and useful, to aid managers
Regulation	Regulated by General Accepted Accounting Principles (GAAP), rules established in international financial reporting standards (IFRS) and specific International Accounting Standards (IAS)	No regulation, or requirement to use

1.2.1   Financial accounting

Table 1.1 identifies that financial accounting is concerned with reporting the organisation's financial position and performance on an annual basis for external users. It is mainly at the level of the company as a whole. It is recording what has happened in the past year, so is historic in nature. The key point is it is a legal requirement, in some form, for all businesses.

1.2.2   Management accounting

In contrast, management accounting is focused on providing data and information to aid managers inside the organisation to make better informed decisions. It is therefore forward looking, previous trading period data may be used, but only to aid future decision making. The function of 'control' reviews past financial information, but only to learn from it for the future of the company. Unlike financial accounting, a business has total control in what it decides to do (or not do) with regards to management accounting. A business decides which tools and techniques to use, how to use them and the frequency appropriate within the specific business. This is sometimes described as being like a 'sweet shop' you

1

can pick and mix techniques. The key issue is business can get stuck doing things they have always done and not be open to newer developments in management accounting (these are discussed at some length throughout this textbook).

Management accounting aims to provide managers with necessary information to plan, monitor and control organisation operations. It encompasses a range of techniques which support a range of decisions such as: whether to start a business, what prices to set for services and products, how much investment will be required and how much it will cost to produce/deliver a product or service. The extension to the strategic level is discussed in more detail in the next section.

Finally it is worth noting that the term 'cost accounting' is sometimes used synonymously with management accounting, this is because the management accounting techniques of today evolved from the cost accounting that was developed in the manufacturing environments of the early 20th century. However, costing is now more accurately considered as an aspect within the broader definition of management accounting.

1.2.3 Financial management

Financial management is another discipline within accounting and finance, which shares data and terminology. However in this area the focus is on planning and controlling financial resources, so the financing of a business rather than its operation. Financial management thus focuses on such matters as, complex arrangements for raising finance and valuing business, it overlaps with management accounting in areas such as long-term decision making and working capital management.

1.2.4 Strategic managerial accounting

Strategic management accounting (SMA) extends management accounting as it is externally (market and competition) focused and extends the use of data from purely financial to include financial and non-financial data to provide information to support management decisions. Give the focus it is strategic in nature, whereas management accounting can be more operational and tactical (short-term) in focus.

Strategic management accounting is the accounting discipline. This textbook is concerned with a management perspective, the managerial use of SMA, alongside more traditional management accounting techniques. Hence strategic managerial accounting can be defined as:

The use by managers of strategic management accounting to support their decision making in a competitive environment.

In this textbook where the boundaries between accounting and finance discipline areas overlap chapters have been included to aid the reader in understanding strategic managerial accounting more clearly by explanation of these supporting aspects of accounting and finance. Chapter 13, 'Business finance', provides an overview concerning sources of business finance with a hospitality, tourism and events specific focus. Chapter 2 includes details related to financial accounting statements as the terminology is shared with management accounting and can be used in management accounting focused financial performance analysis.

1.3   The hospitality, tourism and events focus

The focus of this textbook is the application of strategic managerial accounting to hospitality, tourism and events; these represent three important sectors of many nations' economies and those studying in these fields will know the statistics and definitions related to their specific focus (hospitality, tourism or events). A broad overview definition of hospitality, tourism and events is given here so all readers have a basic understanding of all three sectors.

■ Hospitality involves being 'hospitable' and usually refers to areas where there is a 'host' and 'guest' relationship through the provision of food and/or accommodation on a commercial or non-commercial basis. This can include for example (not an exhaustive list), restaurants, hotels, hospitals, clubs and contract catering provision.

■ Tourism involves people travelling away from home for at least one night and can involve travel for business or leisure purposes. An individual staying away from home for 24 hours, by definition, is a tourist and the tourism industry is concerned with the provision of goods and services to tourists. This can include the provision of: travel and transportation; tour services; accommodation; meals; and entertainment for example.

■ The events industry is just as wide and diverse as hospitality and tourism. Event management is the process of planning, running and reviewing 'an event'. By definition an event is an 'occurrence', it will have a beginning, middle and an end, so is discreet in a way not usually associated with hospitality and tourism. The events sector includes: corporate events, exhibitions, festivals, sporting events, music events, weddings, mega events and civic events.

There are situations where it is quite easy to determine from an activity in which one of these three sectors it sits, however at other times, due to overlaps and complexity they can merge. This is illustrated within Figure 1.1.

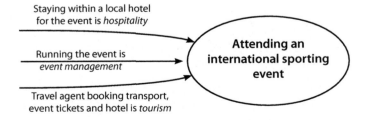

Figure 1.1: How hospitality, tourism and event management can serve one customer

In certain marketplaces there are many overlaps, but this is not always the case. A contract caterer running a company's staff restaurant is firmly within the hospitality sector, this does not have a link to tourism, or events. However, it is argued that such provision can be 50–60% 'retail' in nature, selling prepackaged drinks and sandwiches, plus vending machine services that are akin to purchasing these products in a supermarket, the point being, there are no hard boundaries more generally between sectors. There will be examples where provision to a customer firmly sits in hospitality, tourism or events and times when one customer is utilising products and services across two or three of these areas combined, Table 1.2 illustrates this point.

Table 1.2: Customer provision combinations in hospitality, tourism and events

	Hospitality	Tourism	Events
Hospitality	Contract catering	Hotel accommodation as part of a tour package	A wedding, including the provision of specialist catering services
Tourism	A business tourist, booking his hotel through a travel agent	A water sports business at a tourist resort	A charity international trek event
Events	Provision of accommodation for those that attend a trade show/exhibition	The booking of holidays to international sporting events	Running a local civic event (that does not include hospitality provision)

It can equally be argued that the diversity within each of these areas is also vast, often leading to them having more in common with like providers across these sectors, than within their own sector. For example a luxury 5* hotel may have very little in common with a budget hotel provider. They both provide accommodation, but their product and services will differ considerably, as will selling prices, market segment, and customer expectations. A 5* hotel may have greater alliances with tour operators also serving the same market (customers), or those running a sophisticated event and needing a high quality venue than with a budget hotel that is within hospitality.

Another example could relate to asset value, a city centre hotel can be notoriously expensive as a property asset, likewise an airplane, or a cruise ship within tourism. However, a fast food restaurant is likely to have a lot lower asset value than the hotel. So whilst it can be argued that hospitality, tourism and events are 'not the same', it is equally true that there are differences within these individual sectors. These three sectors can display different cost structures and business models, but all display to lesser or great extent a set of characteristics that allow them to be studied together from the perspective of strategic managerial accounting.

It is not suggested here that every tool and technique in this textbook is equally applicable across all three sectors, and equally it is not true they all can be used despite the size of the organisation, or whether it is in the commercial sector, or the not-for-profit sector. This textbook focuses on strategic managerial account-ing techniques that can be used across the range of organisations that operate in these sectors, as opposed those tools and techniques specific to manufacturing environments. As individual techniques, concepts and tools are discussed, their applicability within hospitality, tourism and events is discussed. Some strategic managerial concepts equally apply across these sectors, whilst others are more sector-specific and this is clearly identified and discussed in the text.

Even if an event is using contact caterers when food and beverage provision is required for an event, an event manager still needs to know enough about hos-pitality management accounting to ensure he is maximising his profits, likewise tour operators when negotiating room rates with hotels. Hence even when a technique is highlighted as useful related to food and beverages, or to events, or air transport, awareness of this from the perspective of a manager in any of these three sectors is valuable.

1.4   Characteristics of hospitality, tourism and events

As already stated, certain characteristics are displayed in organisations across these sectors to a lesser or greater extent. These are discussed here in that they have great relevance to the strategic managerial accounting approach managers may take and what will be key aspects to maximise financial returns in given situations. These characteristics are discussed by others, including Harris (2011) in relation specifically to hospitality and tourism.

1.4.1   Fixed capacity

Whether it is: a hotel having 100 rooms available per night; or an events venue having a seating capacity of 2000; or a plane seating 400 people, all these are fixed capacity. In the medium to long term more hotels can be built, a different venue used, or an additional plane added to the route.

This has operational implications, there may be a demand tonight for 120 room sales, or 2500 concert tickets, or 500 plane tickets, but that demand cannot be filled, the fixed capacity restricts business. Is it worth increasing capacity? A major horserace, the Cheltenham Gold Cup, takes place every year at Cheltenham. It is the highlight of a festival of four days' racing which creates such demand for accommodation that it is difficult to book a room within a 30-mile radius of the event. Does this mean it is worth building more hotels in Cheltenham? If the extra demand is only for four days a year and there is not a capacity issue year round, increasing capacity by adding permanent extra facilities is not appropri-ate. If capacity is not increased then there will be points in the year where demand outstrips supply.

This prompts the need to use strategic managerial accounting information in a number of ways: to predict demand; to price according to demand (high demand = high price, low demand = low price); to budget and forecast so a financial plan is in place for 'peaks and troughs' in the business; in times of low demand reducing costs; and using revenue management to maximise sales revenue. All these techniques are explored within this textbook.

1.4.2 Changeable demand

Some of this is predictable, but quite often unavoidable. On a rainy day in June, some hardy customers will still attend an outdoor agricultural show, whilst others will be put off due to the weather. Likewise, a theme park can be weather dependent in relation to customer demand. Other aspects of changeable demand are predictable such as: the greater demand for holidays during the summer school holidays; business travel demand being higher weekdays than at weekends; demand for weddings being higher on Saturdays than other days of the week.

There are specific strategic managerial accounting approaches to aid with this, whether it is predict the impact of weather on demand (i.e. rain = 30% reduction in sales revenue) and using this financial analysis alongside weather forecasts to change staffing levels in the next few days, or using sophisticated revenue management systems that aid price setting based on previous demand patterns and advance booking. These approaches are all explored within this textbook.

1.4.3 Perishability

The concept of perishability is clear to identify with a physical product with a short shelf life; you buy strawberries and they will last two days, or fresh meat with a use-by date. In these situations if a shop is 'over-stocked', once the use-by date is reached it cannot be sold, whilst frozen strawberries and meat have a longer shelf life so are less perishable. Perishability also applies to services and in some ways can be seen as having 'absolute perishability'. An unsold hotel room, venue seat, or plane seat is a sale lost forever, once it becomes the next day it is a new set of rooms that are for sale. Compare this to a clothes shop, they can sell this season's clothes over a few months, any that are left at the end of the period can be sold in a sale. A service cannot be 'stockpiled' in this way. You cannot say last week 200 rooms were not sold and retrospectively sell them.

This perishability is the opposite side of fixed capacity in some ways: too much demand and fixed capacity stops us selling more than 100 rooms; but too little demand and due to perishability a sales opportunity is lost forever. In the same way as above forecasting, planning and responding to changing demand patterns is crucial. Is it better to let a plane fly with an empty seat, or offer a discount and make some 'contribution' towards your costs? There are management accounting tools to aid in these situations.

1.4.4   Range of products and services offered

There are two aspects of this, first, from a consumer perspective and second, from an operations perspective. First, in such markets customers rarely buy one product or service: tourists buying accommodation, transportation, food, and entertainment from the tour operator; a hotel guest using a hotel room, eating breakfast, drinking in the bar and using the golf course; a music festival goer buying a ticket, parking, food on site, a tee shirt and programme. This gives opportunities of packaging individual products and services into a combined single price, or viewing profitability at the level of the customer, as opposed to individual product or service profitability.

The second aspect is in 'full service' operations the variety of products and services provided can cause specific operational issues. For example 'fine dining' where a wine list can run into 100s of different wines has implications for cost of holding stock, and security.

1.4.5   Concurrent production and consumption

Within manufacturing it is possible to have a factory in a low-cost area; control product quality before delivery to the customer; and distribute the product through various channels (High Street and online). Within service industries, production and consumption are concurrent; the quality relies on staff in face-to-face contact with the customer; the service is sold where it is made and experienced by the consumer.

This leads to alternative quality control processes, as mentioned in Chapter 8, and the fact 'back-of-house' space, such as kitchens are situated in areas with high property values, unlike manufacturing factories.

1.4.6   A real-time activity

All customers arriving at the same time demanding service can be a problem. As part of the Olympics preparation in London they tested traffic flows getting people off trains and into venues, the paper predictions didn't match the live test – the reason? The hadn't allowed for what happened when people got off a train and had their first glimpse of the venue they would stop to have photos taken with family, hence slowing down flows. Identifying such peaks in demand in advance they can be planned for. If a restaurant is very busy after 7.30 in the evening, offering an 'early bird' discount could spread demand. If an event knows between acts the bar will be in great demand, or a theatre during an interval then staffing and preparation can be done to manage the situation.

Having data of demand patterns and knowing the techniques that can be used to overcome the 'instant demand' expectations in some environments is key. Going to a bar and being told they can fit in serving you in 30 minutes wouldn't be an acceptable level of service.

1.4.7   Business size

Even with large well-known brand names in these sectors, compared to manufacturing, the potential for 'mass production' are limited. It may be more cost-effective to run one 500-bedded hotel than 5 that have 100 beds, in manufacturing centralising production is a real possibility, but in these environments the hotel location has to be focused around customer location requirements, hence business units being many and dispersed. This in itself demands specific management and control techniques to deal with them effectively.

It is also important to note the number of SMEs and micro business in these sectors, which is discussed within this textbook.

1.4.8   Nature of labour in hospitality, tourism and events

Service products that have a high level of customer/staff interface are labour-intensive. The level of service offered is an integral part of the product/service offered so it is difficult to cut staffing costs without impacting on service delivery to the customer. This needs to be managed financially, but in an operationally sensitive way. 'What if?' analysis is one way of modelling this, deskilling menus, changing service delivery, and using contract staff for events are all approaches where management accounting information could be used to aid decision making.

1.4.9   Location implications

Location has been mentioned in relation to other aspects; customer demand dictates the location. Some types of events are more conducive to changing locations, using alternative venues than for example a hotel. Prime locations come at high costs, so business financing implications come in to play.

1.4.10 Capital-intensive

Permanent exhibition sites, event venues and hotels can be considered capital-intensive, with a comparatively low ratio for sales to capital employed. As discussed earlier customer demand dictates locations, which dictate some capital-intensive locations for such business investment. This can be a challenge in these sectors. The separation of hotel property ownership from management, through the use of management contracts is becoming more common because of this and has implications for strategic managerial accounting practices. Likewise local-authority-owned town halls and events venues are often contracted out to events firm for operational management. Equally the leasing of planes can cut capital costs within tour operations.

1.4.11 Operating cost structure

This is discussed in a number of chapters of this textbook, whilst not universal, a number of operations across these sectors have a high fixed costs/low variable costs structure. The impact of this is that even before a customer comes through the door the business is saddled with many costs to pay, but as more customers arrive the additional cost is very small. This has implications for business orientation and understanding cost structures can aid business decision making in a number of ways in order to maximise financial returns.

1.5   The role of managers in strategic managerial accounting

As has been stated throughout this chapter, the purpose of strategic and traditional management accounting is to provide information to aid management decision making at all levels throughout the organisation. Where does that leave the manager? The role of the manager is to understand appropriate management accounting tools and techniques, and how to use such information to make fully informed decisions, whether these be operational or strategic management decisions.

As this textbook is written from the perspective of managers using these techniques, tools and concepts in hospitality, tourism and events sectors it should be seen as a 'toolkit' for those studying management, or working as a manager in these sectors.

Once the different aspects of the subject are developed, the final chapter (Chapter 20) reflects again on the role of the manager in relation to strategic managerial accounting.

Summary of key points

This chapter has given a broad introduction to what strategic managerial accounting is and how it fits within the general field of accounting and finance. The chapter explains the tourism, hospitality and events focus of this textbook, alongside characteristics of these sectors. The key points from this chapter are:

- Accounting and finance is split into three key areas.

- Management accounting provides managers with information to aid decision making.

- Strategic managerial accounting is the management use of a range of financial and non-financial data, with an external perspective for strategic decision making.

- The nature of hospitality, tourism and events provides a number of key characteristics that impact on appropriate managerial accounting techniques that are useful.

Reference

Harris, P. (2011) *Profit Planning for Hospitality and Tourism*, 3rd edn, Oxford: Goodfellow Publishers.

Further reading

At the time of writing, no other textbooks exist that focuses on strategic managerial accounting across these three sectors. As discussed in Chapter 20, even research into management accounting across tourism and events sectors is almost non-existent. However many operational management textbooks applied to these sectors individually do offer brief chapters relating the accounting and you may find these of some use in your sector focus, hospitality, tourism, or events.

Self-check student questions

1   What are the key differences between financial management, financial accounting and management accounting?

2   How might aspects of hospitality, tourism and events overlap or work together?

3   What are the key characteristics associated with businesses within these sectors?

4   What is the manager's role in relation to strategic managerial accounting?

Further questions and problems

1   From the perspective of either a hotel manager, events manager, or a tour operator discuss the role strategic managerial accounting can have in aiding management decision making.

2   'It is impossible to have a standard management accounting system as it needs to match the needs of an operation.' Discuss this statement from the perspective of hospitality, tourism or events perspective.

2 Financial Statements for Decision Making

2.1 Introduction and objectives

This chapter introduces the various types of financial statements used for internal and external financial reporting. There has been much change in the international external reporting regulations in recent times and this has caused some changes to terminology and internal reporting changes. Traditionally the terminology used within the UK and the USA has been very different, but a number of terms are becoming more internationally utilised industry-wide. This chapter explores the basics of reports and financial information reporting in the context of their use in management accounting. This textbook focuses on management accounting, so the annual financial accounting reports are considered from a management use perspective only, the further reading section gives further guidance for those needing information concerning detailed financial accounting concepts and approaches.

After studying this chapter you should:

- Have a better knowledge and understanding of a variety of accounting statements

- Be able to critically evaluate the usefulness of such information to managers, and other statement users

- Have a better knowledge of alternative accounting terminology used within financial reports

- Have a working knowledge of the concepts of profit and cash in the business context.

2.2 Alternative accounting statements

Companies' year-end accounts are a legal requirement for external reporting purposes and are regulated by rules and statement formats that need to be followed. However, management accounting is not a legal requirement for organisations; it is an internal tool to aid managers in performing their roles and responsibilities. Given this, a variety of different reporting structures and accounting statements exist, the key being they need to be 'fit for purpose' for the style, orientation and size of the organisation using them.

It is also important to understand that in management accounting it is not a case of ignoring annual financial reports and only focusing on management accounting reports. Externally focused financial statements can aid managers by giving an overview of competitors and be useful as a benchmark (comparison) for evaluating your own organisation's performance, particularly at the higher, more strategic level in the organisation.

Throughout this textbook a variety of management accounting reports and formats are used for specific purposes and with specific management accounting technique. Every organisation will do things slightly differently and over time, formats and terminology change within financial statements reported externally. The fact that there are many financial statement formats and frequent change can lead to frustration with those studying management accounting; one report talks about 'stock' and the next 'inventories'; the terms 'fixed assets' and 'non-current assets' have the same meaning; and a 'profit and loss statement' is the equivalent of an 'income statement'. This chapter gives a broad overview of some key financial statements and the alternative terminology used.

2.3 The difference between profit and cash

The difference between profit and cash is an important basic accounting concept that often causes much confusion – they are not the same and both are important in an organisation.

Profit = the surplus of value between sales revenue and associated costs for the same period

Sales revenue – Costs = Profit

In commercial operations income statements use an accounting system known as 'accrual accounting', which 'matches' sales generated and costs incurred over a specific period of time. Accrual accounting requires sales to be 'recognised' when the sale takes place, not when cash changes hands. If someone stays in a hotel tonight, but their company is to pay on account in 1 month's time accrual accounting would state this is a sale today, not when the cash changes hands. Likewise, gas used to heat the hotel room today, for today's sale means the hotel is committed to pay that cost in the future. In accrual accounting the expense of gas would be costed when it occurred, not when it is paid.

There are also 'non-cash' expenses, such as depreciation, a cost that is an internal accounting transaction, but not a cash item. An example would be buying equipment that has a life of 5 years. In cash terms this could be £10,000 going out of the business on the day of purchase, then having it to use for 5 years. For profit purposes the cost is effectively 'shared' over its operational life of 5 years by charging depreciation to the income statement. In this example, using the 'straight line method of depreciation', £10,000/5 years = £2,000 per year would be charged as a depreciation cost under accrual accounting.

2.3.1   Example: difference between cash and profit

Cultural Events is a small local events company, its operating information for one month, April is:

- Sales for the period are £40,000, which includes £10,000 invoiced and yet to be paid by the customer.
- Cost of sales, £12,000, which includes £6,000 still to be paid to the supplier.
- Expenses for the month are £20,000, but this includes £4,000 paid previously and £6,000 not to be paid until the next month.
- At the start of the month the bank balance (cash) was £5,000.
- A cash payment of £15,000 is paid in April related to last month's expenses.

Table 2.1: Differences between profits and costs

Cultural Events	Profit		Cash
		Opening cash	£5,000
Sales revenue	£40,000	+ cash from sales	£30,000
– Cost of sales	£12,000		£35,000
= Gross profit	£28,000	– Expenses for March	£15,000
– Expenses	£20,000	– Expenses for April	£10,000
Profit	£8,000	Closing cash	£10,000

Table 2.1 is a very simplified example of the concept, but highlights the differences between profit and cash positions.

Profit tells a manager 'if' all sales revenue came in and 'if' all costs and expenses related to April (the same time period) were paid, a profit (surplus on sales after all costs) would equal £8,000. That £8,000 profit is just a paper financial value, it is a statement of 'value', but not a statement of how much physical cash is available at the end of April. This is the matching concept of accrual accounting.

Cash is the physical amount of money, in this case £10,000 in the bank of Cultural Events. This is money that is available as a resource to the company. Over time, theoretically cash and profit should always match, but in an ongoing business there are always timing difference between them unless it is a full cash-based business, both for sales and expenses.

As a manager understanding the difference between profit and cash is important. Both are key to a business's long-term survival, but should not be confused. Throughout this text issues related to profit and cash are explored from a management perspective.

2.4 Key external financial reporting frameworks – IFRS

Throughout the 20th century the key focus for financial standards was at the national level, with individual countries setting accounting frameworks for use in their own country. Approaches to financial reporting can be 'rule-based' or 'principle-based'. Rule-based approaches provide a list of rules that must be followed, these can be very detailed and complex, but some argue they require less 'judgement' and are less open to interpretation. Financial Accounting Standards Boards (FASB) tend to follow a principle-based approach, that is more conceptually based by offering guidelines to sound reporting, as opposed a more detailed rules-based approach. Principal-based approaches provide broad guidelines that are adaptable to many different situations. This allows accountants to use professional judgement in preparing the accounts. Generally Accepted Accounting Principles (GAAP) are the key to such stands, but 'GAAP', could refer to UK GAAP, US GAAP, or International GAAP, each have differences in precise accounting requirements.

There are a number of accounting 'concepts', more explicit in the older UK GAAP, but the key two to mention are the 'going concern' concept and the 'accruals concept'. The accruals concept of recording sales and costs in the period in which they are occurred has already been discussed in relation to the difference between profit and cash. The going concern concept assumes the company is on-going, never-ending. The earlier example of depreciation is an example of going concern. If an asset has a useful life for the company of 5 years and the business in continuing that cost does not all have to be covered in one year, depreciation is effectively how this is recognised in the accounts.

As trade has become more international, with many large international corporations trading over national borders, the use of national accounting standards has led to different requirements in different countries and an argued difficulty for such organisations. This has led to calls for an international financial reporting standard (IFRS). The goal of the IFRS foundation and IASB has been to develop a single set of enforceable and internationally accepted financial reporting standards, based on clear principles (IFRS, 2012).

The international convergence of accounting standards has been supported by 'G20' countries. Many countries have now adopted the IFRS based standards.

Table 2.2 shows some examples of international standards, IFRS, usage, though more countries are constantly being added.

Table 2.2: Some examples of IFRS standards usage (Data from IFRS, 2012)

Australia, European Union countries (incl. France, Germany, Italy, United Kingdom – UK), South Africa, Turkey	Use of IFRS since 2005, some countries for listed companies only
Argentina, Mexico, Russia	2012
Brazil	2008 or 2010, depending on type of company
Canada	2011, plus allowed for not-for-profit organisations
China	Broad convergence with national standards
India, Indonesia	Planned convergence
Japan	Allowed for some international companies since 2010, further adoption under consideration
Republic of Korea	2011
Saudi Arabia	Required in banking sector, under consideration more generally
United States (USA)	Allowed for foreign company users since 2007, aiming for substantial convergence

The reason for highlighting this is that the international reporting standards are leading to a convergence of terminology, some of which is more akin to that traditionally used in the USA than was used previously used in the UK. However, when reviewing older financial statements, academic texts, journals and practically working in industry, managers need to understand a range of terminology – just because on a financial report 'stock' is now called 'inventory', doesn't stop managers talking about 'stocktakes'.

2.4.1 Statement of comprehensive income

The 'statement of comprehensive income' is the IFRS equivalent of an 'income statement' or a 'profit and loss account'. The terminology is consistent with equivalent previous statement. The statement covers the trading side of the business, it summaries revenue coming in from sales and the costs going out to calculate company profit. It then continues by identifying how the profit is used, such as paying tax and dividend and what is retained in the business.

Whilst management will use more frequent (weekly, monthly) management accounting operating statements to consider profit on a more regular basis, by department, unit, or division the annual report gives an overview for the whole year (see Table 2.3). It can aid a strategic overview of the business as a whole and provides the opportunity to be able to compare data with competitors to aid strategic decision making. For operational management the report lacks the detail required to aid with specific decision making lower down in the organisation structure.

Table 2.3

Statement of income for the year ended 31st December XXX2

	31st December XXX2	31st December XXX1
	£	£
Revenue	6,900	7,400
Cost of sales	(710)	(680)
Gross profit	6,190	6,720
Other income	700	670
Distribution costs	(80)	(72)
Administrative expenses	(3,450)	(3,708)
Other expenses	(690)	(740)
Finance costs	(40)	(60)
Profit before tax	2,630	2,810
Income tax expense	(790)	(843)
Profit for the year	1,840	1,967

(Note: data for format illustrative purposes only)

This statement is either added to by another section related to 'other comprehensive income' and then becomes a 'comprehensive income statement'; the alternative is that this additional section is presented as a separate, 'other comprehensive income statement'. For management accounting purpose, 'profit for the year' is usually as far down as is needed from such a statement, the follow-on statement is shown in Table 2.4, just for information.

Table 2.4

Statement of other comprehensive income for the year ended 31st December XXX2

Other comprehensive income for the years, after tax:	£
Gains on property revaluation	xx
Exchange difference on translating foreign operations	xx
Income tax on other comprehensive income	(x)
Other comprehensive income net of tax	xx
Total comprehensive income for the year	xxx

A further statement, 'Statement of changes in equity' shows the changes in share capital and dividends amongst other elements du ring the year and the retained profit to be shown on the statement of financial position under 'retained earnings'. This is not related to the needs of management accounting, so not detailed here.

2.4.2 Statement of financial position

The 'Statement of financial position' is the IFRS equivalent of a 'balance sheet'. It is a 'snap shot' in time as it shows the financial position on a specific date 'as at XXX2'. It shows what the company owns and owes. The information shown on this statement is utilised in a number of chapters of this book. This information can be used by managers to explore in more detail the financial position of the company, how effectively it is using its assets and controlling its liabilities. Comparisons to competitors can be made using their annual published reports. It can aid in decision making both in long-term strategic financing decisions and aid in operational working capital (current assets – current liabilities) management.

Some key definitions of terms on this statement and their alternatives are given in Table 2.5 to aid understanding of alternative terminology.

Table 2.5: Definitions of key terms

Accounting term	Alternative term	Description
Statement of financial position	Balance sheet	A statement that shows what a company owns and owes at a given point in time
Assets		Something the company owns, or has use of
Non-current assets	Fixed assets	Assets that usually have a useful life for the company longer than 12 months, e.g. owned property, machinery, equipment
Current assets		Assets that are short-term, usually have a useful life for the company shorter than 12 months, e.g. cash, inventory, trade receivables
Inventories	Stock	The value of the stock of goods for resale, e.g. food, drink, merchandising, shop stock
Trade receivables	Debtors and prepayments	Money outstanding from sales, customers to pay in the future and things paid for but still to 'use', e.g. customers with credit terms still to pay, and a year's insurance paid at the start of the year (prepayment)
Equity	Shareholders' funds	The owners' value in the business, e.g. value of shares, retained profits, reserves
Liabilities		An obligation to be met in the future
Non-current liabilities	Long-term liabilities	Liabilities, usually over 1 year, e.g. bank loans
Current liabilities		Short-term liabilities, to be met within 12 months
Trade payables	Creditors and accruals	The amount you owe to your suppliers, e.g. for stocks already purchased, but not yet paid for, or electricity that you are invoiced for after consumption (an accrual)

For those that need a deeper refresher of these terms used in financial statements or more details on international terminology see the 'Further reading' section for guided reading.

Table 2.6

Statement of financial position as at 31st December XXX2

	31st December XXX2	31st December XXX1
ASSETS		
Non-current assets	£	£
Property, plant and equipment	750	740
Intangible assets	100	100
	850	840
Current assets		
Inventories	85	80
Trade receivables	140	160
Cash and cash equivalents	300	270
	525	510
Total assets	1375	1350
EQUITIY AND LIABILITIES		
Equity attributable to owners		
Share capital	850	700
Retained earnings	180	140
Total equity	1030	840
Non-current liabilities		
Long-term borrowings	150	244
Deferred tax	10	30
Total non-current liabilities	160	274
Current liabilities		
Trade payables	150	194
Short-term borrowings	10	12
Current tax payable	25	30
Total current liabilities	185	236
Total liabilities	345	510
Total equity and liabilities	1375	1350

(Note: data for format illustrative purposes only)

2.4.3 Statement of cash flows

There are two methods of calculating cash flows, the direct and indirect method (see Tables 2.7 and 2.8). The direct method records cash transactions directly, whilst the indirect method 'adjusts' the profit figure to generate a cash figure.

Table 2.7: Direct method: cash flow statement

Cash receipts from customers	xxx
Cash paid to suppliers	xxx
Cash paid to employees	xxx
Cash paid for other operating expenses	xxx
Interest paid	xxx
Income taxes paid	xxx
Net cash from operating activities	**xxx**

Table 2.8: The indirect method: cash flow statement

Profit before interest and income taxes		xxx
Add back depreciation		xxx
Add back amortisation of goodwill		xxx
Increase in receivables		xxx
Decrease in inventories		xxx
Increase in trade payables		xxx
Interest expense	xxx	
Less interest accrued but not yet paid	xxx	
Interest paid		xxx
Income taxes paid		xxx
Net cash from operating activities		**xxx**

The importance of cash is discussed in detail within the working capital chapter from a management accounting perspective.

The financial statements so far in this chapter represent external financial reporting formats, but for comparing financial information externally are important, particularly at the corporate and strategic level. Such statements will be utilised in Chapter 10, on financial measurement, where ratio analysis is used to interpret such statements.

2.5   Key management accounting reporting framework – USALI

As previously stated, there is no legal standard form of internal management accounting reporting, however the Uniform System of Accounts for the Lodging Industry (USALI) is quite unique in that it has been providing a hospitality-specific reporting framework since the 1920s. Within hospitality and associated sectors, it is well used and has a number of uses and benefits (Kwansa and Schmidgall, 1999). It was first designed in New York to give local hotel association members guidance on financial reporting, using the terminology of the industry and specific hotel-related needs. At its time it was ground-breaking, being the first such guide for any industry in the USA (Kwansa and Schmidgall, 1999). The 10th edition was published in 2006, over the years it has led to variant guides for small hotels, motels and restaurants but in more recent times these have been drawn into the one guide to the lodging industry. It not only covers rooms, food and beverages, but provides department reporting guidance and formats for: golf courses; golf pro shop; tennis; tennis pro shop; health centre; swimming pool; gaming operations (casinos); as well as functional support departments.

USALI is in a 'responsibility accounting' (see Chapter 9 on budgeting for explanation) format, which gives a detailed reporting framework by department in a way that aids operational managers in using the reports to aid planning and control. It provides detailed guidelines for every line on the financial statements, what to include and what not to include. The complete expenses dictionary gives specific details of what expenses to record where, so whether it is: food costs; a boiler inspection; a box of matches for guest use; contract entertainment costs; or tour agency commissions, it informs the accountants where to record it in the accounts. In this sense it is seen as a 'turnkey' solution for new properties, giving very specific guidance that is easy to follow. It also covers industry-specific ratios and provides guidance across a range of management accounting tools, such as budgeting, and breakeven analysis.

The fact the USALI started in the 1920s and is still in use supports its usefulness in the sector. Each updated new edition is developed by a committee made up of key industry members, international accounting firms, consultancy firms, and academics. Beyond the turnkey internal management accounting use it provides other benefits which have led to its key positioning in the hospitality sector and being widely used and recognised. Benefits of USALI include:

- It provides guidance for a complete internal management accounting reporting system in a responsibility accounting format.

- It is a turnkey system, useful for new entrants to the market that is adaptable to different size and types of property.

- It allows opportunities for benchmarking as, if comparing data with other USALI users, you are comparing 'like-with-like' as all items are recorded in the same way.

- It provide benefits to industry specific consultancy firms when conducting feasibility studies by providing comparable data.
- It is used as the standard built in reporting framework of many computerised property management systems (PMS) software packages.
- It is used as the format for many 'industry studies', regional specific reports on key industry performance which provide a useful external benchmark; and
- It can form the basis of the accounting requirements in hotels run under management contracts (see section 13.6.2).

A number of large international hotels are run under a 'management contract' (operating agreement). The owner of the physical building (hotel asset) contracts out the running of the operation to a hospitality firm – this could be a 10-year agreement or even 50 years. Terms vary, but operators can receive a 'base fee' for running the operation, plus 'incentive fees' based on profits. It is common therefore, in management contracts, to detail aspects of accounting to ensure the profit is shown in a consistent agreed format. Operational reports can be stipulated as using USALI in these situations.

As USALI is used so widely, PMS systems can adopt this format in standard packages, although individual company bespoke reporting is also possible. Another important area is that of external benchmarking opportunities. This can work by a hotel company who is using USALI format agreeing to share key data, on an anonymous basis, with a company that produces hotel benchmarking data. The benchmarking companies get data from thousands of hotels in different locations, ownership and market segments. The data has to conform to their reporting guidelines to be acceptable. Key statistical data can be collected on a daily, weekly or monthly, with more detailed data on an annual basis. In return for supplying data the hotel organisations get free access to market performance reports generated from the combined, anonymous data. Additional 'competitor analysis' reports can also be obtained that group together hotels with similar characteristics to provide a more focused anonymous report. Such data can include ranking, so in your data set you can see in the last week where you ranked with other similar hotels on key statistics. The benchmarking companies can then use the combined hotel data to write industry reports for sale, use the data to model future industry predictions and for consultancy and feasibility study purposes.

For hotel management using USALI the ability to gain such industry benchmarking data online on a daily, weekly and monthly basis is a powerful management accounting tool that allows them to respond rapidly to market.

2.5.1 Example: USALI department statement

To understand the format of an individual department report and how it can aid managers the example of a swimming pool is used and this is a discrete and straightforward report.

Figure 2.1: Swimming pool department financial statement

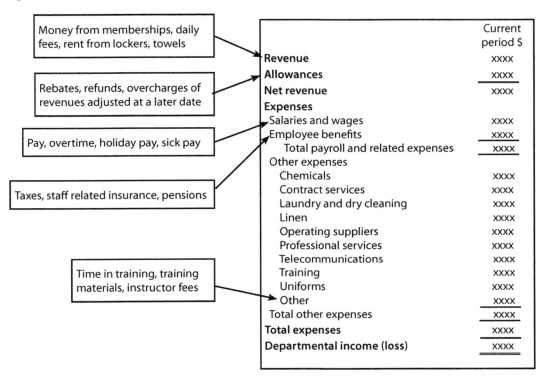

The department report illustrates the detail, not only in the breakdown of items in the report, but the illustrative examples of the guidance notes that give full details of what is included in each line heading. As the operational manager for this department the report would give a detailed breakdown of costs for analysis and decision making. If this was part of a resort hotel chain, comparative data for analysis could also be compared between individual units across the chain.

2.5.2   Example: USALI summary statement of income

The individual department reports link together to provide a 'summary statement of income', which is useful for hotel general management purposes. It shows the summary data for the main departments and the minor departments combined, plus the hotel level costs.

Table 2.9: Summary statement of income

Operated departments	Net revenues	Cost of sales	Payroll and related expenses	Other expenses	Income* (loss)
	$000s	$000s	$000s	$000s	$000s
Rooms	6,000		1,080	480	4,440
Food	1,900	665	570	152	513
Beverage	700	145	100	72	383
Telecommunications	205	175	18	8	4
Rentals and other income	170				170
Total operated departments	8,975	985	1,768	712	5,510
Undistributed operating expenses					
Administrative and general			205	290	495
Marketing			105	390	495
Property operation and maintenance			186	155	341
Utility costs				500	500
Total undistributed operating expenses			496	1,335	1,831
Totals	**8,975**	**985**	**2,264**	**2,047**	
Income after undistributed operating expenses					**3,679**
Rent, property taxes, and insurance					580
Income before interest, depreciation and amortization, and income taxes					**3,099**
Interest expense					410
Income before, depreciation and amortization, and income taxes					**2,689**
Gain on sale of property					2
Income before income taxes					**2,691**
Income taxes					430
Net income*					**2,261**

* Income – in this American terminology 'income' relates to what in the UK would be termed 'profit'

This report provides a summary of individual departments' revenue, departmental costs and 'income' (departmental profit). If a hotel general manager reviewed this report and wanted to investigate the rooms department in more detail they can investigate the full rooms report. The data highlighted in the summary tables matches key data in the rooms report.

Figure 2.2: Rooms report. .

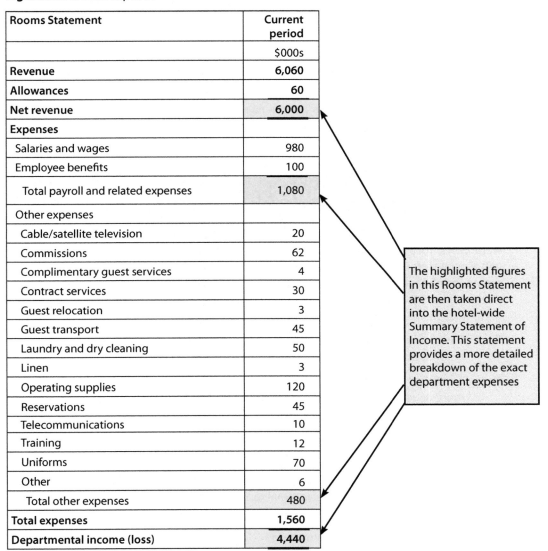

Rooms Statement	Current period
	$000s
Revenue	6,060
Allowances	60
Net revenue	6,000
Expenses	
Salaries and wages	980
Employee benefits	100
Total payroll and related expenses	1,080
Other expenses	
Cable/satellite television	20
Commissions	62
Complimentary guest services	4
Contract services	30
Guest relocation	3
Guest transport	45
Laundry and dry cleaning	50
Linen	3
Operating supplies	120
Reservations	45
Telecommunications	10
Training	12
Uniforms	70
Other	6
Total other expenses	480
Total expenses	1,560
Departmental income (loss)	4,440

The highlighted figures in this Rooms Statement are then taken direct into the hotel-wide Summary Statement of Income. This statement provides a more detailed breakdown of the exact department expenses

All the revenues and expenses in the rooms report are 'controllable' by the rooms division manager, therefore they can be held accountable for them and their financial performance can be measured against targets set for the rooms division.

These examples show the depth of information available in USALI reports for management use and the detailed instructions for their preparation to assist management accountants.

2.6   The purpose of such statements in aiding managers

In this textbook a number of chapters consider how financial information aids managers in performing their roles and responsibilities and aids a better understanding of financial performance. It is important that managers understand the terminology of these reports in order to fully utilise tools such as ratio analysis and fully understand the cause and effect relationships between different aspects of the business financially.

Summary of key points

This chapter has provided a refresher on the format of external financial reporting statements, focusing on the more modern terminology likely to be encountered in financial statements prepared using IFRS formats. The utilisation of these statements in management accounting and the alternative internal reporting framework provide by USALI have helped to set the scene for future chapter within this textbook. The main points are:

- Cash and profit refer to different elements of the accounts and should never be used interchangeably, they are different.

- A number of different 'GAAPs' exist, international GAAP, using IFRS are used more widely than other 'national' country-specific GAAPs.

- External reporting statements can be utilised internally for management accounting analysis purposes, but are too general and far-reaching for operational decision making.

- USALI is well utilised as a reporting framework within hospitality and is one of the oldest sector-specific internal reporting frameworks in the world.

- USALI serves many purposes for internal reporting and external benchmarking for decision making.

References

IFRS (2012) www.ifrs.org

USALI (2006) *Uniform System of Accounts for the Lodging Industry*, 10th edn, Hotel Association of New York City. Published by: American Hotel and Lodging Educational Institute, with support from Hospitality Financial and Technology Professionals.

Kwansa, F. and Schmidgall, R. (1999) 'The Uniform System of Accounts for the

Lodging Industry: its importance to and use by hotel managers', *Cornell Hospitality Quarterly*, December, 40 (6) 88–94.

Further reading

In addition to reading of those texts in the referencing section, for those wanting a deeper understanding of basic financial accounting there are many textbooks to refer to, more recent ones will generally use the IFRS standards and format. The following text is recommended as a good introductory text to financial accounting:

Thomas, A. and Ward, A.M. (2012) *Introduction to Financial Accounting*, 7th edn, McGraw-Hill Education.

Self-check student questions

1 What is the difference between cash and profits?

2 How can external annual financial accounting statements be used by managers within an organisation?

3 What are the benefits of having international financial report standards?

4 Explain the main purpose of the income statement, cash flow statement and the statement of financial position.

5 As a manager, what could be the benefits of using the USALI?

6 What industry advantages are there if using the USALI?

Further questions and problems

1 For a listed company in either hospitality, tourism or events review a set of their accounts. How does their reporting format link to IFRS format. Apart from the financial statements named in this chapter what other elements make up the whole annual report?

2 Having read the article by Kwansa and Schmidgall (1999) in the reference section, review how USALI usage was reported at that time and how could this have changed since that date.

3 Costs and their Behaviour

3.1 Introduction and objectives

Managers need to be able to understand costs and how costs behave to be able to appreciate the consequences of their decisions. They need to be able to make informed decisions and choose between various alternative courses of action. The term 'cost' can be defined as the monetary value of the resources used, or consumed, in the process of manufacturing a product or serving a customer. There are so many different costs incurred in business, so many different situations where costs need to be understood, and so many different ways of analysing them, that it can be quite confusing. As a result the term cost is nearly always preceded by another word which helps clarify its meaning, such as variable cost or opportunity cost, each of these costs carry different meaning and are used in different circumstances.

After studying this chapter you should be able to:

- Understand a range of cost concepts that underpin decision-making
- Identify the elements of cost and the main ways of classifying costs
- Understand what is meant by direct/indirect; variable/fixed costs
- Be able to apply these cost concepts
- Understand the implications of different cost structures.

This chapter will provide the underpinning for later chapters covering cost volume profit analysis, decision making, pricing and budget preparation so is an important starting point.

3.2   Classifying costs

It is important to recognise that there are different ways of classifying costs, Figure 3.1 provides a summary of the main ways of classifying costs, and these will be explained and discussed in more depth throughout this chapter.

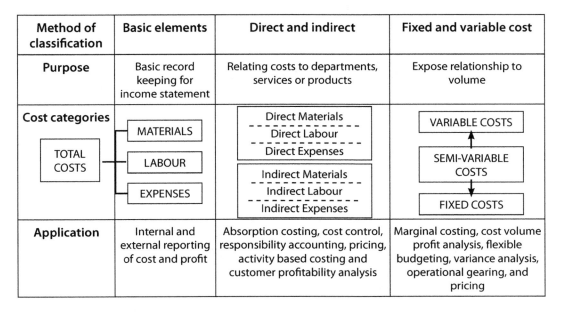

Method of classification	Basic elements	Direct and indirect	Fixed and variable cost
Purpose	Basic record keeping for income statement	Relating costs to departments, services or products	Expose relationship to volume
Cost categories	TOTAL COSTS — MATERIALS, LABOUR, EXPENSES	Direct Materials, Direct Labour, Direct Expenses / Indirect Materials, Indirect Labour, Indirect Expenses	VARIABLE COSTS ↑ SEMI-VARIABLE COSTS ↓ FIXED COSTS
Application	Internal and external reporting of cost and profit	Absorption costing, cost control, responsibility accounting, pricing, activity based costing and customer profitability analysis	Marginal costing, cost volume profit analysis, flexible budgeting, variance analysis, operational gearing, and pricing

Figure 3.1: Three cost classifications

This chapter considers how costs can be classified for use in management decision making. In later chapters, costs will be further analysed in relation to specific decision making such as short-term or long-term decisions.

3.2.1   Basic cost elements

This represents the most fundamental form of classification. Here costs are identified in terms of the basic resources of materials, labour and expenses necessary to produce a product or service. Thus, in the case of a hotel, materials in the form of food are purchased and transformed to provide breakfast, labour is utilised to clean rooms and provide reception services and general expenses (including electricity, insurance, marketing) are amongst other vital inputs to the process of providing guests with a good night's sleep. This method of grouping costs has been developed to provide useful information on the resources that are used in the production process and is considered as a convenient way of assembling costs for the presentation of profit statements (i.e. the income statement and other internal management reports).

3.2.2 Direct/indirect costs

The second method of classifying costs relates to whether they can be attributed or assigned to a specific product or service. This method of classification is used for management control purposes. Direct costs are those that can be directly identified with, or linked to, a particular product, department or saleable service and can sometimes be called traceable costs. Direct costs are further broken down into the three key elements creating direct materials, direct labour and direct expenses.

Examples of direct costs for an event would be:

Direct materials	Food and beverages
	Tickets
Direct labour	Bar staff
	Artists' fees
Direct expenses	Event licence
	Event insurance

Indirect costs cannot be easily identified with a particular product, department or service. They can also be broken down further in the same way as direct costs.

Examples of indirect costs for an event would be:

Indirect materials	Cleaning materials
Indirect labour	Event organiser's annual salary
Indirect expenses	Vehicle running costs
	Head office heating and lighting

Generally within the hospitality, tourism and events industries there are numerous costs that fall into the indirect category, however there are exceptions and variations, an example of a direct expense, which may be considered indirect normally, is rent, in this case, the one-off rental by a hotel of audio-visual equipment for a specific conference would be a direct cost of that conference. It therefore becomes apparent that the classification of costs into direct and indirect groups is dependent on the context and/or the type and scale of the business activity. Look at the examples below to see how costs can be categorised in different circumstances.

Table 3.1: Cost classification in business context

Cost	Context	Classification
Food	Restaurant	Direct – food cost of meals sold to customers
		Indirect – food cost of meals provided for staff
Fuel costs	Airlines	Direct – fuelling a plane
		Indirect – fuelling ground vehicles
Energy	Hotel	Direct – metered gas in kitchens
		Indirect – general lighting of public areas
Marketing and advertising	Event	Direct – advertising specific one-off event
		Indirect – company promotion at wedding fair

Importantly the classification between direct and indirect provides a basis for assigning cost responsibility and accountability to departments or segments of a business and thus is important to maintaining control over costs. There are several publications that address the issues of management control systems in more detail, for example, Anthony and Govindarajan (2007).

In service provision it is the identification of direct costs which is of key importance, however a business must ensure that its indirect costs are also covered by its sales and allocation of indirect costs to products and services is required for external financial reporting purposes.

3.2.2.1 Absorption costing

Absorption costing is an approach to costing that attempts to identify the full cost of a product or service. Determining full costs requires the identification of direct costs and the allocation of indirect costs. This can be used to help set prices and evaluate profitability. The direct costs are easily attributable to the product or service but there needs to be a systematic process to attach the indirect costs in an equitable manner to units of output. For example allocating the annual cost of insurance to cabins on a cruise ship could be undertaken per cabin or per metre squared of cabin space. Both of these would result in an allocation of indirect cost but the exact amount would be different.

Example

The insurance cost is £60,000. There are 2,500 cabins. The total space occupied by cabins is 30,000 m^2 and standard cabin occupies 10 m^2 whilst a deluxe occupies 15 m^2.

If the insurance is absorbed by cabin, the cost absorbed by each type would be:

£60,000/2,500 = £24 per standard or deluxe cabin

If the insurance is absorbed using metres squared, the cost absorbed by each type of cabin would be:

£60,000/30,000 = £2 per m^2

A standard cabin occupies 10 m^2 so would absorb £2 x 10 = £20

A deluxe cabin occupies 15 m^2 so would absorb £2 x 15 =£30

Whilst the total indirect cost has remained unchanged at £60,000, the cost associated with a deluxe cabin varies from £24 to £30 and shows the method of absorbing the indirect cost will impact on decision making and this is why absorption costing is often considered an arbitrary method of allocating indirect costs.

The greater the proportion of indirect costs that exist in the business, the more allocated cost will make up the full costs of the product or service. Also the more the complex the product or service is the more difficult it is to identify reliable allocation methods. As a result, service businesses tend not to engage in absorption costing due to the difficulty of establishing reliable and equitable allocation methods linked to the characteristics of services discussed in Chapter 1, plus, there is less need to understand individual product/service costs because pricing is often externally determined and market orientated rather than cost orientated.

As a result of the difficulties implementing absorption costing in increasingly heterogeneous business settings, where service and information costs far outweigh direct costs of materials, activity-based costing (ABC) was developed to provide a more practical approach to assigning indirect costs to products and services. Activity-based costing focuses on the activities that drive cost and assigns overheads to activity centres rather than departments. In this way the allocation or assignment of costs to products or services can be more accurate.

Full consideration of ABC is given in Chapter 8.

3.3   Behaviour – fixed, variable and semi-variable costs

This final classification into fixed and variable, relating to behaviour is probably the most useful and important for managers, it is primarily used for management planning and decision-making. It is important because it provides an insight into how costs behave in different circumstances.

The classification of costs into fixed and variable is used within marginal costing, in this approach the focus is on the value of costs that are incurred as a direct result of producing one unit of a service or product. Grounded in the economic concept of marginal cost, accountants often treat this as synonymous with variable costs, but it can be defined as the additional cost associated with the next unit of output, thus in some circumstances it will not be the same. Arguably if a firm sells a product or service anywhere above the marginal cost it will be better off. However this implies that overheads and fixed costs are not incurred in this process, which is obviously not correct. Marginal costing has an important role to play and underpins CVP analysis, pricing decisions and revenue management.

3.3.1   Variable costs

A variable cost in total tends to vary in direct proportion to changes in volume of activity[1] during a period, e.g. cost of food and beverages or commission on ticket sales. So, in the case of a restaurant business where the food cost is £2 per meal the variable cost of 5,000 and 10,000 meals sold will be £10,000 and £20,000 respectively. If the commission on the ticket is £1.00 per ticket and 40,000 tickets are sold the total commission will be £40,000, if ticket sales increase to 65,000 then the commission will increase to £65,000. We can see that there is a *direct link* between the total variable cost and the volume of sales. We can represent this cost function in a graph (see Figure 3.2) here it is clearly shown that there is a linear

---

1   The term 'activity' refers to productive outputs such as dishes prepared, meals sold, rooms occupied, inclusive coach tours or passengers transported.

relationship between the costs and the volume of meal/tickets because the line is straight.

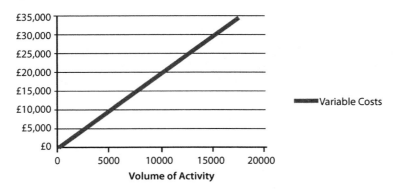

Figure 3.2: Cost function for variable costs.

3.3.2   Fixed costs

In contrast, a fixed cost is one which in total accrues in relation to the passage of time and that, within limits, tends to be unaffected by fluctuations in activity (output or turnover), e.g. rates, insurance and salaries. So fixed costs are not immediately affected by fluctuations in volume. Thus assuming the above restaurant pays rates of £1,000 per month the cost will remain constant over the period regardless of whether the volume of meals sold is 5,000 or 10,000 and the cost of insurance for an event will remain unchanged by the volume ticket sales, providing the organisation remains broadly within planned activity levels (see relevant range discussion, 3.4.1). The cost function for fixed costs (shown in Figure 3.3) displays a very different pattern, remaining horizontal thus unaffected as volume rises. So to summarise, variable costs vary in direct proportion to sales, fixed costs are unaffected by changes in sales.

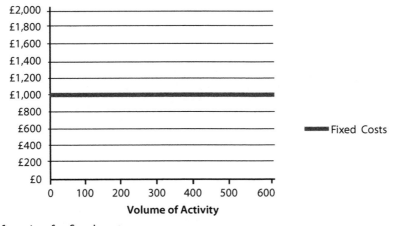

Figure 3.3: Cost function for fixed costs

3.3.3   Semi-variable cost patterns

In addition to the wholly fixed and variable costs there are semi-variable (or mixed) costs that contain both fixed and variable elements. This kind of cost is partly affected by fluctuations in volume during a period, but not proportionately so, for example, labour, electricity, and insurances. Therefore, if the restaurant incurs an electricity cost of £1,000 at an activity level of 5,000 meals sold, then it may incur a cost of (say) £1,250 at a level of 10,000 meals. Although the cost has changed when volume changed, importantly it has not changed in direct proportion to volume or sales. We can see that the volume of meals sold has doubled, but the cost of electricity has not doubled and only increased by 25%. This shows that although activity affects electricity, there is a residual amount of electricity cost that is incurred no matter how busy the restaurant is and this is why the cost function in Figure 3.4 does not start at zero.

There are many semi-variable or semi-fixed costs in most businesses, for example labour costs, usually called wages and salaries, will include the cost of managers who need to be on duty when the business is open regardless of how busy it is (fixed) and hourly-paid staff who will be employed in shifts to meet demand peaks and troughs (variable). Telephone costs usually include a line rental and a usage charge, in call centres and box offices, these are likely to be semi-variable costs. Costs can also change in a staged fashion, an event company may need to employ a set number of security and safety staff relative to the number of event customers, but this will not change in direct proportion to sales, but as the event moves from 20,000 to 30,000 attendees the security contractors will have to scale up the number of staff, resulting in a stepped cost function (also see Figures 3.5 and 3.6).

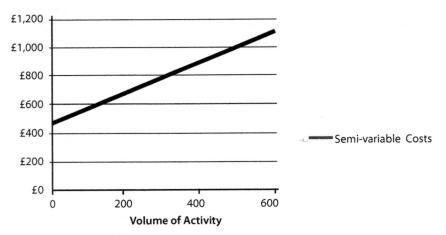

Figure 3.4: Semi-variable cost function

The examples in Figures 3.4 and 3.5 have highlighted two semi-variable cost patterns (one linear, one stepped) but there are an infinite number of different cost profiles that could be identified. The benefits and application of identifying the cost profiles are numerous, such as CVP analysis and pricing, however to utilise these techniques all costs must be separated into two categories, namely, fixed and variable. Therefore, for decision-making purposes the third category, i.e. semi-variable (or semi-fixed) costs, must be separated by dividing them into their fixed and variable components. The next section will explain how this is done and introduce key concepts and definitions that facilitate the analysis and use of cost data for management decision-making and provide key concepts that will be utilised in subsequent chapters.

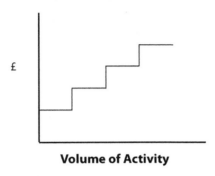

Volume of Activity

Figure 3.5: Stepped semi-variable cost function

3.4   Cost concepts, analysis and applications

The cost functions above are a simplified version of real life, yet the process of estimating and classifying costs is not simple. Assumptions about cost behaviour are based upon past experience, analysis of costs from previous years and norms in the industry; this can be intuitive for small businesses or very scientific with systematic use of regression analysis of historic data for larger businesses (see subsection 3.4.2.4). Also similar cost items can exhibit different cost behaviour in different contexts, for example in the airline industry labour costs can display different cost behaviour, cabin crew on a scheduled aircraft will be fixed regardless of the number of passengers, but in a restaurant business with hourly-paid staff and shift-working, non-managerial staff wages can be treated as variable. So the classification of costs will be affected by the operational factors, such as flexibility, contracts and safety as well as the nature and size of the business.

3.4.1   Relevant range

The classification and estimation of costs is carried out within the constraint of limiting, or simplifying, factors, the most important of which is the relevant range. It is important to recognise that assumptions about cost behaviour can only be reliable within specific circumstances and particular range of activity, because as a business changes its scale of operations it is likely to benefit from economies of scale driven by bulk purchases or efficiencies in operational set ups. Thus the assumptions about cost behaviour can only apply within a specific range of activity, called the relevant range. The behaviour of costs outside this range of activity is unknown and likely to change. For example, in the case of fixed costs such as salaries, they may be applicable to an activity range of 5,000 to 10,000 meals sold per month, but it is possible they may change substantially if business increases or decreases beyond that range. The effect of this on the cost pattern is illustrated in Figure 3.6. The recognition of the relevant range concept is critical when management is contemplating significant reductions or increases in activity levels and should be borne in mind when applying cost functions in CVP analysis, pricing and short-term decision making.

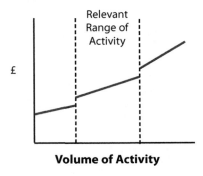

Volume of Activity

Figure 3.6: Graph showing the relevant range

3.4.2 Cost functions and cost estimation

An assumption frequently made in investigations of cost behaviour is that the cost functions are linear, i.e. take the form of a continuous straight line. If cost functions are curvilinear then cost computations can become extremely complex. Partly as a result of this, linear approximations, within the relevant range of activity, are often used to simplify the calculations. Furthermore, the practice is not unreasonable, as a number of statistical studies have shown linear approximations to be realistic interpretations of cost behaviour patterns.

It is important to understand what the independent variable is. In the context of cost behaviour we are focusing on sales (volume) as the independent variable driving our costs, but other factors can also affect costs. For example, ambient temperate or weather conditions can affect the heating costs for outdoor event marquees or swimming pools. The market price of raw materials can affect food costs even when the amount of ingredients is stable; the effects of such changes are discussed in Chapter 9. For the purposes of decision making and separating fixed and variable costs, the independent variable is assumed to be volume of activity (sales) unless otherwise stated.

3.4.2.1 Separating semi-variable cost techniques

When separating costs into their fixed and variable components from a semi-variable cost, there are a number of methods that can be used. These methods include: the high/low method, scatter graphs, and the use of linear regression. Each of these methods has advantages and disadvantages, but the same basic principle applies to each method, they aim to identify the element of the cost that is fixed and the value (per unit) of the variable element.

3.4.2.2 High/low method

From the financial data there will be a range showing the semi-variable costs at different levels of activity (units). With this method, two sets of data are used; first, the highest level of activity (units) and the second at the lowest level of activity (units). As the fixed element of the cost will not change with levels of activity any changes have to be due to variable cost changes in direct proportion to the change in activity (units).

Simply, the difference costs/difference in units = variable cost element per unit

A worked example of the high/low method is given later in this chapter. Where there is little variation in the data sets the high/low method works fine, however it only uses the two extreme points of data so where the data set contains more variations it may not be as reliable as other methods (see Figure 3.7).

3.4.2.3 Scatter graph method

This method plots the data on a graph and a line of 'best-fit' is drawn, so the fixed element can be separated and read off the graph. This is illustrated in Figure 3.7 highlighting how, in some circumstances, it may give a better estimate than the high/low method.

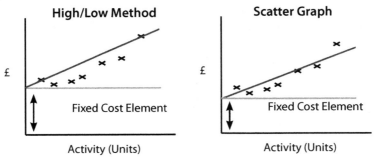

Figure 3.7: Comparison of high/low and scatter graphs

The graph on the left of Figure 3.7 shows the use of the high/low method, only the two extreme points are used, but when these two points are not the norm for all the data the estimation could be inaccurate, in this case too high. The graph on the right uses the scatter graph method. It shows a similar cost pattern, but all points of data have been used to estimate the average data, the scatter graph method draws a line of 'best fit' through all the data points to estimate the fixed cost element. When the activity level equals zero (no sales) the only costs are fixed costs. Where the line of best fit crosses the Y axis, represents the estimated value of the fixed cost element. As can be seen between the two graphs the estimate of fixed costs would be different, due to the method used, in this situation.

3.4.2.4 Linear regression

This is a more sophisticated method that effectively allows an accurate averaging of the data to be obtained, better than drawing a line on a scatter graph by eye. This is a more complex method, but can be made easier by the use of spreadsheets. Within industry linear regression has been utilised when needing accurate data for calculating costs, such as in customer profitability analysis (CPA), which is discussed in more detail in Chapter 8.

3.4.3 Total costs and unit costs

Another important aspect worthy of attention is the way in which costs are presented and interpreted. Until now discussion has centred on costs in 'total'. Fixed cost and variable cost imply 'total fixed cost' and 'total variable cost'. Interest has focused on how fixed and variable costs respond in total to changes in activity level. In addition, costs may be presented in terms of a single 'unit', e.g. cost per meal. So what are the implications of total cost and unit cost determination? This can be considered by utilizing data from the previous examples in Table 3.2.

Table 3.2: Total and unit costs

No of meals sold	5,000	Unit cost	10,000	Unit cost
Variable	€25,000	€5	€50,000	€5
Fixed	€15,000	€3	€15,000	€1.50

Observation of Table 3.2 shows that over the relevant 5,000 to 10,000 range of activity, variable costs increase, whereas fixed costs remain constant. However, over the same range, variable cost per unit remains constant at €5 per meal, but fixed cost per unit reduces from €3 to €1.50 per meal. The variable cost per unit, e.g. food cost, remains at €5 per meal regardless of the number of meals sold. In contrast, the fixed cost per unit, e.g. salaries, becomes smaller as it is spread over a larger number of meals. It is possible to summarize the total and unit fixed/variable costs responses to changes in volume as shown in Figure 3.8.

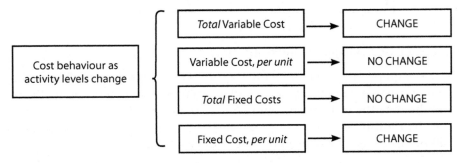

Figure 3.8: Total and unit cost behaviour

The recognition of 'total' and 'unit' costs is essential to the decision-making process, but care should be exercised in assessing and evaluating opportunities, there is a danger that variable costs and fixed costs will get compounded into total costs and then this figure used in calculations. It is important to remember that unit costs are average costs and there is the danger of interpreting total unit cost, i.e. fixed plus variable unit costs, as if they are exclusively variable, this is not the case. Thus, in a case where activity is increasing then the total unit cost will reduce to the extent by which the fixed cost element is shared by a greater number of products or units of service. In other words, it is not possible to take the total unit cost predicted for one level of activity and simply multiply it by another level of activity and expect to obtain a meaningful cost prediction. The important point to bear in mind when dealing with unit costs is that they should be handled with caution. The next section will utilise concepts and knowledge explained in the previous section in the context of an illustrative example.

3.4.4   Illustrative example – Paris Tours

Paris Tours is a small business that offers full-day coach trips around Paris city centre and the surrounding area. The standard guided tour includes full-day coach tour around Paris, with access to the Eiffel Tower, lunch and entry to the Louvre in the afternoon. The following forecasts have been prepared for the forth-coming year at varying volumes of activity; low, medium and high. From the data in Table 3.3, it is possible to:

1   Identify variable costs, fixed costs and semi-variable.

2   Separate out the fixed and variable element of the semi-variable costs

3   Work out what the profit would be if they sold 15,000 tours.

Table 3.3

No of tours sold (@ €30)	12,000	14,000	16,000
	€	€	€
Sales revenue	360,000	420,000	480,000
COSTS			
Entrance fees	108,000	126,000	144,000
Food and refreshments	144,000	168,000	192,000
Wages and salaries	78,000	86,000	94,000
Overheads	28,000	28,000	28,000
Total cost	358,000	408,000	458,000
Operating profit	€ 2,000	€ 12,000	€ 22,000

3.4.4.1   Identify variable costs, fixed costs and semi-variable costs

Careful observation of the figures will reveal that overheads are fixed as they do not change at all; all other cost items change so they must be either variable or semi-variable.

Variable costs change in direct proportion, so divide the cost by the number of tours sold on the low forecast and multiply by the medium to see if figures are correct. Entrance fees are variable because there is a direct change €108,000 ÷ 12,000 = €9.00 x 14,000 = €126,000. The unit cost is consistent at €9.00. Food and refreshments also change in direct proportion, working from high forecast to medium €192,000 ÷ 16,000 x 14,000 = € 168,000 (the medium cost for F&R).

Wages and salaries are not variable (€78,000 ÷ 12,000 x 14,000 = €91,000 ≠ €86,000) so these costs do not change in direct proportion, so they must be semi-variable.

3.4.4.2 Separate out the fixed and variable element of the semi-variable costs

To separate out the fixed and variable elements, it is necessary to focus on what changes between the different forecasts, using the high/low method discussed in 3.4.2.2. At 12,000 tours, wages and salaries (W&S) are €78,000, when the number of tours is increased to 16,000 (an increase of 4,000 units) W&S cost increased to €94,000 (an increase of €16,000), therefore the unit cost of W&S must be €4.00 (€16,000 ÷ 4,000). So the variable element of W&S is €48,000 at 12,000 tours (€4.00 x 12,000). Now that the variable element has been identified it is possible to isolate the fixed costs element (€78,000 – €48,000 = €30,000), see Table 3.4 for full breakdown of W&S costs.

Table 3.4

Number of units	12,000	14,000	16,000
	€	€	€
Variable W&S	48,000	56,000	64,000
Fixed W&S	30,000	30,000	30,000
Total W&S	78,000	86,000	94,000

3.4.4.3 Work out what the profit would be if they sold 15,000 tours

Now it is fairly simple to multiply the unit costs by the number of units for each cost element to calculate the profit. For example entrance fees €9.00 per tour x 15,000 = €135,000 (you can check the figures in the same way for food and refreshments and wages – Table 3.5).

Table 3.5

	€
Sales revenue	450,000
COSTS	
Entrance fees	135,000
Food and refreshments	180,000
Wages (variable)	60,000
Salaries (fixed)	30,000
Other costs	28,000
Total cost	433,000
Operating profit	17,000

With a full understanding of cost behaviour managers can calculate the effect of different scenarios and different planning assumptions, also carry out CVP analysis, understand the effect of different pricing decisions and support a range of short-term decision making, these topics are covered in Chapters 4, 5 and 6.

3.4.5 Cost structure and operational gearing

This chapter has explained the various ways of classifying costs, but has mainly focused on classifying costs into fixed and variable and the application of this. The relative importance, or mix of, fixed and variable costs that a business experiences is a major issue and has significant implications. This next section will explain the implications of costs structures on operational gearing and business risk.

Cost structure refers to the relationship between fixed and variable costs, some businesses costs are mainly variable and other businesses exhibit a majority of fixed costs. This is derived from the nature of the business itself and the way that organisations set up their businesses. This is a *relative* scale, where the focus is on the proportion of total costs that are either fixed or variable. A firm that has a large proportion of fixed costs relative to total cost is said to have a high fixed cost structure; correspondingly, a firm that has a small proportion of fixed costs is referred to as having a low fixed cost structure. An understanding of the influence cost structure has on profits is a crucial element in management decision-making.

When a business has a high proportion of fixed costs relative to variable costs it is described as having high operational gearing or leverage. The higher the gearing the more sensitive profits are to changes in volume, Table 3.6 will demonstrate.

Table 3.6

	Co A Low FC £	Co B High FC £
Sales	150,000	150,000
Variable costs	75,000	30,000
Fixed costs	45,000	90,000
Profit	30,000	30,000
Profit as a % of sales	20%	20%
If sales increase by 15%:		
Sales	172,500	172,500
Variable costs	86,250	34,500
Fixed costs	45,000	90,000
Profit	41,250	48,000
Profit as a % of sales	24%	28%

In this example Company A has relatively low fixed costs (38% of total costs) and Company B has high fixed costs (75% of total costs). When sales increase, the increase in profit for Company B is larger than company A, so when things are going well they do better. However when sales decrease the picture is different Table 3.7 will show the effect of a 15% drop in sales.

Table 3.7

	Co A Low FC	Co B High FC
If sales decrease by 15%:	£	£
Sales	127,500	127,500
Variable costs	63,750	25,500
Fixed costs	45,000	90,000
Profit	18,750	12,000
Profit as a % of sales	15%	9%

When sales decrease, Company B profits fall much more than Company A, thus when things are *not* going well they do far worse. This is the volatility effect of operational gearing, the higher the gearing the greater will be the volatility of profits, thus the greater the business risk. A general conclusion that can be drawn from this illustration is that profits in firms that have high fixed cost structures are relatively more sensitive to changes in critical factors. This in turn would suggest that their profits are potentially more at risk than for firms with low fixed cost structures.

Table 3.8: How business can differ in their costs proportions

High fixed costs proportion:	
Airlines	*High fixed* cost of fuel and crew for each flight
	Low variable cost per passenger for meals and other extras
Luxury hotels	*High fixed* cost due to location, space and staffing levels
	Low variable costs of consumables
Major event venue	*High fixed* cost due to location, space and staffing levels
	Low variable costs of consumables

Low fixed costs proportion:	
Restaurants	*Low fixed* costs as property is usually rented
	High variable costs of food and drink costs relative to prices
Retail outlets	*Low fixed* costs as property is usually rented, flexible staffing
	High variable costs of cost of goods relative to prices
Events operations	*Low fixed* cost as venues hired or at client's premise and outsourcing key inputs, e.g. security or catering
	High variable costs due to number of costs specific to an individual event, such as contract staff and material/artist costs

However it is important to note that not all businesses can have low operational gearing. There are many reasons why businesses differ, such as the location and property running cost, level of staffing to provide services and cost of capital (interest payments) which result from financing decisions (discussed in Chapters 11 and 13). Examples of this are given in Table 3.8.

Management decisions such as outsourcing in events and establishing management contracts in hotel industry can shift costs from fixed to variable (i.e. gear down costs) and thus it is possible through choices of business set up and strategic management decisions to change the operational gearing of a firm.

3.4.5.1 Cost versus market orientation

As mentioned earlier, service firms have varying cost structures; firms which have a relatively low proportion of fixed costs, are usually associated with higher volumes of lower priced products and services, e.g. fast food outlets, chain restaurants, and some tour operations. On the other hand, firms with high proportions of fixed costs are associated with relatively lower volumes of more expensive and commercially targeted products, e.g. luxury hotels, full service airlines and cruise ships.

Apart from the more explicit consequences on a firm's profitability, cost structure has implications on management decision-making. Travel agents, event operators, chain restaurants, with their relatively low proportions of fixed costs are said to be 'cost oriented', whereas hotels, major event venues and long haul/ full service airlines with their high proportions of fixed costs are referred to as 'market oriented'. An example of this is a horseracing venue. Racing may only take place less than 20 days in the year and yet the infrastructure costs are all year, so being market orientated to sell the space for other purposes is key. For an event operator, not owning their own venue the focus is about the cost of hiring at the best price to keep costs down. Whilst all service firms need to be customer focused and, due to competition and customer empowerment, all firms have to set competitive prices, the orientation and emphasis of management will differ from cost control to customer service.

Briefly, the significance of this is that in the case of a cost-oriented firm, where demand may be less critical, the large variable cost presence provides management with the opportunity to improve profits by placing greater emphasis on cost-control techniques than would otherwise be justified. This does not imply that marketing should be disregarded, but simply suggests that it may be more profitable to concentrate additional resources on cost reduction and control procedures. In contrast to this, in the market-oriented firm, the emphasis should be different. The lower levels of variable costs experienced by this type of firm means there is less latitude to improve profits by cost-control techniques. Instead, profitability may be better served by emphasizing the market in order to generate additional revenue. Again, it is not a case of disregarding cost-control procedures, but merely diverting more resources into or emphasizing the marketing effort.

3.4.5.2 Wychwood musical festival

Wychwood Festival is an annual music festival that takes place on Cheltenham racecourse (see textbook cover photo). It is often in the top five family-friendly festivals and would be considered small size (around 6,000 people). Whilst the company is involved in some other event management the company mainly focuses on this one annual event. Examples related to pricing and cash flow using Wychwood appear later in this text. Given a good estimate of numbers attending, many costs for the event are fixed, they are incurred for the event irrespective of additional customers (within the relevant range).

If you view their website (www.wychwoodfestival.com) you will find links to pictures and videos from the event as well as links to prices, volunteering and camping. Using this data you can get a clear picture of some of the costs of running this, or an equivalent event. If you search 'Bmn211' on YouTube you will find a video that shows the event in progress, but also gives a clear view of many of the hidden costs in running a green-field event. Artists' costs are large, but are still a smaller proportion of the costs than many people imagine. Items such as generator hirer (and fuel), lighting, tenting, toilets are just a few costs to consider. The video identifies many costs, but also revenue opportunities at such an event.

Summary of key points

This chapter has explained how to understand and analyse costs, providing an vital foundation of later chapters covering CVP, pricing, short-term decision making and customer profitability analysis, some key points to remember are:

- Costs are the value of resources used up in the production of products and services and there are several ways of subdividing costs.

- Analysing cost behaviour reveals variable and fixed costs, which are fundamental to many management accounting techniques.

- A variety of costing techniques have been developed, including absorption and marginal costing, which are utilised in different decision contexts.

- Costs can be reported as unit values or in total, it is very important to understand the difference and the nature of any data used in decision making.

- The cost structure of a firm has significant impact on the market orientation and risk of the business.

Reference

Anthony, R.N. and Govindarajan, V. (2007) *Management Control Systems*, 12th edn, Boston, MA: McGraw Hill.

Further reading

3

For further detail regarding cost allocations and absorption costing see:

Drury, C. (2009) *Management Accounting for Business*, 4th edn, London: Thomson Learning.

Generic management accounting textbooks tend to focus around manufacturing organisation and have a heavier emphasis on absorption costing, but still provide a worthwhile source of cost-related data.

www.wychwoodfestival.com provides a good example of an event for considering the costs associated with such an event.

http://youtu.be/Zqu4k9To-j0 This is the direct link to a video highlighting costs, revenue and pricing at the Wychwood Festival.

Self-check student questions

1 Explain what you understand by the 'elements of cost'.

2 Distinguish between 'direct' and 'indirect' costs and give examples of each.

3 Define 'fixed' and 'variable' costs, what is the main difference between them?

4 What is a semi-variable cost?

5 A banqueting suite is trying to ascertain the cost structure for a single menu:

Standard menu 'D'	Cost per head (fixed and variable)
100 covers	£25.30
150 covers	£20.90
200 covers	£19.75

Portion size and quality of the food and service were the same in all cases. Calculate the fixed and variable portions of the total cost (note: same process as for semi-variable separation). Estimate the cost if 175 covers were sold.

6 From the data and your answers from question 5, sketch two graphs showing the following against level of activity:

(i) variable cost; and

(ii) fixed cost.

Clearly label each line on your graphs.

7 How can you identify semi-variable costs and separate them into the fixed and variable elements?

8 What does the term 'operational gearing' refer to and why is this important?

Further questions and problems

1   (a) 'Fixed costs are really variable. The more you produce, the less they become.' Do you agree? Explain.

(b) 'In the long term, all costs are variable.' Explain with reference to the relevant range.

2   Below are details of a number of costs, please categorise them into the various categories (fixed, variable, semi-variable):

- Food served at an event as part of the attendance fee per person, prepared and served to standard portion sizes.
- Food provided in the staff canteen of a service business.
- Electricity charge consisting of a flat basic charge plus a variable charge after a minimum number of units have been used.
- Depreciation of equipment where the charge is calculated by the straight line basis.
- Salaries of maintenance staff where 1 member of staff is required for 150 bedrooms or less, 2 members of staff for 151–300 bedrooms, 3 members of staff for 301–450 bedrooms and so on.
- Aircraft maintenance staff working for an airline based at one hub airport.

4 Cost Volume Profit Analysis (CVP)

4.1 Introduction and objectives

Cost volume profit analysis is a technique used to explore the relationship between the three elements of financial performance; the volume of activity (sales), the costs associated with them, and the profit (the difference between them). A key aspect of this is to be able to understand how costs respond to changes in level of activity and to use this awareness in the planning and decision making process.

After studying this chapter you should be able to:

- Understand the concept and terminology of CVP

- Have a working knowledge of CVP calculations

- Appreciate the usefulness of CVP to managers as a decision making tool; and

- Explore the use of 'What if?' case scenarios with the aid of computer spreadsheets.

4.2 CVP terminology and concept

At a basic level we know that:

Profit = Total Sales Revenue – Total costs

For planning and decision-making purposes it is important to look at this relationship and how it varies in different situations. For example a manager could ask the questions related to impact on profit, such as:

- What if my sales volume reduces/increases by 10%?

- What if my supplier puts his costs up by 10%?

- What would be the impact of reducing/increasing the selling price by 5%?

- How many sales do I need to make to break even?

- How many sales are needed to produce a given profit?
- What price needs to be charged to return a specific profit from a specific level of activity?

An important aspect in answering such questions is identifying what type of costs you have and how they respond to changes in levels of activity. In the previous chapter it has been identified that variable cost vary in direct proportion to the volume of activity and fixed costs vary with time (no cost remains constant forever). Given this knowledge it is important that fixed and variable costs can be separated if the relationship between costs, volume of activity and the profit achieved are to be explored. Costs cannot be left in the semi-fixed or semi-variable category – such costs have to be split into their fixed and variable components. How to do this is discussed in the previous chapter using methods such as the high/low method, scatter graph approach or by using linear regression.

CVP emphasises the 'contribution margin', which is the contribution made towards fixed costs and profit. The formula for this is:

Contribution margin = Sales revenue – Variable costs

So it is the amount left from sales revenue once variable costs have been removed that is available to contribute towards the fixed costs in the first instance and once fixed costs have been met, it is a contribution to profit. It is important to note that contribution is not profit, there is often confusion and the terms 'contribution margin' and 'profit' should not be confused. The concept of variables costs was discussed in some depth in the previous chapter.

4.2.1   Example: Oriental Delight Restaurant

This restaurant is an 'All-you-can-eat' buffet style restaurant with a set price of £10 per customer (cover). Its 'relevant range' (see previous chapter) in a typical month are sales of between 15,000–30,000 units (meals). Their variable costs are £4 per unit and their fixed costs are £120,000.

Table 4.1: Contribution margin profit statement for Oriental Delight Restaurant

Oriental Delight Restaurant				
Relevant range (meals)	15,000	Unit	30,000	Unit
Sales revenue	£150,000	£10	£300,000	£10
Less: variable costs	£60,000	£4	£120,000	£4
Contribution margin	£90,000	£6	£180,000	£6
Less: fixed costs	£120,000		£120,000	
Net profit (loss)	–£30,000		£60,000	

The contribution statement shows the impact of sales volume on profit. Within the relevant range the selling price and variable costs have remained constant per unit sold, as has the total fixed costs. In effect, what the unit information is telling the manager is for every £10 that comes in £4 goes directly towards covering the variable costs of that sale, in this case food costs. That means for every sale there is a £6 contribution.

Selling price – variable costs per unit = contribution per unit

£10 – £4 = £6 contribution per unit

Each time a unit (meal) is sold there is a £6 contribution towards fixed costs; once those are covered is the contribution goes towards profit. Oriental Delight Restaurant has fixed costs of £120,000, but when it sells 15,000 units the total contributions (£6 * 15,000) only equals £90,000, so a loss of £30,000 is made.

Total contribution – Fixed costs = Profit (loss)

@15,000 units £90,000 – £120,000 = (£30,000)

@30,000 units £180,000 – £120,000 = £60,000

Looking at the relationship between costs, volume and profit it can be seen here that volume of activity has a massive impact on profits when variable costs remain constant per unit and fixed costs remain constant as a total. The situation moves from a loss of (£30,000) to a £60,000 profit. So doubling the volume improves the profit/loss position threefold.

With CVP calculations this information can be utilised further to give deeper insights into the data. And this is discussed in depth in the next sections.

4.3   CVP calculations

There are a number of calculations that can aid us in the decision making process using CVP. The knowledge that Oriental Delight made a loss of –£30,000 when it sold 15,000 units and a profit of £60,000 when it sold 30,000 units is useful, but at what point did it neither make a profit or a loss? The point where neither a profit nor loss is made is called the 'breakeven point'. At this point total sales revenue = total costs. In the example above a £6 contribution is made for every sale and the fixed costs are £120,000. The question is how many amounts of £6 are needed in order to cover the total fixed costs?

4.3.1   Breakeven point (BEP)

There is a formula that is simple to aid managers in calculating when neither a profit nor loss is made:

Breakeven point (BEP) in units = Fixed costs/contribution per unit

£120,000/£6 = 20,000 units

This identifies that they need to sell 20,000 units to breakeven, to neither make a loss or a profit.

The formula can be adapted to show how many units need to be sold to make a given profit.

Fixed costs + Required profit

Contribution per unit

This is one of the basic key concepts in CVP analysis and can be used to judge the value of, for example, accepting a specific contract. The formula can also be adapted to aid understanding how many sales are required to make a predetermined profit as well.

In this example the managers would like a profit of £15,000 – how many units (meals) do they need to sell to get this?

$$\frac{£120,000 + £15,000}{£6} = 22,500 \text{ units}$$

In this situation they need to sell 22,500 units in order to generate their desired profit of £15,000. When deciding to accept a conference or a discounted tour group accommodation in a hotel this can be a vital piece of information to aid the decision making.

Within a scenario where all costs do not have to be covered, for example where you have grant funding towards costs, or in a subsidised staff canteen, so not all costs have to be covered the formula can also be adjusted the other way to allow for the funding subsidy towards the fixed costs i.e. sales revenue does not have to cover the full fixed costs. For example a staff canteen has the following data:

Subsidised staff canteen

Selling price	£3.00 per unit
Variable costs per unit	£1.80
Fixed costs	£30,000
Company subsidy	£10,000

Fixed costs – Subsidy

Contribution per unit

In this situation the managers would like to know: how many units (meals) do they need to sell to cover the cost after the company subsidy is taken into account.

$$\frac{£30,000 - £10,000}{£1.20} = 16,667 \text{ units}$$

They need to sell over 16,667 meals or the sales revenue, plus grant income, will not cover all the fixed costs.

The above examples are simple as there is one set selling price, this is not uncommon in these environments, or if we were looking at a breakeven point for a wedding or conference package related to the number of delegates or wedding guests. However, if we looked at bar sales or a normal restaurant service with various menu items with different prices this isn't as simple. In such situations it is simple to use a 'contribution margin to sales ratio (C/S)' instead – this effectively uses the same principles as above, but instead of calculating units of sales it calculates the monetary value of sales needed.

$$\text{C/S ratio} = \frac{\text{Contribution margin} * 100}{\text{Sales revenue}}$$

If we look back at Oriental Delight this would be:

$$\frac{£90,000}{£150,000} * 100 = 60\%$$

This tells us that for every £1 of sales 60% (60p) is the contribution margin towards fixed costs and profits. This can be used to calculate the breakeven point as follows:

$$\text{Breakeven point} = \frac{\text{Fixed costs}}{\text{C/S ratio}}$$

$$\text{Oriental Delight BEP} = \frac{£120,000}{0.60\,(60\%)} = £200,000$$

If this is compared to the previous calculations that were in units of sales the relationship between the two calculations is clear. It was previously calculated that Oriental Delight need to sell 20,000 units to breakeven, selling at £10 each 20,000 * £10 = £200,000, the same result as when using the C/S ratio above. This proves both ways of calculating breakeven (per unit, or contribution to sales ratio) give the same answer. Just as before, a desired profit can be added to fixed costs, or a subsidy deducted when calculating the BEP using this alternative formula.

4.3.2 Margin of safety

The margin of safety (MoS) is used to determine how 'safe' the business is in relation to changes in sales volume. In the example of Oriental Delight it was identified that they had to sell 20,000 units just to break even. For a specific month, Oriental Delight estimated their sales to be 25,000, given they will make a loss if the number goes below 20,000 how safe is the business? The margin of safety represents the difference between the breakeven point and the estimated sales. It can be calculated in units, £ of revenue or as a %margin of safety, in units =

Estimated sales – breakeven sales = 25,000 – 20,000 = 5,000 units

Margin of safety, in £ revenue = est'd sales revenue – breakeven sales revenue

= 250,000 – 200,000 = £50,000 sales revenue

$$\text{Margin of safety \%} = \frac{\text{Estimated sales – breakeven sales}}{\text{Estimated sales}} *100$$

N.B. Sales can be expressed in units or £s

$$\frac{25,000 - 20,000}{25,000} *100 = 20\% \quad \text{(estimated sales in units)}$$

$$\frac{£250,000 - £200,000}{£250,000} *100 = 20\% \quad \text{(estimated sales in £s)}$$

Whether the calculation is in sales units or sales revenue, the answer is the same, 20% margin of safety. What does this tell the manager? It demonstrates that sales would have to decline by 20% before neither a profit nor a loss is made, i.e. the BEP is reached.

This tells the management that customers can drop by 5,000 before they do not make any profit. By using margin of safety managers can identify how risky a decision is. For example you are costing for a wedding and they currently estimate 80–120 guests (the relevant range), but will not know exact numbers for a couple of months. If you do the calculations and find you make a profit even on the lowest estimate you will be a lot happier than if you find out your BEP is at 100 wedding guests – if this was the case you may not accept the booking, viewing it as too risky, or you may set a minimum chargeable number for the event. This could mean a contract for a set price, requiring payment for a minimum of 110 guests for example. This way you have identified the financial risk and tried to protect against it. The importance here is that CVP analysis gives you valuable information to support your decision, particularly in 'What if?' scenarios, so the decision becomes more informed and less of an educated guess. These ideas are further developed later in this chapter, in Chapter 6 on pricing and in Chapter 10 on events accounting.

4.3.3 Graphical representations of CVP

In the above section, formulae have been used to calculate BEP and MoS, but these can be represented graphically and answers read off the charts (see Figure 4.1). The classic breakeven chart identifies sales, costs, BEP, plus profit and loss.

The breakeven chart in Figure 4.1 shows the information related to Oriental Delight Restaurant, as already calculated. The point where the sales revenue and total costs line cross is the breakeven point, where neither a profit nor a loss is made. Reading from the chart the BEP is at 20,000 volume of activity (units) on the X axis and £200,000 of revenue on the Y axis – this corresponds to the answers calculated using the formulae earlier in the chapter. Up until the breakeven point a loss is made, when nothing is sold the loss is equal to the total fixed costs, each time 1 sale is made £6 contribution goes towards covering the fixed costs, so each sale that is made closes the gap between the total cost line and the sales line, until they cross (BEP) and no loss is made. After the BEP is reached all fixed costs are covered, so the £6 contribution goes direct towards profits – the chart shows the revenue coming in from sales is more than the total costs, the difference equals the profit. The triangle between the fixed cost line and the total cost line represents the total variable costs at any given level of sales – at 0 sales it is £0, at 20,000 sales it is £80,000 (20,000 * £4) and this can be read off the chart.

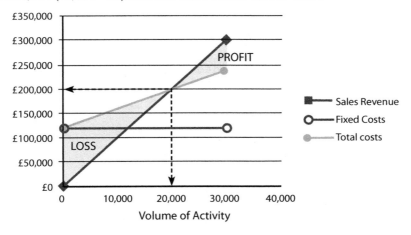

Figure 4.1: Oriental Delight breakeven chart

Such a chart gives managers an overall visual representation of the relationship between cost, volume and profit for the business.

Identifying margin of safety is also possible on a breakeven chart (Figure 4.2) – the difference between expected sales and BEP in sales, in this case the difference between 20,000 and 25,000.

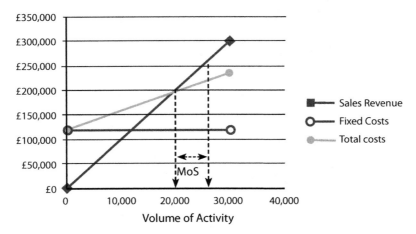

Figure 4.2: Oriental Delight MoS

An alternative to the traditional breakeven chart is called a contribution chart (see Figure 4.3). The main advantage of this is that the total contribution is visible on the chart and it is argue to be more representative in that it shows sales revenue first goes towards covering variable costs and what is left, contribution, first goes towards covering fixed costs and once these are covered is a contribution to profit.

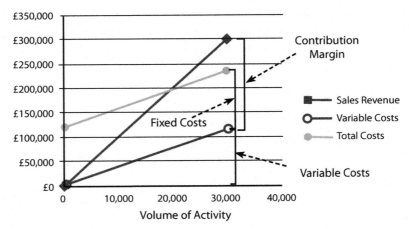

Figure 4.3: Oriental Delight contribution chart

From Figure 4.3 it can still be seen that when no sales are made the total costs equal fixed costs. However, the representation of when revenue starts coming in that it first pays towards variable costs, then fixed costs and lastly profit is more easily represented. On the breakeven chart and the contribution chart the total sales line and total cost lines are exactly the same, what changes is whether the fixed costs or variable costs are represented by a line on the chart.

Another chart that can be useful is a profit/volume chart (P/V chart – Figure 4.4), this chart is simpler than the previous charts in that it shows the clear relationship between activity (units sold) and the profit generated. Using the previous data this can be shown in a P/V chart.

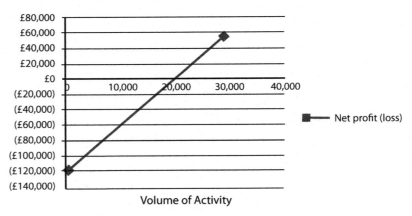

Figure 4.4: Oriental Delight profit/volume chart

Looking back at the previous calculations it is clear to see how this data is derived. If 30,000 units (meals) are sold a profit of £60,000 is generated, if no units are sold there are still £120,000 of fixed costs to cover, so a loss of –£120,000 is made. The point where neither a profit nor a loss is made is when the chart is at £0, this is at 20,000 units and represents the BEP, as previously calculated and shown on the earlier charts. To read the chart either axis can be used, depending on the purpose. For example; how many sales are needed to generate a profit of £60,000? On the Y axis find the profit level of £60,000 and read off the volume required at that point = 30,000 units. Alternatively you could ask; if I sold 25,000 units how much profit do I make? On the X axis identify 25,000 units of activity and read off the profit generated = £30,000 profit.

Charts provide a good visual representation of the data and a good overview. However, their accuracy relies on how accurately they are drawn and the scale used to read off data accurately. The calculation method can give a more accurate answer to a specific question, but obviously each new question requires a new calculation to answer it. Therefore both methods have their place and often they are used together. Later in the chapter both are used together in a spreadsheet, where the chart is directly linked to the data, so as you make changes to the data in 'What if?' scenarios the chart automatically updates as well.

4.3.4 Impact of cost structure

The last chapter discussed 'operational gearing' and this can be illustrated diagrammatically (Figures 4.5 and 4.6).

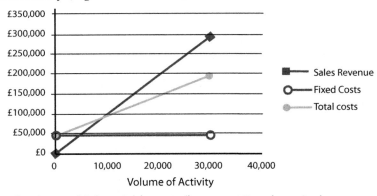

Figure 4.5: Low fixed costs, high variable costs (low operational gearing)

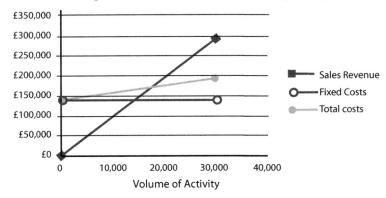

Figure 4.6: High fixed costs, low variable costs (high operational gearing)

You can clearly see the difference between these two situations. In the low-geared example initial losses are lower, but once breakeven is reached it is still slow to generate profits, only a small contribution per unit sold. In contrast, with high fixed costs the loss is more dramatic at lower levels of activity, but given the lower variable costs as soon as the breakeven point is reached profit per unit is far more dramatic. The impact on this is discussed in Chapter 6, specifically related to 'price discrimination'.

4.3.5   Underlying assumption in CVP analysis

It has been demonstrated how CVP analysis can aid planning and decision making, but CVP does make a number of assumptions and it is important managers are aware of these when using the technique. If these assumptions are not considered then serious errors of judgement may be made, resulting in the incorrect conclusions being drawn from the analysis. These assumptions include:

- Revenue and cost behaviour are linear, i.e. are straight lines on the chart
- All variables, other than those under consideration remain constant, such as
  - Selling price per unit will not change
  - Variable costs vary in direct proportion to sales
  - Fixed costs remain constant
- Cost prices remain constant, e.g. food costs and staff wage rates
- Productivity remains unchanged
- Methods of production and service remain unchanged
- It covers a single product, or if multiple products (menu items) the sales mix remains unchanged.
- All costs can be segregated into their fixed and variable components.
- Revenue and costs are related to a single independent variable, which is level of activity (units sold); and
- Volume of activity is the only relevant variable that determines cost behaviour.

This doesn't mean CVP is worthless, but that in using it for decision-making purposes the assumptions have to be reviewed related to the specific organisation circumstances. A more detailed explanation of some of these assumptions follows.

4.3.5.1   Economist's versus accountant's CVP model

Economists would view the use of straight lines for sales revenue and total costs to be inaccurate as they would not see them in such a perfect linear relationship. The economic view point would be, as sales volume increases the unit selling price has to decrease in order to encourage the additional sales to take place – as the selling price decreases the volume of sales increase. The economic view point would also consider purchasing economies of scale. If an organisation buys 2,000 units of a product to sell on (for example bottles of beer) the unit price would be higher than if they were buying 200,000 units – the higher the volume purchased the better the negotiating position on unit price. From an economic perspective, and if looking at the full activity volume range, these arguments are valid. In CVP analysis however, from an accounting perspective, we are only looking at the relevant range. It is therefore argued that within this range the accounting view is representative and appropriate for use. There is also an argument that the benefits which might be gained from the economist's view are outgained by the costs involved – for the accountant's, simple means better in this respect.

4.3.5.2 Sales mix

As previously mentioned, examples of CVP often refer to a singular product, but this can work with multiple products by the use of a C/S ratio, but in doing so this assumes the ratio is constant and this is not always the case. The balance of sales between different products, which generate different contributions, can impact on a calculated C/S ratio. Table 4.2 illustrates this with a simple menu.

Table 4.2: Balance of sales in a simple menu

Menu item	Selling price £	Contribution margin %	Sales volume in units	Contribution £
A	10	70	100	700
B	10	60	90	540
C	10	65	80	520
D	10	65	80	520
E	10	75	100	750
F	10	65	90	585
Average	10		540	3,615
Sales revenue	5,400			
C/S ratio	67%			

In this example there are 6 menu choices and they all have a selling price of £10, due to varying food costs (variable costs) between dishes, they have different contribution margins. The range of contribution margins is from 60–75%. From this information and knowing the expected volume of sales for each dish a weighted average C/S ratio can be calculated.

Menu item A:

selling price £10 @ 70% contribution = £7 contribution (£10 * 70%)

If we sell 100 the contribution is £7 * 100 = £700. If we do that for all 6 items (A–F) the total contribution can be calculated to be £3,615.

C/S ratio = £3,615/£5400, which equals 67%. However if the volume of sales by dish changes, even if total sales volume and price remain constant, the C/S ratio can change.

Table 4.3

Menu item	Selling price £	Contribution margin %	Sales volume in units	Contribution £
A	10	70	80	560
B	10	60	120	720
C	10	65	110	715
D	10	65	80	520
E	10	75	60	450
F	10	65	90	585
Average	10		540	3,550
Sales revenue	5,400			
C/S ratio	66%			

In Table 4.3, the sales revenue is the same, as is the selling price and the total units sold. What has changed is the sales mix – the volume of each dish sold. As there are less sales of higher contribution items and more sales of lower contribution items the overall C/S ratio has declined from 67% to 66%. This illustrates that the assumption of a 'fixed' C/S ratio in CVP analysis is a weakness that managers need to recognise.

4.3.5.3   Volume of activity as the only relevant variable

There are other factors, beyond volume of activity, which impact on revenues and costs, such as:

- Quality of management and staff
- Working methods
- The economic situation
- Staff training; and
- The weather.

In the illustration above it could simply be a hot day and more people ordering the salad than a hot stew due to the weather, and your assumptions are flawed. These considerations are difficult to quantify, therefore the extent of their influence is difficult to measure and they do not form part of the CVP analysis, but managers need to be aware of what CVP doesn't show them as much as understanding its usefulness as a planning and decision making tool.

4.4   CVP in an industry context

The nature of costs and how the proportion of fixed and variable costs varies by industry and industry sector is an important consideration when using CVP. The previous chapter discussed specific sectors having relatively high or low fixed costs. In pure service provision, where there is no 'product' element sold to the customer-variable costs are minimal, or for practical purposes viewed as non-existent. Where a sale is a pure retail product, with minimal service there will usually be clearly definable variable costs. Within hospitality, tourism and events there is quite often a mix of a product and service, to some degree. Classification in specific sectors, such as room sales, food and beverage sales, event ticket sales can all be seen to have different proportions of fixed and variable costs and this can be an influence on management accounting approaches that are suitable for use. At the extremes, if all costs are fixed, or all costs are variable then it is impossible to use CVP analysis.

Later in this text contribution margin and its impact are further explored in relation to yield management, revenue management, contribution pricing decisions and customer profitability analysis – all these have a relationship to cost structures and the importance of contribution.

4.5   Computerised 'What if?' analysis

This chapter has explored CVP and its use in decision making. It is an extremely useful tool in planning and is an aid to managers when looking at alternative scenarios and the impact these could have on the business. One issue is that it can be time consuming – each time a new alternative is posed a new calculation is needed and doing this manually takes time. Using the example previously used in this chapter the following could be questions to ask:

- How much profit will I make if I sell 23,000 units?

- What would be the impact on profits if I increased the selling price to £11?

However time can be saved by putting the initial contribution profit margin statement on to a spreadsheet and using the power of the spreadsheet to do the calculations. The rapid computation of results is instantaneous, so every time a number is changed all the other data is automatically updated. Using the example of changing the selling price on a computer you could see the CVP analysis changes of altering the price 10 times in a minute, calculating manually 1 change could take 10 minutes. Thus the computer doesn't do anything that couldn't be done manually, but it saves time and allows managers to consider far more alternative options in a short space of time. So the use of a spreadsheet:

- Allows rapid computation

- Gives instant feedback

- Provides flexibility as data can be moved after initial entry

- Alternative document forms – viewed on screen, emailed, web uploaded, network file sharing, printed, numerically and/or graphically displayed results, and the ability to automatically produce summary data; and

- Formula presentation – as well as showing the results the formulae used to generate the results can be displayed and printed, 'audit' functions can also identify the relationships between cells visually on screen to assist managers.

It is very easy to prepare a simple spreadsheet for the writer to use themselves, but in a business environment it needs to be recognised that staff change, even if they do not, the initial spreadsheet designer may not be the only user of the spreadsheet, or the person who enters or updates the information. Due to this, more care and attention needs to be given when designing professional spreadsheets, beyond the considerations an individual might give in using a personal spreadsheet at home.

4.5.1   Formal approach to spreadsheet design

In a work environment it is important that spreadsheet design principles are followed to reduce the possibilities of errors. It will also ensure a logical layout and sound data presentation needed in a professional environment. A real-life example of poor spreadsheet design was a restaurant manager using a spreadsheet and not understanding why he wasn't making a profit only to realise a few days later, due to a formula error, all the staffing costs were being deducted from the revenue twice. Every time he spent £1 on staff the spreadsheet deducted £2, so the profit was much lower than in reality.

4.5.1.1   Spreadsheet design guidelines

There are number of basic aspects that if followed can avoid errors.

1 **Prepare an initial spreadsheet design on paper.** It is very tempting just to start on the top-left of a spreadsheet, just like a sheet of paper when writing, however there needs to be a focus on the 'output' you want, not just starting with the first thing in cell A1. The other thing to consider with spreadsheets is they are often three-dimensional, so as well as going across or down a page you can use different 'sheets' within a workbook file. You may want to put input data on one sheet, full output results on another sheet and have a third sheet for summary files. Equally you may want charts and graphs next to data tables, or for them to appear separately on further workbook sheets. Sketching out the design on paper first can greatly save time in the design process.

2 **Identify separate 'input' and 'output' areas of the spreadsheet.** An input is a 'decision variable' – a piece of information you are inputting into the computer. The computer cannot calculate it, it needs to be told the value, plus it is something that could change and may need adjusting in the future. An 'output' is something you want the computer to report as an outcome. In the output section no numerical data is entered directly, all will be cell referenced, or formulae calculated within the spreadsheet. Why keep these two aspects (inputs and outputs) separate? First, it makes the spreadsheet easier to navigate for different users; the person entering data knows all the entries to be made will be in the input screen, whilst a manager want to just review the summary outputs can go direct to that section. Second, it avoids formulae being overwritten or deleted in error – output areas of the file can be 'cell protected' which means only those with the correct authorisation and password can amend those cells.

3 **Enter a decision variable only once.** By ensuring each numerical input is only directly entered once is important. If entering the selling price is £10, if this information is needed anywhere else on the spreadsheet the initial entry should be 'cell referenced'. For example in cell C3 the entry of £10 is made, if this information is needed elsewhere in the spreadsheet cell reference 'C3 should be put in the cell'. That way if the price is changed to £12 only the original cell (C3) needs to change and all other references to it and calculations will automatically change to £12.

4 **Never include a decision variable in a formula.** Formula should only ever include cell reference to numerical data; numerical data never gets added direct into a formula. As an example, if you are trying to calculate the total sales revenue and know the volume sold is 5,000 and the selling price is £10 you should never use the formula '=5,000*£10' as if either of those inputs change the changes wouldn't automatically update in the spreadsheet. If the price is shown in cell C3 and the volume in cell C4 the formula to enter would be '=C3*C4' this means anytime the entry data changes the output will automatically update at the same time.

5 **Include a summary output screen.** Particularly in large spreadsheets, the ability to view the key outputs is helpful to the user.

6 **Incorporate instructions, as needed.** Textbox notes can be added to the spreadsheet to advise and guide users of its operations – the do's and don'ts.

7 **Test the spreadsheet for proper functioning.** This is an important part of designing a spreadsheet. Change selected decisions inputs and review the results in the outputs – all may look fine initially, but entering negative numbers, or certain values may highlight specific issues to be resolved before formal implementation.

4.5.1.2 Spreadsheet design example

Oriental Delight Restaurant has been considering changing its price, as food costs have increased from £4 per unit to £4.50. At the price of £10 they estimated 25,000 customers per month, however if they increase the price they believe customers numbers could decline to 23,500, fixed costs remain at £120,000 – should they change the price? The basic numerical information above is the input data – the decision variables the computer cannot calculate (Table 4.4).

Table 4.4: Input data

INPUT DATA	Current situation	Option 1	Option 2
Selling price	£10	£10	£11
Variable costs	£4.00	£4.50	£4.50
Fixed costs	£120,000	£120,000	£120,000
Units sold	25,000	25,000	23,500

The input area of the spreadsheet will look like this – this includes all the data needed to produce a contribution margin profit statement. Following the manual calculations earlier in this chapter, formulae can be entered into the output screen to do these calculations (Figure 4.7).

Figure 4.7

	A	B	C	D
1	INPUT DATA	Current situation	Option 1	Option 2
2	Selling price	£10	£10	£11
3	Variable costs	£4	£4.5	£4.5
4	Fixed costs	£120000	£120000	£120000
5	Units sold	25000	25000	23500
8	OUTPUT FORMULA			
9	Per unit:			
10	Selling price	=B3	=C3	=D3
11	Variable costs	=B4	=C4	=D4
12	Contribution per unit	=B10-B11	=C10-C11	=D10-D11
13				
14	Total values:			
15	Sales revenue	=B3*B6	=C3*C6	=D3*D6
16	Variable costs	=B4*B6	=C4*C6	=D4*D6
17	Contribution margin	=B15-B16	=C15-C16	=D15-D16
18	Fixed costs	=B5	=C5	=D5
19	Profit	=B17-B18	=C17-C18	=D17-D18

This format shows the formulae entered into the specific cells, usually on the screen you will see the answer, not this information

8	OUTPUT RESULTS			
9	Per unit:			
10	Selling price	£10.00	£10.00	£11.00
11	Variable costs	£4.00	£4.50	£4.50
12	Contribution per unit	£6.00	£5.50	£6.50
13				
14	Total values:			
15	Sales revenue	£250,000	£250,000	£258,500
16	Variable costs	£100,000	£112,500	£105,750
17	Contribution margin	£150,000	£137,500	£152,750
18	Fixed costs	£120,000	£120,000	£120,000
19	Profit	£30,000	£17,500	£32,750

This format shows the data that will appear into the specific cells, when the formulae are entered

The computer allows you to copy formulae from one cell to another, so if you have written the formula for 'Current situation' you can copy it over to the next two columns and do not have to type it in again. Effectively this means you can complete three sets of calculations, just as quickly as one.

What do the results show? They show that currently they make a profit of £30,000. If they chose to just absorb the increased food prices whilst they will still have 25,000 customers the contribution will go down by 50p per customer. The net impact of this is a drop in contribution margin of £12,500, so profit reduces from £30,000 to £17,500. The alternative is to increase the selling price, but this leads to a drop in customers. The results show that the increase in price more than compensates for the drop in customer numbers and alongside the increased contribution per unit leads to an increased profit – going up from £30,000 to £32,750.

Assuming these predictions are accurate the best option for the business would be to increase the price, as shown in Option 2 on the spreadsheet. Of course multiple options could be entered for price and demand to generate further options to consider. Or further CVP calculations could be completed for these options.

You could add the BEP and MoS information to the spreadsheet, as shown below.

BEP	=B18/B12	=C18/C12	=D18/D12
MoS in units	=B6-B21	=C6-C21	=D6-D21
MoS %	=B22/B6	=C22/C6	=D22/D6

BEP	20000	21818	18462
MoS in units	5,000	3,182	5,038
MoS %	20%	13%	21%

This gives more information to support the decision, both in terms of BEP and the risk level from the MoS. It is clear to see how the change in contribution per unit has had an impact on the BEP of the options.

If managers wanted to see this graphically a 'X-Y Scattergraph' can be drawn in the spreadsheet linked to the data. To draw a graph the computer needs 2 points of data, the values at 0 sales and the unit sales value in the option. The computer also needs total costs to draw a total costs line (Figures 4.8 and 4.9).

The graphs can be compared to show a visual representation of the different breakeven points and the varying proportion of variables costs between the two options.

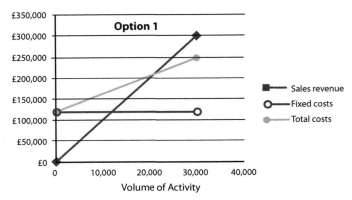

Figure 4.8: Option 1

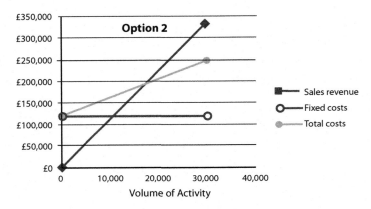

Figure 4.9: Option 2

4.5.2   Additional spreadsheet functions to aid CVP analysis

The above examples use basic spreadsheet functions, over the years spreadsheet software has developed and become more sophisticated. The benefits of 'What if?' analysis is now recognised with dedicated functions in this area that can perform even more powerful analysis. Search for this phrase in a spreadsheet to find the functions available. These allow you to experiment with many different values to aid decision making. The following are examples of some that exist and how they can aid decision making.

4.5.2.1   Scenario manager

In the example above the current situation and options were all shown next to each other. Scenario manager allows you to set up one set of data values in the sheet, for example the current situation and then use this function to substitute alternative data values. This is a quick way of doing the same as in the earlier example. Each option can be shown one at a time on screen, or a summary can be produced showing all the options (Figure 4.10).

4.5.2.2 Goal seek

This is a way of working backwards in your formula, so the computer can tell you the value of the input cell. Looking at the previous example you could work backwards and ask the computer – in order to still achieve £30,000 profit (the goal), given the increased variable costs, what would the selling price need to be. It only looks at one variable at a time, but is a very powerful tool.

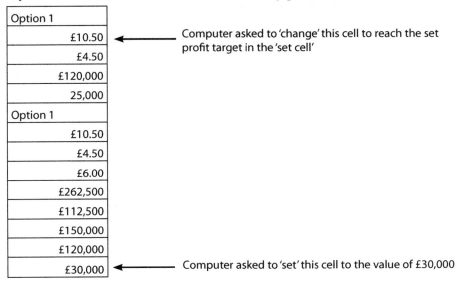

Option 1	
	£10.50
	£4.50
	£120,000
	25,000

Computer asked to 'change' this cell to reach the set profit target in the 'set cell'

Option 1	
	£10.50
	£4.50
	£6.00
	£262,500
	£112,500
	£150,000
	£120,000
	£30,000

Computer asked to 'set' this cell to the value of £30,000

Figure 4.10: Using goal seek to work backwards from desired result.

4.5.2.3 Data table

A data table can give you various 'outputs' for a cell, given different 'input' values for a different cell. Using a similar example to the goal seek in Figure 4.10, the computer can be asked to tell you the profit generated by changes to the selling price, assuming all else remains equal (Figure 4.11).

Selling Price	
£8.00	–£32,500
£8.50	–£20,000
£9.00	–£7,500
£9.50	£5,000
£10.00	£17,500
£10.50	£30,000
£11.00	£42,500
£11.50	£55,000

Figure 4.11: The data table shows, given the value of the cell for 'Selling Price' in option 1, what loss or profit would be generated – this assumes no impact on customer volume.

There are many options that can be used here, any combination of an input cell and an output cell can be interrogated with the goal seek or data table functions illustrated above.

From these examples it can be seen how spreadsheets can add much power to CVP analysis and aid the decision making process.

Summary of key points

CVP analysis is a tool to aid managers in considering the relationship between costs, volume of activity (sales) and the profit. It aids understanding the impact on profit of fixed and variable costs. This can aid managers in the planning phase looking at alternative scenarios, or 'What if?' situations. This is further aided by the use of computer spreadsheets. The key points from this chapter are:

■ CVP is a useful management planning tool.

■ CVP aids the understanding of the relationship of costs to sales volume and profits.

■ Within a service situation with high fixed costs it can aid planning and help in marginal pricing decisions.

■ Computer spreadsheets offer a variety of tools that aid CVP analysis.

■ Specific functions in spreadsheets further support 'what if?' scenario planning.

Further reading

Given the practical nature of this chapter there is no specific referencing.

CVP is covered in most generic management accounting textbook, though not with industry applied examples, but any such text will discuss the general principles and aid understanding of this subject.

For further reading related to use of spreadsheets see Chapter 15, Using Computer spreadsheets, (written by Jones, T,) in Harris, P (2010) *Profit Planning for hospitality and tourism*, Goodfellow Publishers Ltd.

Self-check student questions

1 Define these key CVP terms: breakeven point, contribution margin, margin of safety.

2 How can CVP analysis aid business planning?

3 White Weddings has to decide whether to accept a contract to run a wedding. They want to make £2,000 profit and the fixed costs are £4,000. The contribution per guest (sale) after variable costs is £25. How many guests would there need

to be in order for them to achieve their required profit from the event?

4   Explain the importance of the margin of safety in decision making.

5   What are the lines drawn on a breakeven chart?

6   Explain what a profit/volume chart shows you.

7   What are the underlying assumptions of CVP analysis?

8   Describe the phases in the design of a computer spreadsheet.

Further questions and problems

1   Given the following data for Day Tours, calculate:

2   The breakeven point

3   Number of sales needed to make £5,000 profit

4   The margin of safety

5   Draw a breakeven chart from this data.

	Day tours
Selling price	£12
Variable costs	£5.00
Fixed costs	£130,000
Units sold	25,000

6   Using the following extended data from question 1, consider the three alternatives using CVP. Prepare your answer by designing a computer spreadsheet to model the data.

DAY TOURS	Option 1	Option 2	Option 3
Selling price	£12	£12.50	£13
Variable costs	£5.00	£5.50	£6.00
Fixed costs	£130,000	£130,000	£130,000
Units sold	25,000	25,000	23,500

5 Short-term Decision Making

5.1 Introduction and objectives

Previous chapters have focused on the nature of costs and how they behave in relation to changes in activity and over time. The nature of costs is an important factor to consider in decision making. Types of decisions are usually split into short and long-term. Chapter 14 (Capital Investment Appraisal) considers the longer-term decision-making process, whilst this chapter focuses on the short-term.

After studying this chapter you will be able to:

■ Understand costs that are relevant to the decision-making process in different circumstances

■ Demonstrate working knowledge of typical short-term decisions managers have to make and how financial data can support these decisions

■ Recognise the issues of managing scarce recourses in decision making; and

■ Appreciate the implications of outsourcing in a business context.

5.2 Relevant costs in decision making

Relevant costing is a management accounting term and relates to focusing on only the costs relevant to a specific decision being made. It simplifies the decision-making process as it ignores cost data that is 'irrelevant', or will not have an impact on the specific decision being made. When making a particular decision-relevant costs are those that may change, depending on the decision taken.

Relevant costing is often used in short-term decision making and a number of specific practical examples are illustrated later in this chapter. A typical decision could involve, a venue has been hired for a commercial event to take place in two weeks' time, unfortunately ticket sales have been very slow and it looks as though the event will be run at a loss. The manager of the events company needs to make the decision: 'Should the event be cancelled or not?' from a financial perspective he would need to look at the 'relevant' costs to see which costs would be 'relevant' to his decision (Table 5.1). What would these be?

Table 5.1: Example relevant costs for an event

Venue hirer costs	Irrelevant – already paid in full, with a 100% charge if cancelled
Printing tickets	Irrelevant – tickets already printed and cannot be reused
Performing artists' fees	Irrelevant – already paid in full, with a 100% charge if cancelled
Permanent event company staff salaries	Irrelevant – they have to be paid even if the event doesn't run
Casual staff employed for the event	Relevant – if the event is cancelled these won't have to be paid
Food and beverage material costs	Relevant – the food hasn't been ordered as yet, if the event is cancelled there are no F&B costs
Merchandising costs	Irrelevant – programmes and tee shirts already printed
Event publicity costs, flyers and posters	Irrelevant – already printed and distributed

5

For this specific decision the balance is:

- Decision A – the event goes ahead – if it does there is some income, but all the 'relevant' costs will be incurred.

- Decision B – the event is cancelled – in this situation the 'relevant' costs would not be incurred, but refunds would need to be issued (another cost) and there would be no income.

When using relevant costing in this example it is already accepted this event will not make a profit, the decision is about which option, running the event, or cancelling will make the least loss. It is a decision about mitigating losses. Irrelevant costs are still incurred by the events company, but the key point here is that they do not impact on the specific decision being made – whether it is decision A or B, all irrelevant costs will still be incurred, so they are ignored in relation to the specific decision.

5.3 Opportunity costs

These are decisions that are made where they are mutually exclusive alternatives. Imagine two potential customers (Jones and Smith) want to book your conference suite for a wedding at the same day and time. You only have the capacity to take one wedding on a specific day and both have confirmed dates that cannot be moved. From a financial perspective you would accept the booking that would give you the best financial return, maximises the contribution from the event, in this case accept the booking for Mr and Mrs Jones.

The opportunity cost is the value of the 'opportunity' lost for the next best alternative in making a specific decision. In this case the opportunity cost is the potential contribution from Mr and Mrs Smith's booking that has been lost through taking Mr and Mrs Jones' booking. Opportunity costs need to be considered when making decisions, particularly where there is a 'scarce' resource (in this case physical space). Whether the 'scarce' resource is physical space/capacity, a raw material/ingredient, or staff availability it restricts a manager's ability in some way to meet all customer needs. In such situations managers have to make decisions about how best to use their scarce resources, and what they cannot do, will be an opportunity lost and therefore an opportunity cost.

5.4   Differences between short-term and long-term decisions

The obvious difference between short-term and long-term decision making is the timeframe involved. In reality they have different purposes in the organisation, but both are important to maximising returns for the organisation (see Table 5.2).

Table 5.2

Short-term decisions	Long-term decisions
Operational, tactical in nature, meeting short-term goals, or reacting to a crisis, i.e. making the best of resources in the short term	Strategic in nature, impact on corporate level objectives and goals i.e. making the best of resources in the long term
Each decision involves relatively small amounts of monetary value	Each decision can involve large sums of monetary value
Relatively easy to change decision, withdraw from activity if the business environment changes	Making wrong decisions can have a major financial impact on the firm

All decision making is concerned with making the best choices for the organisation, in financial decision making this is about the financial impact of the decisions made. Later chapters discuss the decision making process and the relationship to information needs in more detail, and Chapter 14 on capital investment appraisal focuses on the long-term decision-making process.

Decision making costs money; management time is a basic cost, but long-term decisions can be very expensive to make. Decisions with multimillion pounds being invested may take several months, feasibility studies, information costs, etc. In short-term decision making speed is of the essence, both to keep costs to a minimum and because delaying a decision (slow reaction) could have financial implications for the organisation.

5.5   Types of short-term decisions

Short-term decisions could include whether to resolve staff shortages by using agency staff, to make something in-house or buy it in, to offer special packages/reduce prices to boost short-term sales or to accept a booking/one-off contract.

Within short-term decision making the understanding of relevant costs, and opportunity cost is important. The use of contribution margin and CVP analysis are also useful tools in short-term decision making.

5.5.1 Example: make or buy decision

At the moment the kitchen of Island Resorts Hotel makes its own bread for all its restaurants and for use in its many conference and banqueting venues. This amounts to an average production of 30,000 bread rolls a week. They have been approached by an industrial baker who can guarantee supply, as needed, on a daily basis and will charge 15 cents ($0.15) per roll.

The current costs of making rolls per week are as follows:

Island Resorts Hotel

Variable material cost	$1,800
Variable labour	$1,200
Fixed costs avoided if not making	$1,300

If not producing the bread rolls the 'relevant' costs are that the variable costs would no longer exist. When looking at the fixed costs, the specialist bread oven leasing and maintenance contract could be avoided, so these costs are relevant to the decision. Other fixed costs will still be incurred, so these are irrelevant to the decision-making process (Table 5.3).

Table 5.3: The make or buy decision, at 30,000 rolls

Island Resorts Hotel	MAKE	BUY
Bread rolls	30,000	30,000
Purchase price		$0.15
Variable material cost	$1,800	
Variable labour	$1,200	
Fixed costs avoided if not making	$1,300	
Total relevant costs	**$4,300**	**$4,500**

When comparing the data it shows that, considering all relevant costs it is still more cost-effective to make bread rolls than to buy them in by $200 ($4,300 – $4,500). With this data the management could make the informed financial decision to continue to make their own rolls.

If the situation was different and they only needed on average 24,000 bread rolls a week the decision may be very different (Table 5.4). When the data is compared now it would financial be a better decision to buy the rolls. The difference ($3,940 – $3,600) means it is $340 cheaper to buy in than to make yourself. On a purely financial basis you would decide to buy in, however you may also consider other 'non-financial' information in making the decision, such as the customer (market) expectation of having homemade bread as an example, or the quality of the rolls.

Table 5.4: The make or buy decision, at 30,000 rolls

Island Resorts Hotel	MAKE	BUY
Bread rolls	24,000	24,000
Purchase price		$0.15
Variable material cost	$1,440	
Variable labour	$1,200	
Fixed costs that can be avoided if not making	$1,300	
Total relevant costs	$3,940	$3,600

5.5.2   Example: decision to cease tour destination

A small tour operator (Peace Yoga Retreats) currently runs specialist overseas yoga retreats to three destinations. The head office has reviewed the information and is considering ceasing its Indian tour operations.

The information they have is as shown in Table 5.5:

Table 5.5: Peace Yoga Retreats, revenue and costs

Peace Yoga Retreats	India	Portugal	Turkey	Totals	Notes
	£000s	£000s	£000s	£000s	
Revenue	400	700	500	1600	An all-inclusive price covering plane, transfers, accommodation, full board, local representative and yoga teacher
Variable transport costs	80	35	75	190	Includes plane and transfers per person
Variable hospitality costs	200	420	225	845	Includes resort accommodation and meal costs
Fixed resort cost	30	40	35	105	Local representative and yoga teacher
Fixed head office costs	100	100	100	300	Fixed HO costs shared by 3 locations
Total costs	410	595	435	1440	
Operating profit/ loss by location	–10	105	65	160	

When looking at this information, at first it seems they are losing money on their Indian operation, as it shows an operating loss of –£10,000. If they simply closed the Indian operation the figures for Peace Yoga Retreats would change as shown in Table 5.6.

Comparing the two sets of data the managers are shocked that when they closed the 'loss-making' operation the profits at the other two locations have decreased and the total company operating profit has fallen from £160,000 to £70,000.

What was wrong with their decision making?

Table 5.6: Peace Yoga Retreats, revised revenue and costs projection

Peace Yoga Retreats	Portugal	Turkey	Totals	Notes
	£000s	£000s	£000s	
Revenue	700	500	1200	All-inclusive price
Variable transport costs	35	75	110	Includes plane and transfers per person
Variable hospitality costs	420	225	645	Includes resort accommodation and meals
Fixed resort cost	40	35	75	Local representative and yoga teacher
Fixed head office costs	150	150	300	Fixed HO costs shared by 2 locations
Total costs	645	485	1130	
Operating profit by location	55	15	70	Profit is much lower without operations in India

They have looked at the total cost, not just the relevant costs to the decision. The Head Office costs of £300,000 have to be paid whether their yoga retreat operates in India or not. Relevant to this decision is the loss of revenue from India and the cost saving of operating in India. If the original data was amended to only show the relevant costs for each location the amended data would be as shown in Table 5.7.

Table 5.7: Peace Yoga Retreats, costs assigned by relevance

Peace Yoga Retreats	India	Portugal	Turkey	Totals	Notes
	£000s	£000s	£000s	£000s	
Revenue	400	700	500	1600	All-inclusive price
Variable transport costs	80	35	75	190	Includes plane and transfers per person
Variable hospitality costs	200	420	225	845	Includes resort accommodation and meal costs
Fixed resort cost	30	40	35	105	Local representative and yoga teacher
Fixed head office costs				300	Not a location operating cost
Total costs	310	495	335	1440	
Operating profit by location	90	205	165	160	All locations make a positive input to company profits

Taking only the relevant costs into account, the data, and the decision, would be very different. This shows the revenue from India, less the costs associated with the Indian operation make a £90,000 input into the company as a whole. It is the arbitrary allocation of head office costs to locations in the first statement that confused the managers in making the decision.

This example highlights the importance of using only relevant costs in short-term decision making and of using management accounting information in the decision-making progress. It also clearly identifies the importance of looking at the 'correct' (relevant) costs that are related to the specific decision only.

5.6   Long-term implications of short-term decisions

Long-term impacts of short-term decisions may sound like a contradiction in terms, but this needs to be considered. Heavy discounting may financially maximise returns in the short term, but can have long-term impacts that are detrimental to the business. An example of this is short-term price slashing that may increase customer volume in the short term, but long term can impact on buyer behaviour leading to the lower (slashed) prices becoming the norm. Long term this could reduce financial returns.

5.6.1   Example: ducks, dogs and teddy bears

This an old but real hotel-based example, back in the early 1990s, recession was hitting some hotels and discounting room rates (selling price) to increase occupancy rates (sales volume) became the norm in the 4* hotel market. In order to still make a profit with the reduced rates hotels focused on cost control, reducing costs given the reduced selling prices.

Some hoteliers were rightly concerned that once rates had been reduced to meet today's short-term profit needs it would be hard to push rates back up and still keep customers in the longer term (the long-term impact of the short-term decision). One hotel, to save costs, considered stopping their 'turndown service'. This is where housekeeping would go into rooms in the early evening and 'turndown' the side of the bed sheets ready for the night and place a mint on the pillow. As room cleaning takes place in the morning, staff were employed specifically for a couple of hours each night just to do this turndown. So the potential cost saving (relevant costs) to the decision were the saving in staff time and the cost of mints. Strategically they considered this and felt 'cutting corners' would impact on the quality of the customer experience. To position themselves in the market they wanted to maintain the level of service and not discount as heavily as other hotels, so following the recession their selling prices would be optimised.

What did they do? Replace the mints with teddy bears. A number of customers were business customers staying away on business, often leaving families at home. The turndown service continued, but teddy bears were placed on pillows in place of the chocolates. Each bear could be purchased for a mere £4.99 each – a great present to take home to the family from a business trip! Soon across the hotels teddy bears were being sold in the thousands. It actually reached the point where sales of teddy bears covered the cost of the turndown service! So whilst other hotels slashed selling prices and cut service to maintain profits the decision was made to compete by keeping a full service operation, but adjusting the service to make it more profitable.

Ducks and dogs? These were not quite the same as the introduction of teddy bears, but in hotels you may also find ducks and dogs in hotel rooms for sale.

Rubber ducks by the bath that you can buy to take home. One hotel, in place of 'Do Not Disturb' signs used toy dogs instead and these could also be purchased to take home. There is a saying 'Let sleeping dogs lie', if you didn't want to be disturbed you simply place the toy dog outside your room door.

This is a frivolous example, but clearly shows that when making short-term financial decisions there are other operational considerations and long-term implications that need to be considered.

5.7   Scarce resources

Scarce resources were mentioned earlier in the chapter in the discussion of opportunity costs. In generic management accounting literature the key focus of scarce resources relates to raw materials for making products. In a service environment, given the perishable nature of 'space' this can be important to consider in a similar way. There are only four Saturdays in June, the peak time for wedding bookings; the 'limiting factor' which will stops selling more weddings could easily be physical space in which to hold them. A short-term decision may be to erect marquees over the summer months to increase the scarce resource of space. A full cost–benefit analysis of the financial and market implications of this decision would need to be made.

Another example of a scarce resource important within service industries is staff. Over a number of years in a number of countries around the world, from UK to USA to Australia there have been reports identifying the scarcity of highly-trained skilled chefs. This is an example of a scarce resource in this sector where managers would need to look the financial data to review their options and the best use of resources. It may be they have to increase the staffing costs to increase the Head Chef salary to attract staff of the calibre required; employ agency staff at even higher cost; or 'de-skill' the menu so a less skilled chef can deliver it. This is an operational decision with many implications, but management accounting information can aid this decision-making process by identifying the financial implications of the alternatives.

If you type, 'Portaloo shortage London 2012' into any web search engine you will be amazed at the number of hits you will get. The demands due to the London 2012 Olympics, not just onsite, but around London and other venues associated with the Olympics created an unprecedented demand for temporary toilets. This is an example of the impact of a 'scarce resource', it has been referred to as, 'Great Olympian London Portaloo Shortage' and has been quoted by many as one of the key reasons for the Glastonbury music festival being cancelled in 2012. This has not just been in the national news, but reported internationally as a major issue. Business news pages reported this as an opportunity to set up new companies due to the demand. To identify something as basic as a portable toilet in running a 'green field' event as a scarce resource can have a major impact in decision making, as has been identified with Glastonbury 2012.

These examples identify the need for operations to consider the availability of resources, where scarcity is an issue, even if the issue is resolved it could be at a higher cost, so management accounting information is critical in review such issues. Limiting factors are discussed, with calculations by Drury (2012).

5.8   Uncertainty

The financial examples used in this chapter could imply that financial data is simple to identify and clear information always exists to aid decision making. Uncertainty is a consideration in the decision-making process and is usually viewed alongside risk in the decision making process. In the last chapter, when using CVP analysis, 'best', 'expected' and 'worse case' scenarios were suggested. This helps in making decisions where there are uncertainties, whether these relate to the market and sales or to costs. The probability of each outcome could be identified and added to this information to review the likely weighted outcome to make a more informed decision.

Attitude to risk is also part of decision making. Once you have the data, if it shows that the 'worse case' scenario is a loss of –£2,000 and there is a 20% chance of that happening, does the manager take the risk? A 'risk taker' may look at the data and see there is an 80% chance of making a profit and take the risk. A 'risk adverse' decision maker may look at the same data and decide if there is any chance of making a loss to not go ahead with the project. In Chapter 19 concerning not-for-profit organisations, the specific issue of being risk adverse due to public accountability in this sector is discussed in more detail. A charity does not want to run a fundraising event, only for it to make a loss, so can be more conservative in their decision making.

5.9   Outsourcing

Outsourcing is where an organisation 'outsources' specific jobs or activities to an outside firm to undertake on their behalf. This can be a strategic, long-term decision, or a short-term one. It is dealt with here as it is usually a cost-based decision, so income statement related, as opposed a high value asset based decision, as dealt with in the later long-term capital investment appraisal (CIA) chapter.

Outsourcing can cover numerous situations such as:

- Hiring a security company to supply event or site security staff
- Contracting out hotel window cleaning
- Hiring a cleaning services company
- An event company outsourcing food and beverage provision for an event, hiring caterers

- Call centre company used for reservations
- Maintenance contracts, including IT
- The supply of crockery, cutlery and linen
- Accounting or human resource functions
- Monthly stocktaking by a specialist firm; and
- Laundry of table linen, and hotel room towels and bedding.

A decision to outsource has to be considered carefully from both an operational and financial perspective. Invariably, the decision to outsource is driven by the drive to reduce costs. It allows managers to focus efforts on core business activities and allow 'specialists' to perform other support functions. It can reduce overheads and give greater flexibility in only paying for service when needed, thus reducing associated costs.

Early perceived financial benefits may not last, or changes in volume of activity (sales volume) alter the costs of outsourcing. There are also risks associated with giving 'control' of some critical aspects of service delivery to an outside company. The financial decision-making process in much the same as with 'make or buy decisions' explored earlier in this chapter and should use relevant costs. When space is at a premium there may also be an 'opportunity cost', by freeing up space that can then be put to a more profitable use.

Clearly a decision to outsource (or not) needs to be made based on sound financial information for the manager to be fully informed of the full implications of the decision.

Summary of key points

Short-term decisions can be of key importance to maximising revenues and profits in the short term. They are generally operational and tactical in nature, whilst long-term decision making is more strategic in nature.

- Relevant costs are those that are relevant to a specific decision being made.

- An opportunity cost is concerned with the 'missed opportunity' when deciding between mutually exclusive options.

- There are various types of short-term decisions – each may have a slightly different focus or role within the organisation.

- Short-term decisions can have long-term implications for an organisation.

- Scarce resource can lead managers to focus on how to use them to maximise the return for the organisation.

Reference

Drury, C. (2012), *Management and Cost Accounting*, 8th edn, CENGAGE Learning.

Further reading

A number of management accounting textbooks cover short-term decision making, but often from the perspective of a traditional manufactured product perspective. Some marketing books consider pricing, but not in the detail covered here related to a specific industry context.

Self-check student questions

1 Discuss why only relevant costs need to be considered in a short-term decision.

2 List and describe the main categories of short-term decisions.

3 Why do short-term decisions have long-term implications for an organisation?

4 How might a manager mitigate against the impact of scarce resources?

5 Take a specific sector with which you are familiar (events, hospitality, or tourism) and consider what opportunities exist for outsourcing and what the implications of this might be.

6 Using the data from the Peace Yoga Retreats example in this chapter, explain how relevant costing impacts on the decision-making process.

Further questions and problems

1 At the moment the kitchen of Tubby Tea Rooms makes its own cupcakes for use in the tea rooms and for sale to a number of events companies. This amounts to an average monthly production of 3,000 cupcakes. They have been approached by an industrial baker who can guarantee supply, as needed, on a daily basis and will charge £0.40 (40p) per cupcake.

The current costs of making cupcakes per month are as follows:

Tubby Tea Rooms	
Variable material cost	£400
Variable labour	£400
Fixed costs avoided if not making	£500

Given your calculations for Tubby Tea Rooms, what 'non-financial' considerations could be important?

6 Pricing Decisions

6.1 Introduction and objectives

Pricing decisions are among the most important decisions management has to make. Formulating an effective pricing policy is a complex and delicate matter which needs to consider the economic environment, competitor, financial and psychological factors. Setting the 'right' price is a constant challenge in a changing marketplace and is essential to long-term business success. This is made even more complex when pricing services and packaged products.

After studying this chapter you should be able to:

- Understand the importance of the pricing decision and its impact on the business

- Develop a working knowledge of pricing methods

- Consider pricing from a financial, economic and market perspective; and

- Reflect on the specific issues within hospitality, tourism and events sectors.

6.2 Pricing approaches

The three key approaches relate to pricing from a financial, economic, or market perspectives. Each of these has different merits and within these three broad approaches there are different techniques that can be used.

6.2.1 Financial approach to pricing

This is often referred to as the traditional approach to pricing. Although there are a number of variations the basic traditional approach is simply:

Costs + Mark-up = Selling price

Mark-up is a predetermined amount added to the costs to calculate the selling price. Given the calculation, this approach is known as Cost-plus pricing. There are variations to the cost base in this formula that lead to variations to this approach – these are summarised in Figure 6.1 and then discussed in more detail.

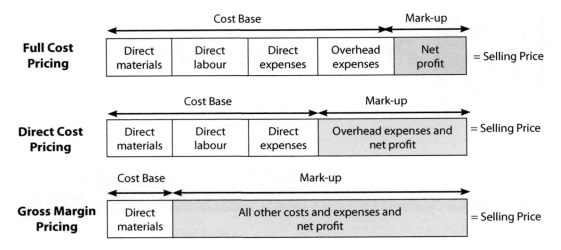

Figure 6.1: Cost-plus pricing variations

6.2.1.1 Full cost pricing

This basic 'cost-plus' approach, known as full or total cost pricing, entails establishing the total cost of individual products or services and then adding a mark-up to that to cover the required profit.

As an example, a company has estimated the following data:

Direct materials = £60,000

Direct labour = £30,000

Direct expenses = £15,000

Overhead expenses = £25,000

Desired profit = £30,000

The above data can be displayed as follows to show the total cost and the desired profit (Table 6.1). On this basis the desired sales revenue becomes £160,000. From this data the percentage mark-up can then be calculated.

Table 6.1: Total costs and desired profit

	£
Direct materials	60,000
Direct labour	30,000
Direct expenses	15,000
Overhead expenses	25,000
Total costs	130,000
Desired profit	30,000
Sales revenue	160,000

The following formula is used to calculate the mark-up needed on costs to reach the desired profit.

Formula using full cost pricing

$$\frac{\text{Profit}}{\text{Total costs}} * 100 = \text{Mark-up \%} \qquad \frac{30{,}000}{130{,}000} * 100 = 23\% \text{ Mark-up}$$

How does this help in setting a price for individual products? If for an individual item (unit) we have calculated the total costs to be £10 the price would then be:

£10 + 23% = £10 + £2.30 = £12.30 Selling price

If another item (unit) had a total cost of £15 the price would be:

£15 + 23% = £15 + £3.45 = £18.75 Selling price

If you can easily establish all the costs then this total cost (absorption costing) base for pricing can work. Based on space/time usage for a conference, however, across events, hospitality and tourism sectors given the service element this is not always as easy to do, so an alternative cost base may be more desirable.

6.2.1.2 Direct cost pricing

In this approach only the direct costs are calculated and then a mark-up is added to cover the desired profit and the overhead expenses. Within events and banqueting, or even tourist packages it may be possible to identify all direct costs. If a conference has been be requested for 150 people with a set menu these direct costs can be readily calculated, i.e. food and drink costs, direct labour for the event and specific expenses. Taking the previous data, this is how direct cost pricing is calculated.

Formula using direct cost pricing

$$\frac{\text{Overheads and profit}}{\text{Direct costs}} * 100 = \text{Mark-up \%} \qquad \frac{25{,}000 + 30{,}000}{105{,}000} * 100 = 52\% \text{ Mark-up}$$

If the direct costs for an individual unit were calculated at £8 the selling price would be:

£8 + 52% = £8 + £4.16 = £12.16 Selling price

Or if the direct costs were £12:

£12 + 52% = £12 + £6.24 = £18.24 Selling price.

There are many situations where calculating all direct costs can be difficult, in this case gross margin pricing could be a better option.

6.2.1.3 Gross margin pricing

In a factory situation it is reasonably easy to establish for an individual product being made how much direct labour is involved, i.e. how many minutes a specific task takes. This isn't always so easy with a service encounter. Imagine two individual customers come in to a restaurant, they order the same food and drink.

One of them is in a hurry, eats quickly and leaves in 30 minutes. The other person, who has ordered the identical items takes an hour and requires more time from the service staff helping them select the food and checking ingredients in the dish. So, two identical products have different direct staffing costs in this situation. In a factory, if you make 2 identical products it is more likely the direct labour will be similar as it is more routine and controllable.

In gross margin pricing it is only the direct material costs that are used as a base; a mark-up is then added to this to cover all other direct costs, overheads and required profits.

Formula using gross margin pricing

$$\frac{\text{Other costs and profit}}{\text{Direct materials}} * 100 = \text{Mark-up \%} \qquad \frac{70{,}000 + 30{,}000}{60{,}000} * 100 = 167\% \text{ Mark-up}$$

If the direct material costs for an individual unit were calculated at £5 the selling price would be:

£5 + 167% = £5 + £8.35 = £13.35 Selling price.

Or if the direct material costs were £10:

£10 + 167% = £10 + £16.70 = £26.70 Selling price.

In all the above examples, using 'cost + mark-up' it is the cost base that represents 100%, not the selling price. Taking the example above:

Direct material costs	+ Mark-up	= Selling price
£10	+ £16.70	= £26.70
100%	+ 167%	= 267%

Within the food and beverage sector the gross profit percentage is used as a key performance indicator, so using the above example this can be turned around to express the elements in relation to a selling price of 100%, this then becomes a 'gross profit margin'.

Direct material costs	+ Gross profit	= Selling price
£10	+ £16.70	= £26.70
37% *	+ 63%	= 100%

* Rounded to nearest 1%

So when seeing a mark-up %, the 100% base is the cost, when seeing a gross profit % it is the selling price that represents 100%. It may be that the required GP% has been set at 70%, knowing that requirement and the food cost of £10 the selling price would be calculated as follows:

100% – 70% = 30% food cost, therefore 30% = £10,

so 100% selling price = $\dfrac{£10}{30}$ * 100 = £33.33 selling price

6.2.1.4 Applied cost-plus pricing considerations

In food and beverage areas it is usually the gross margin variation that is used. In contrast to manufacturing, these operations can be described as having short runs or erratic activity cycles. Particularly in a hotel providing breakfast, lunch and dinner, the restaurant has three set production cycles a day, each comprises a variety of different dishes. In this situation it becomes impractical to build up full or total product (dish) costs by allocating and apportioning associated costs so gross margin pricing is used to recover wages, indirect costs and profit. There is a similar situation in bars.

As total cost (and even prime cost) is often uneconomical to ascertain, material (food and beverage) costs provide the only suitable base on which mark-up or gross profit percentage can be applied. This means that, in comparison to manufacturing, the link between costs and price are more tenuous. The further up market you go the weaker the link becomes as the material costs pale into insignificance in the selling price set.

In one-off events, such as weddings, banqueting, or in large-scale catering organisations with centralised food production facilities (including hospitals, welfare catering and airline catering) it does become possible to ascertain a higher proportion of total costs per unit. Direct labour is an example where in these situations, with pre-known customer numbers, production and service is more standardised making a stronger link between price and costs.

In 'pure service' operations the case for traditional cost-plus pricing is even less convincing than in food and beverage operations. A hotel room effectively constitutes a rental or hirer charge and does not have a material (product) cost. This, alongside the fact that other identifiable costs (laundry, cleaning, bathroom disposables) are insignificant in relation to the selling price stretches this tenuous link between costs and price even more – for practical purposes the relationship becomes meaningless.

6.2.1.5 Contribution margin pricing

Whereas full cost-plus pricing aims to cover total costs and a target profit-contribution pricing seeks to achieve a target contribution towards fixed costs and profit. This works on the premise that the minimum price should never be lower than the variable costs and the highest price is the maximum the market will bear – anything between these two figures will make a 'positive contribution' to the business. The philosophy behind the approach is that although individual sales may not achieve a net profit the sum total of the contributions from all sales will be sufficient to cover fixed costs and provide an adequate net profit.

Contribution margin pricing can serve as a particularly useful approach in service industries, where there is a relatively high proportion of fixed costs and demand at a specific price can vary significantly by time of day, day of the week, time of the year. As an example, there is frequently discussion in the press about the 'price hike' in holiday packages during school holidays – are the supply costs in August in reality significantly different to those in January? The answer is no, but using contribution margin pricing you could argue the maximum the market will bear in January is very different to August. So you make a small contribution in January, by selling at a lower price to encourage sales, and in August when you know demand is strong you vastly increase your price and make a significant contribution. In this way over the year you maximise your sales, therefore contribution, so maximise the net profit over the year.

An example of this related to selling a hotel room is illustrated below:

Selling price		£150
Less: Variable costs		
Direct labour	£10	
Variable overheads	£5	£15
Contribution margin		£135

Provided the room is sold above the variable costs, £15, it is making a contribution, however at the full tariff price of £150 a contribution of £135 can be generated, but would we sell any rooms at this price out of season?

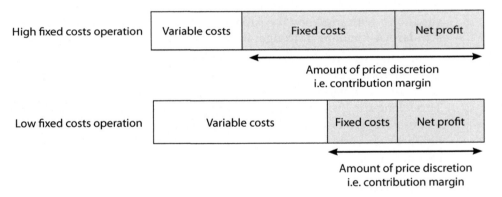

Figure 6.2: Price discretion

As can be seen in Figure 6.2, where variable costs are a smaller proportion of overall costs the price discretion (ability to change selling prices) is considerably more. Examples of using this price discretion in selling services are extensive:

- Selling holiday packages in different seasons
- Entry by day of the week e.g. theatre, cinema, clubs cheaper Monday to Thursday
- Midweek or Sunday weddings cheaper than Saturdays
- Business hotels offering cheaper weekend deals
- Leisure based hotels offering cheaper mid-week deals; and
- Travel costs (rail, air, coach, buses) vary with peak/off-peak times.

These ideas also relates to the concepts of yield management and revenue management, discussed in later chapters. It also needs to be considered that in such business situations customers are likely to buy multiple products, for example:

- Buy a festival ticket, but during the weekend by merchandise, food and drinks
- Buy a hotel room, but also drink in the bar and eat in the restaurant
- Buy a package holiday and then optional excursions, upgrades; or
- Buy a cinema ticket, and then purchase a drink and popcorn.

This gets into another subject discussed later in this book, customer profitability analysis (Chapter 8). A hotel room could be sold to two different customers. Customer A pays for their room and eats out all the time, customer B however pays the same for the room, but has breakfast and dinner in the hotel restaurant, pre-dinner drinks in the bar, pays extra to use wi-fi in their room. Customer B in this situation will generate far more revenue and profit for the business than customer A. If we have spare capacity then we would be happy to sell to both these customers, but if we had just one room vacant we would prefer customer B. So pricing an individual product, in this case a hotel room, is far more complex than it first appears.

6.2.1.6 Cost-plus v. contribution margin pricing

There are arguments for and against these two cost based approaches to pricing are shown in Table 6.2.

Table 6.2: Comparing two cost approaches

	Cost-plus pricing	Contribution margin pricing
Arguments for	Forms a logical basis to recover total costs	It allows scope over the pricing decision between a floor and ceiling price
	Simple to understand and safe to use	It maximises contribution where price is elastic; and
	It provides a 'fair' profit; and	
	It encourages price stability, whereas constant short-term price changes may prejudice long-term objectives.	Marginal costs are said to more accurately reflect the future.
Criticisms against	Ignores what customers are prepared to pay, suggesting the 'correct' price is costs plus assumed mark-up.	Practical difficulties encountered with establishing the demand curve (setting price too high or too low)
	It involves circular reasoning – costs depend on volume, but volume is influenced by price.	Difficulty in separating fixed and variable costs
	Having multi-products/services renders allocation of fixed costs meaningless.	Constant price changes could affect stability; and
	It ignores competitors' prices, sales will normally go to the lowest priced provider if product/service is comparable; and	Competition could lead to low margin returns, so fixed costs are not covered.
	It exaggerates the precision by which costs may be allocated.	

Even if a 'cost-plus' approach is adopted a contribution margin model might still be utilised for secondary pricing decisions, such as low-season holidays, special weekends, prestige functions and when national or international events are taking place in the local area.

6.2.1.7 Pricing, using target costing

This is an approach to costing used in pricing products and services, initially designed for use at the product development phase of new products, but now used for existing products as well. With this approach when conducting market research in developing a new product a 'market price' is identified. From this the profit required is deducted and what you have left is the 'target cost'. For example, market research tells us that for our standard wedding package the market will bear a price of £50 per head. For our company we wish to generate a 65% contribution towards fixed costs and profit.

Selling price = £50

Contribution = £50*65% = £32.50

Target variable costs = £50 – £32.50 = £17.50

In this example the final decision would be can we supply the package keeping to a variable cost of £17.50? It may be we adjust portion size, substitute dishes, or ingredients so we can design a package that fits both the customer's budget and our desired profit in selling the product. So whereas cost-plus pricing builds up to a price, ignoring the customer, this approach works the opposite way. It starts with what the customer is prepared to pay and works back to the maximum the costs can be.

For existing products and services it can be used to review the costs for an existing product. An example would be we are currently selling a particular dish at £8.99, but our raw material prices have gone up, to keep our profit margins the selling price would need to be increased to £9.50. However, market research identifies that the market will not accept a price increase. Using target costing we can work backwards to what our maximum costs can be. In this situation we may adapt the recipe, change portion size, etc. so the dish is adapted so it meets both the internal cost requirements and the market selling price demanded.

During times of recession this has happened a lot in retail. Examples include: a chocolate bar being reduced in size, but sold at the same price; and fruit juices and smoothies sold at the same price, but with 10% less volume. This is an approach where costing meets market-based approaches so is seen as having many merits.

6.2.2 Economist's view of pricing

The key to an economist's view of pricing is the idea that there is one 'best' price to charge which will generate the maximum financial return. Having a price higher or lower than this will generate a lower percentage return. This is shown graphically in Figure 6.3.

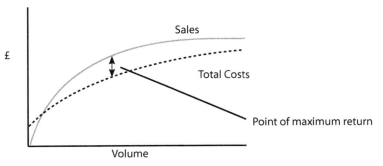

Figure 6.3: Economist's view of pricing

The economist's view is that to increase the volume of sales, price per unit needs to be reduced – the higher the volume sold the lower the unit price, hence the curved line. Equally total costs are shown as a curved line as volumes increase economies of scale mean the unit cost of buying from their supplier goes down. The economist's view of price is to set it at where there is the maximum distance between the sales and cost lines, i.e. where the profit is maximised.

6.2.3   Market-based approaches to pricing

As mentioned at the start of this chapter, the market, including the psychological aspects of pricing can be important. When considering the market competition is a key aspect – when setting a price not only does it need to be something a potential customer is prepared to pay, but it has to be considered what competition there is for that customer and how the price compares to competitor. The strategic positioning of the organisation and specific products and services offered are essential to success. The stage in the lifecycle for a specific product/service can also be a major consideration in the pricing decision.

6.2.3.1 Penetration pricing

Penetration pricing is an approach that can be used when introducing a new product or service. In this situation you are trying to penetrate an existing market. An unknown new service or product is initially priced low to gain market share i.e. to get potential customers interested in trying the product. Once the new item has a market share then the price is increased in the hope that once customers are loyal to the new product/service they will still but at a higher price. This is what you might call 'an introductory offer'. This is shown in Figure 6.4.

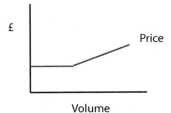

Figure 6.4: A penetration price starts low and increases after initial introduction.

6.2.3.2 Price skimming

This is another approach to selling a new product or service, particularly where there is a high initial demand for a new product or service. Just as you skim the cream off the top of milk, this strategy is to recoup development costs as quickly as possible by charging a high initial price to recoup costs as there is a high demand for the product or service. As time moves on to encourage more customers, who may be price sensitive, the price is reduced to maintain sales demand. This is frequently used within the entertainment industry – a film can be a multi-million investment, first it is released in the cinema, only after cinema sales have been exhausted will it be released on DVD, etc. Video gaming is another classic example of this. When a new edition of a known game is released many gamers will pre-order or happily pay full price to be one of the first to play the game. Six months later they move on to the next new game, but there is another audience, happy to buy a game that has been in the market some time at a lower price.

This is a strategy when the market isn't sensitive to price. As well as new products this can also be used as a short-term strategy when demand is high. Examples of this could include hotel accommodation close to major events or exhibitions. Each year during the four-day Cheltenham racing festival it is practically impossible to get accommodation within a 50-mile radius of Cheltenham. For these four days hotels will charge full tariff rates, insist on a minimum 4-night stay, or a minimum of half board to accept a booking, see Figure 6.5.

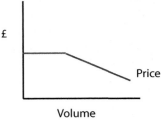

Figure 65: A skimming strategy starts high and reduces after initial introduction.

6.2.3.3 Loss leaders

A 'loss leader' is selling a headline product at a low price, possibly just above marginal costs. This can be done for a number of reasons: to attract customers, who then buy other products and services at the same time, for example reducing a hotel room price or discounted event tickets in the hope they will also buy food and drink at the venue, or event merchandise. In this way whilst one product or service is sold as a loss leader the customer becomes profitable due the additional range of products and services they purchase. This could also be used as a technique to dispose of surplus stock that otherwise is slow moving.

6.2.3.4 Psychological pricing

This pricing strategy takes into consideration 'pricing barriers'. In marketing literature research is often reported on the use of '9' – £7.99, as opposed £8.00, is only a penny different but psychological could have a big impact on the consumer buying decision. Prices ending with a 9, 5, 0 are far more common than those ending in other numbers. Within the budget hotel sector adverts will state 'rooms from £29', not £30. Whatever other pricing methods are being used this can be used in combination. Even if using cost-plus pricing, if the calculated selling price comes out at £87.14 it is likely this will be rounded to a more 'attractive' exact advertised selling price. Chapter 10, on events, discusses the opposite advice, on crowd control grounds, that a round price reduces queuing when people are paying on arrival at the event.

6.2.3.5 Competitor-based pricing

Competitor-based pricing is having a pricing strategy that considers the prices being charged by competitors and pitching your price against them to signal your product in the market. Purposefully setting a price above competitors is a strategy used to signal a product or service of a superior quality in the marketplace. An alternative can be to match competitor prices, thus taking price out of the decision-making process for the consumer and selling on your unique selling point (USP) – within the service sector very few products and services are truly identical when you consider venue, location, service quality, etc. The third option is to pitch your product or service as the value option, thus below the cost of competitors. Each of these three are valid options and the strategy of the organisation will clearly influence the pricing strategy adopted.

6.2.3.6 Flash sales

Although not directly a pricing method 'flash sales', holding a sale for 1–2 days is becoming increasingly popular within the retail sector. There are examples of this also in low-cost airlines, selling a certain number of seats at a very low price (sometimes 1p, plus taxes) for a short period of time. Some evidence suggests it has been used be a number of hotels as well, but revenue managers have concerns of the long-term impact of such drastic price cuts.

6.3   Relationship of cost/cost structure to price

As has been highlighted in much of the discussion in this chapter, plus in the previous chapter that considered cost-volume-profit (CVP) analysis there is a relationship between costs, the type of costs and the selling price. It has been identified that the relationship between cost and price is far more pronounced where there are high direct costs or high variable costs. Where an organisation is selling a service-based product with a high proportion of 'period' costs (fixed costs) then the causal relationship between costs and pricing is not as strong.

In more recent times, traditional manufacturing environments use of traditional cost-plus pricing has also been seen to lead to problems, with recognition of the 'suicidal spiral' when price is focused too close to costs in isolation. The strategic needs of setting an appropriate price in a modern competitive environment are far more complex and demand a multidisciplinary team to consider both internal costs and strategic perspectives, as well as looking externally at what the competition are charging and what the customer is prepared to pay.

6.4   Developing a pricing strategy

Developing a pricing strategy is a critical part of an organisation's general strategy development. From this chapter it is clear pricing is not a simple task. There are many decisions in the pricing decision, long-term in a commercial operation, strategically the aim is to maximise financial returns for the owners of the business. To achieve this, the relationship between selling price and costs needs to be a consideration, however this should not be viewed in isolation. The external environment is essential, so understanding competitors' pricing approaches and strategically deciding where to position your own products and services is critical. Understanding the consumer, their purchase behaviour and influences on their decision to buy is important in pricing to attract customers.

Specific techniques discussed in other chapters are also helpful to consider when pricing. Revenue management (yield management) can be particularly useful in service industries when trying to sell the right 'product' to the right customer at the right price to maximise revenue. Customer profitability analysis (CPA) aids an understanding that when considering pricing it is not just pricing individual products and services that has to be considered. In events, hospitality and tourism customers are often buying multiple products and services or packaged bundles and that can have a major influence on how things are priced and sold to consumers.

Summary of key points

This chapter has considered a variety of different pricing approaches, both from an accounting and from a non-accounting perspective. Price is an important element in any business as it will impact on the volume of sales and the total sales revenue generated. The key points from the chapter are:

- Traditional accounting-based approaches are cost-based, 'cost-plus' so add a 'mark-up' to cover profit and any costs not in the 'cost base'.

- Contribution margin pricing is useful where there are high fixed costs, therefore a high level of price discretion.

- Target costing uses costs in a market-orientated approach to pricing.

- The economist's perspective is that one 'best' price can be established for optimising returns.

■   Market-based approaches consider what the market is prepared to pay for a product, this can vary with point in the product life cycle and market positioning of the product/service.

Further reading

The later chapters covering revenue management and customer profitability analysis further explore pricing in the context of hospitality, tourism and events and provide this industry-based focus.

For more generic pricing reading the recommended text is:

Drury, C. (2012) *Management and Cost Accounting,* 8th edn. CENGAGE Learning.

6

Self-check student questions

1   Explain the different cost bases available when using cost-plus pricing.

2   Explain the difference between 'mark-up' and 'gross profit margin' when pricing.

3   What is contribution margin pricing?

4   What is meant by 'price discretion'?

5   How can target costing aid pricing?

6   The market will bear a price of £120 day delegate rate for conferences. The company wish to generate a 60% contribution towards fixed costs and profit. Use target costing to calculate the target costs per person.

7   Explain the economist's view of pricing.

8   Discuss the alternative market-based approaches to pricing and how they may be utilised.

Further questions and problems

1   Prepare a report for your manager that discusses the strengths and weaknesses of cost-plus versus contribution margin pricing.

2   Given the following data, using all the alternative cost-plus methods, calculate the mark-up percentage.

Direct materials = £90,000

Direct labour = £500,000

Direct expenses = £25,000

Overhead expenses = £30,000

Desired profit = £45,000

7 Revenue and Yield Management

7.1 Introduction and objectives

Yield management, and more recently revenue management have gained in popularity within hospitality, tourism and events sectors. Initially a technique used within the airline industry it has been adapted and products and services offered have been adapted to maximise the potential of this approach.

After studying this chapter you should be able to:

- Understand the concepts of yield/revenue management

- Appreciate the characteristics needed for successful revenue management within organisations

- Develop knowledge of revenue management calculations and processes; and

- Identify revenue management limitations in different environments, including profit maximisation issues.

The difference between yield and revenue management are dealt with within this chapter, in general the wider term, 'revenue management', will be used to encompass both terms. 'Revenue management' is used as a specific term in the context of this chapter, but readers need to be aware the term is also used more generally in relation to the manipulation of revenues in annual financial accounting reports. This other use of the term relates to manipulation, or 'managing' revenue so it is reported in a specific accounting year, or sales managed so it falls within the following financial year – this can sometimes be confusing when conducting a general Internet search – reader beware!

7.1.1 Difference between yield management and revenue management

Yield management arrived first and very much focused on maximising the revenue yield from the combination of selling price and volume of activity. In some respects, early yield management could be seen as tactical, rather than strategic and had a narrower focus – for example selling a plane seat, event ticket, or a hotel room, but not considering 'secondary' spend in other areas (food, drink, merchandising, additional baggage allowance), or the costs associated with the sale. Revenue management is seen as a development of yield management, in some ways that is considered more strategic and looks at 'the bigger picture', considering the fuller implications from a strategic perspective, so has a broader focus.

7.2 The concept of revenue management

The predicament in many service-based industries is that different buyers have different behaviour and it is not always the customer willing to pay more that books the longest in advance – this can cause issues. Imagine the situation, the summer flight schedule is released and a tour operator wants to book 50 seats each week over June–August, but given the size of the booking they want a substantial discount. As an airline company, do you take the booking? The problem is you could book this business eight months in advance, but then the planes become full and an independent traveller wanting to book at the last minute, at full price, has to be turned away. The same scenario can happen in other environments – a coach tour operator wanting to book 30 rooms weekly at a seaside hotel a year in advance, but wanting a discount. Does the hotelier take bookings and allow discounts, or do they keep to their full (tariff) rate and hope other people will book nearer to the time of arrival?

Traditionally, before revenue management there were two key elements monitored, independently, when monitoring sales revenue. Sales revenue is made up of price achieved multiplied by number of units sold. Traditional measurement has therefore been around average spend, or average achieved price and percentage of capacity utilised. In hotels these would be the average room rate (ARR) and the occupancy %, the percentage of room stock used. In airlines it is the average ticket price and % seat usage per flight. For events, again average ticket price and the % of capacity usage, whether this be festival space, seating capacity or venue capacity, depending on the type of event.

Even using these traditional mechanisms, managers would have experience from the past to know key points when to discount and when not to discount, but this could be ad hoc and when a new manager is appointed they may not have the same understanding of the local environment.

It is clear in service based situations there are points where discounting, and offering lower prices, is needed to encourage activity (units sold). Depending on the service being sold when this discounting is can vary – for a seaside hotel it may be the winter, for a business hotel the weekends, for a country house hotel mid-week, for a wedding venue mid-week, for a holiday package out of season and so on. In some environments, such as summer holiday trade there is a peak season, shoulder seasons around this and an 'off-season' period. In the middle of winter in Cardiff, Wales, one day, hotels can be offering their lowest rates, but 24 hours later offering their highest tariffs – why? One day it is just a cold February day out of season; the next day there is a major international rugby match at the Millennium Stadium bringing 70,000 people to the event in Cardiff, many wanting overnight accommodation.

There are many definitions of revenue management, but generally they relate to:

Selling the right product, to the right customer, at the right time, at the right price.

From the examples given above it is clear different types of customers exist, with different buyer behaviour and in order to maximise revenue returns on any given day there needs to be awareness of this. As a manager you may ask, can a premium be charged today, or do we have too much spare capacity and need to offer discounts to attract other types of customers to buy our services? Revenue management goes beyond a manager's experience, it is a more structure way of tactically predicting the market based on sophisticated modelling of past buyer behaviour to make predictions about the future. The system effectively 'allocates' saleable units to specific market segments, based on predictions of the future, often with the use of very sophisticated revenue management computer software. The key to revenue management is that it is systematic and evidence-based, grounded on more than an individual's human judgement.

7.2.1 Yield management formula

The basic yield management formula for identifying the yield achieved is simply comparing the revenue achieved with the maximum potential revenue.

$$YM\% = \frac{\text{Achieved revenue}}{\text{Potential revenue}} * 100$$

Example

On a specific night a hotel has 100 rooms available, with a full tariff rate of £120 per room, therefore its maximum potential revenue is 100*£120 = £12,000. However, on that night it sold 70 rooms and achieved an average room rate of £90, therefore its achieved revenue is 70*£90 = £6,300.

$$YM\% = \frac{£6,300}{£12,000} * 100 = 52.5\%$$

The YM% shows the hotel, on this specific night, achieved 52.5% of its maximum potential revenue from rooms.

Whether this is a hotel, event ticket, airline seat, train seat, spa treatment the same principle of calculating the potential maximum revenue (selling full capacity at full rate) and comparing achieved revenue as a percentage of this maximum always applies.

Revenue management is not something that is appropriate for every product and service in every industry. To gain maximum benefit from it, certain characteristics need to exist.

7.3   Characteristics for revenue management

Revenue management has a long history in the airline industry and has been evident in other sectors for a couple of decades now. There are certain characteristics of services that make them suited to using this tool, or even adapting so revenue management can be useful. To achieve a significant advantage from a revenue management system the following characteristics are required.

7.3.1   Product/service is perishable

This is often referred to as 'perishable inventory'. This relates to the fact the 'product/service' cannot be stockpiled, once a sale has passed it is gone forever. A manufacturing business could be making 100 products a day, 700 a week, it may sell only 50 one day, but the next day sell 200. This isn't an issue as production and product selling can happen independently. What if this was a hotel with 100 rooms? If only 50 are sold Sunday night there are still only 100 to sell Monday night. You cannot save the room stock for another day; a sale lost is lost for ever in these circumstances.

In the UK it is sometimes estimated that 50% of perfume sales occur in the month of December, so only 50% for the other 11 months of the year, but manufacturers can produce it all year long and hold the stock for when they know there is demand. Whether it is the number of rooms in a hotel, seats at an event, seats on a plane, capacity in a theme park, tables in a restaurant, the same limitation applies that any spare capacity today is lost forever, tomorrow is another day with a new capacity to fill.

7.3.2   Relatively fixed capacity

In the longer term, extra hotel rooms can be built, additional venue capacity created, more (or bigger) planes flown, but in the short to medium term such services have a fixed capacity. If a plane has 200 seats we cannot take 220 customers on the flight, however much they are prepared to pay. This necessitates, when demand is high, selection of customers prepared to pay the most is critical in maximising revenue returns. It is not, in some circumstances impossible to change capacity, but where it is possible there is a high cost to achieve this. A concert may be selling well, so an additional one is added, on a different day. This may double capacity, but equally doubles the venue hire costs. With scheduling, plane availability, route limitations, even if financially it was viable you may not be able to simply add another plane to a route at short notice.

7.3.3 Fluctuating demand

If there was a steady trade for the service 7 days a week, every week of the year, revenue management would not be needed. Realistically this does not fit the pattern across hospitality, tourism and events sectors. Here are some basic examples:

- Music festivals take place in summer months
- Weddings are most popular on Saturdays
- Business travel is mainly taken Monday–Thursday
- Holidays peak in summer months
- Short-break travel is mainly at weekends
- People go out more (events, restaurants, visitor attractions) on non-work days/ weekends
- Business travel and conference trade slackens in the summer, as workers take holidays
- Those with children generally holiday in school holiday periods
- Major local, national and international events impact on demand in the vicinity
- Public holidays reduce business trade and increase leisure trade.

Depending on what segment of the industry an organisation focuses on, they will see peaks and troughs at different times. For the use of revenue management to work these trends need to be identifiable and predictable. This allows organisations to maximise revenue through high prices when demand is high and maximising sales and through low prices when demand is low.

7.3.4 Suitable cost structure

Revenue management works well in situations where there are relatively low variable costs and high fixed cost structures. If 10% of the seats are empty at a concert what costs still need to be paid? The answer is almost all the costs as artist costs, venue hire, lighting, sound equipment still have to be paid. It is therefore best to sell those seats at a reduced cost, than to not sell them at all. The nature of cost structure has been discussed in previous chapters, notably in Chapter 6, on pricing. There are fewer benefits to revenue management where there are high variable costs, as there is limited price discretion in such markets.

7.3.5 Duration control

When you book a hotel room you have rented it for a given time, check-in after 2pm, check-out by 10am. When you pay for a music festival your ticket covers a set period of time, arrive after noon Thursday and leave by noon Monday. The same applies to a plane seat, conference booking, and venue hire. This is another factor which is important in revenue management. Generally in a restaurant you are paying for menu items, not the time you are in the restaurant. Two groups could order identical food, but one could be out in 50 minutes and the table available for resale, whilst the other group takes over an hour – in such environments revenue management is not as workable, unless duration control can be added (discussed later in the chapter).

7.3.6 Advanced sales are common

Revenue management works on monitoring and predicting the future based on past customers' behaviour. If it was a situation where no customers booked in advance it would be difficult to predict future demand and to adjust prices accordingly. On a low-cost airline the first seats are cheap and it is the later seats, as the plane fills up, that are more expensive. For some popular routes/flights 6 months in advance there may only be 10 seats at a high cost left, yet a week in advance, where there are many seats unsold, a seat could be relatively cheap.

Computer modelling revenue management systems can look at advance booking and previous buyer behaviour to decide rates that should be offered to someone wanting to book today. For example, if someone searches to book a hotel for a Sunday night in February the revenue management system make look back and see in the past 4 years the hotel has never sold out on a Sunday night in February. It then looks at advanced bookings and discovers these are no higher than usual. The revenue management system then knows it wants to encourage a sale by offering a lower rate which it predicts would be accepted. On the same day someone makes an enquiry for a room for 2 days in the middle of August. The revenue management system looks at previous sales and identifies in the past the hotel has been full at this time and knows some people book only a month in advance and pay the full price. Advance reservations are then consulted; numbers are already up on last year. Given this, the revenue management system predicts the room can be sold at full price, if this potential customer is not prepared to pay the full price it believes another customer booking later will be prepared to.

The above example makes it clear that without patterns of future demand available it would be difficult to operate a revenue management system.

7.3.7 Ability to segment the market

Very few businesses serve just one market – a plane company or hotel that only dealt with business customers exclusively would close down at weekends. In most marketplaces more than one customer group exists and each has different characteristics and buyer behaviour. For revenue management to work effectively these differences are utilised – maximise high spending customers when they are available, utilise price sensitive customers when there is spare capacity to fill. The important aspect here is not just their attitude to price, but how far in advance they are prepared to book. The market segment that generates the most money may only book a few days in advance, so capacity has to be held open for them and other potential customers turned away to keep this availability open for those prepared to pay the price. A few stereotypical examples include:

- Those travelling for business want a train/plane early in the morning despite the price, a leisure user is happier with a less crowded, cheaper train at 10am.

- A family ski holiday can only take place in the February 1 week holiday, they will pay the price as they cannot be flexible on dates, but a couple are happy to be flexible on dates to get a better price.

- Someone booking a budget hotel is prepared to be flexible on dates/location to get a £29 bargain room and pay in full in advance, but another customer booking at the same hotel for the same night wants the flexibility to change/cancel the booking if needed and is prepared to pay £49 to have this flexibility.

- A festival goer is prepared to buy tickets 10 months in advance, before the line-up is confirmed, at a reduced price, or with staged payments, whilst another person wants to see the line-up before making the decision to go, but is prepared to pay a higher price if they do buy.

Markets can be segmented by other ways, such as by transaction type, how far in advance booked, not just by traditional customer segmentation.

7.3.8 Overbooking policy

This is not a requirement for revenue management, but can be a consideration. In many areas customers pay in full at the time of booking, but this is less common in some sectors. In a number of hotels you could cancel with no financial loss at 24 hours' notice. For a packaged holiday payments can be taken over time, with final payment 8 weeks in advance. A restaurant reservation can usually be cancelled without penalty. This can cause a problem with the principles of revenue management. If a hotel knows that regularly 4% of bookings get cancelled last minute should they overbook by 4%, so they end up at 100% capacity? Strategically an organisation needs to consider this and the implications of any decision. What happens if everyone does arrive and you have more customers than capacity? If a non-refundable deposit is charged how does that impact on customer relations? Do you ask for full payment on booking, so whether they arrive or not the sale has taken place?

Revenue management relies on predictability, so being able to understand consumer behaviour and make clear predictions is critical to the system working.

7.4 Revenue management in different environments

Airplane tickets and hotel rooms match well with the characteristics needed for using revenue management. Within both these areas highly sophisticated revenue management software is available and many organisations employ a revenue manager to manage this area specifically.

Work on this has been completed by Kimes and Chase (1998) who identified the two strategic drivers for revenue management as duration control and ability to have many alternative prices. They argue that airlines and hotels meet these drivers, but others could be repositioned to benefit from revenue management. They represented certain industries as fitting 'quadrants' related to these two dimensions (see Figure 7.1).

	Few prices	Many prices
Controlled duration	QUADRANT 1 Conference centres Cinemas, Spas Stadiums, Venue hire	QUADRANT 2 Airlines, Hotels Cruise liners Car rental
Uncontrolled duration	QUADRANT 3 Golf courses Restaurants	QUADRANT 4 Private hospitals Private care homes

Figure 7.1: Drivers for revenue management. (Adapted from Kimes and Chase 1998)

Quadrant 2 represents products and services where there is a controllable duration and many prices. It is argued that whilst traditionally some service provision falls outside the desired quadrant 2 more could be done to shift these products and services towards quadrant 2 to make them more conducive to revenue management. For example a typical restaurant has a menu including set prices and people can use the table as long as they like – how could this be changed? The initial introduction of 'bundled' meal deals in fast food chains came about to increase revenue per customer as the meal was better value. At the same time it was identified that every saving of 15 seconds in the queuing added 1% to revenue, so the 'meal deal' increased revenue two ways, by customers buying more and making quicker meal choice decisions. At the extreme in efforts to control duration some restaurants now set a maximum duration time, but that could have a negative impact in some situations. More subtly duration management can be managed internally through efficient service, or taking bookings at times that will allow tables to be reused during an evening – a booking at 7pm, followed by 8.30pm is better than one booking at 7.45pm that blocks the table for the whole evening. So in some environments it is possible to move position, if seen as useful to revenue generation, whilst maintaining customer satisfaction. Managing customer arrival is a simple adaptation that can be made is these environments. Bundled discounted menus for 'early bird' diners are an example of varying pricing. A carvery chain is known for a fixed price Monday–Saturday, but charging a higher price on Sundays, just because it is Sunday.

Research into golf courses has looked at managing tee times in a similar way to managing restaurant table bookings, likewise varying prices related to popular and less popular tee times to maximise usage and price, thus maximising revenue.

Spas have a controlled duration, as a particular treatment has a specific time attached, but traditionally set pricing – why should a premium Saturday afternoon slot cost the same as Monday morning? Some have looked at these opportunities to move to a more flexible price so revenue management can be used more fully.

Within events, particularly in venue hire, time is controllable, paying by the hour or day. However, as with spas, traditionally they have had set rates, so having a more dynamic pricing strategy could lead to better revenue management in this environment.

7.5 Revenue maximisation or profit maximisation?

Most of the academic literature on revenue management is written from an operational or marketing perspective. One issue raised is whether maximising revenue actually maximises profits. Work related to customer profitability analysis (CPA) addresses this in more detail. Another powerful tool related to this is direct relationship marketing – it is quite possible, if a customer has logged in to a website seeking a price to adjust the offer based on their individual buyer behaviour. One customer is known when staying in a discounted room to then purchase food and drink in-house, use the spa and book a round of golf. However a second customer may book the room at the same discounted rate and check out, not having spent any more during his stay, so there is an argument that revenue management needs to go deeper in order to move more towards maximising the profit than purely maximising the revenue, without considering the costs, or the opportunity costs of alternative sales. This is addressed in more detail in Chapter 8.

Summary of key points

Given the service nature of these sectors, with bookings often being taken months, if not years in advance generally revenue management provides many advantages as a technique in maximising the revenue of an organisation. The key points from this chapter are:

- Revenue management is about selling the right product to the right customer for the right price at the right time.

- The yield management formula can be used to combine the impact of volume of sales and selling price in one measure.

- Revenue management is not suited to every situation and works best when certain characteristics are present.

- Products and service can be adapted to make them more conducive to using revenue management.

- Concern needs to be given to ensuring revenue maximisation is not at the cost of profit maximisation.

Reference

Kimes, S.E. and Chase, R.B. (1998) 'The strategic levers of yield management', *Journal of Service Research*, **1** (2) 156–166.

Further reading

Yeoman, I. and McMahon-Beattie, U. (eds) (2010) *Revenue Management: A Practical Pricing Perspective*, Palgrave Macmillan.

This text gives many illustrative industry examples related to hotel room sales, golf courses, car parks, menus, airlines, to name put a few and contains many chapters written by different researchers in the field of revenue management.

Hayes, D.K. and Miller, S. (2010) *Revenue Management for the Hospitality Industry*, John Wiley and Sons.

This text is specific to hospitality and includes many real-life examples and is a detailed account of revenue management in a specific context.

Self-check student questions

1 Define what is meant by the terms 'yield management' and 'revenue management'.

2 On a specific flight there are 240 seats available, at a maximum price of £200 per seat. However only 180 seats are sold, with an average achieved ticket price of £110. Calculate the yield management % from this data.

3   Describe the characteristics required for revenue management to be of significant value.

4   Two customers stay in identical budget hotel rooms in the same hotel, on the same night; one has paid £29, whilst the other has paid £59. Using revenue management explain this situation.

5   Why might revenue management not be appropriate in retail product sales with a long 'shelf-life'?

6   Define the two strategic drivers of revenue management.

7   Explain revenue management drivers in relation to Kimes and Chase's four quadrants model.

8   Why does revenue maximisation not always lead to profit maximisation?

7.10   Further questions and problems

1   Within an environment with which you are familiar (hospitality, tourism or events) analyse how revenue management could be applied.

2   Discuss this statement. 'Revenue management does not always lead to profit maximisation so should not be used'.

8 Costing and Customer Profitability Analysis

8.1 Introduction and objectives

Traditional 'cost accounting' was product driven and internally focused. Modern strategic managerial accounting focuses more strongly outwardly and recognises the important role the market and customers have in making an organisation successful and profitable. This chapter explores a number of management accounting tools that aid this modern view of organisations. The notion that: 'It is customers, not products and services, that generate profits for organisations' is key to this market emphasis.

After studying this chapter you should be able to:

- Understand the relationship between the marketing and management accounting functions

- Understand and use activity-based costing (ABC) and activity-based management (ABM) to support management decisions; and

- Critically evaluate the use of; market segment profitability analysis, customer profitability analysis, and profit sensitivity analysis as tools to aid managers' in hospitality, tourism and events environments.

8.2 Market decisions

An external focus of an organisation leads to decisions as to:

- Which specific market are we in?
- Who is our customer?
- What do these customers want?
- Can we deliver what they want?
- Will this make us a profit?
- Could other markets offer a better profit potential?

If an organisation is to maximise its returns to its shareholders such strategic questions have to be addressed. To do this both marketing and accounting functions need to work together to generate the management information needed to answer these questions.

8.2.1   Market and customer examples

General industry sectors are easy to identify, but within those there are a lot of variations, subsectors and different customer needs to consider.

Table 8.1: Markets, customers and their needs

What market are we in?	Who are our customers?	What do they want?
Events – weddings	Those who want a bespoke service	Something designed specifically for them, a 'one-off' event, but prepared to pay for this 'uniqueness' desired from the event.
Events – weddings	Those on a budget, but wanting a special day	They want a memorable day, cost is a concern so they want to select from pre-set all-inclusive packages that they can budget for.
Events – music festival	18–25 year olds with a passion for contemporary music	Top artists, mixing with like-minded individuals, basic camping facilities, bar facilities and a simple food provision.
Events – music festival	Families	A safe friendly environment, with good music for the adults, but also entertainment for the children, with workshops and family-focused camping facilities, quality food and drink provision.
Hospitality 5* hotel (international airport)	Airline crew and air passengers	A one-night stay with easy access to the airport, possibly parking whilst away, 24 hour services so they can arrive, eat and leave at a time convenient to flight needs.
Hospitality 5* hotel (city centre)	Overseas travellers at the 'high end', and corporate executive travellers	Traditional hospitality, opulent surroundings, attention to service details, traditional hotel styling and atmosphere, like-minded customers
Hospitality 5* hotel (city centre)	Entertainment and creative industry executives, younger celebrities, 'young money'	Want 5* facilities, but with a lively, vibrant modern atmosphere in a hotel with a contemporary style and modern service and up-to-the-minute gadgets and technology.

The list of examples in Table 8.1 could go on and on, but just these simple examples illustrate the point of how different customers influence the product/service offered, even in what is perceived to be a single market.

8.2.1.1   London 5* hotel market example

Consider two well-known London 5* hotels: the Dorchester and the Metropolitan. Both are the same star rating, on the same street, in the same city. If you look at their respective websites you will quickly identify very different imagery, styling, facilities and descriptions. This is not to say their customer groups never overlap, but they are 'targeted' in very different ways. The Dorchester offers the traditional grandeur and opulent styling, whilst the Metropolitan focuses on its minimalist contemporary styling and has its own exclusive nightclub, 'The Met Bar'.

Whilst both serve a 5* hotel market in the same location their 'offering' (products and services) are quite distinctive from each other. Both these hotels have survived over the years, but clearly have made distinct market positioning decisions. It could be argued, this 'works' as they each take the customers the other 'doesn't want', fill specific niches in the marketplace. To do this accounting and marketing functions have to work closely together, not only to identify markets, but to consider which markets will maximise profitable returns (see Boston Consulting Group BCG discussion in Chapter 16 on strategic management accounting, which can be linked to this point).

8.3   The accounting/marketing interface

There are a number of research papers in this area, including that of Phillips and Halliday (2008) that looks specifically at the interface during planning. A number of authors draw a similar conclusion that these two functional areas have to work together to maximise organisational performance and shareholder wealth. However, authors also agree that there is often insufficient combined working between marketing and accounting, leading to potential organisation performance issues. There are calls for a holistic view of performance which needs a combined approach.

8.3.1   Problem examples of lack of marketing/accounting interface

The examples in Table 8.2 highlight how basic operational decisions can cause conflict between these two functions, where a holistic 'joined up' approach would better serve the organisational needs.

The illustrations in Table 8.2 identify that working together and thinking through the decision from both perspectives gives a better decision than one on its own. There are a number of costing techniques and market based analysis approaches that provide valuable information to assist in such decision making in organisations.

Table 8.2: Conflicts between functions

Scenario	The events sales team meet with a potential customer wanting to arrange an evening ball for next December (150 people at £40 per head). However, they have an issue with the set menu options and would like to change the salmon for rump steak on one of the two main course options and insist on fresh strawberries for dessert.
Issue	The event sales team are rewarded on sales generated, the date is available for the event, the space needs to be filled and this booking will generate £6,000 sales revenue. The accounting perspective is that steak costs more than salmon and strawberries will be expensive out of season. This change to the set package costs more, which will reduce the contribution margin, thus profits.
Combined solution	Working together the new contribution could be calculated and from this an informed decision taken: Explain to the customer their requirements can be accommodate, but at an extra charge; Accept the lower contribution, it will be difficult to fill the space to make a greater contribution; or Given it is for December and in the past the space has filled with Christmas functions and customers turned away, with revenues of £8,000, do not accommodate this booking.
Scenario	A coach tour operator contacts the hotels central reservation team, they want to book 30 rooms in your hotel for next March for Saturday night. The numbers of rooms are available to be booked and you have a special discounted rate with this tour operator.
Issue	The reservation team are rewarded on the number of rooms sold, the rooms need to be filled and, even at the discounted rate, 30 rooms @ £50 each represents £1,500 sales revenue.
Combined solution	From the accountant's perspective financial data might show: There is a buoyant weekend break market, booking these rooms for Saturday night will make them difficult to sell Friday for one night – an opportunity cost. This tour operator has been very slow to pay its bills in the past, requiring a lot of chasing and there is concern over their credit rating. This could lead to cash flow problems as the amount of trade receivables (debtors) increases or bad debts in the future; or This is a great opportunity and these customers tend to have a high 'secondary spend' in the bar and spa facilities making this a good opportunity.
Scenario	A new spa treatment is priced by the accounting department using a cost-plus approach and calculates the 1 hour treatment should be sold at £65.
Issue	The accounting team are taking no account of the market, what the customer is prepared to pay or the completion.
Combined solution	The marketing department establish that there is competition locally offering the same treatment (customers can go elsewhere) and the prices range from £52–£62. Given this market data the product price can be set considering the market: Set at the lower end of the market, £55 to attract customers in to try the new product Given the quality and reputation of the spa, priced at £65 to identify it as a premium product in the market; or Set at the psychological price of £59, being under the £60 boundary.

8.4   Activity-Based Costing (ABC)

Traditional, total absorption costing was discussed in Chapter 3 and was seen to have a number of limitations when being applied in these service sectors. In total absorption costing, 'direct' costs are easy to allocate to units of production, other (indirect) costs are more arbitrarily 'shared' amongst units of production. Indirect costs for a period of time are calculated and then an 'absorption' rate identified, for example per labour hour.

8.4.1   Total absorption costing example

A souvenir tee shirt and sweatshirt are produced for a tourist venue. The cost breakdown using total absorption costing is as follows:

Absorption costing	Tee shirt	Sweatshirt
Direct costs	£4.00	£8.00
Indirect costs	*£2.00	**£3.60
Total costs	£6.00	£11.60

In this example the total indirect costs were divided by staff time in production to get to an 'absorption rate' of £8 per direct labour hour. The tee shirt takes 0.25 of an hour to produce and the sweatshirt 0.45 of an hour.

*Tee shirt absorption calculation = £8.00 * 0.25 = £2.00

**Sweatshirt absorption calculation = £8.00 * 0.45 = £3.60

In this example the tee shirt 'absorbs' £2 of indirect costs, whilst the sweatshirt 'absorbs' £3.60 – but why? It is a simple process and all costs need to be covered, but it is not viewed as being accurate, or useful in the service sector due to its limitations.

8.4.2   ABC principles

As the name suggests, this costing method considers activities in proportioning costs. ABC assigns costs to activities consumed.

> *A system of management which uses activity based cost information for a variety of purposed including cost reduction, cost modelling and customer profitability analysis.*

> (CIMA official terminology, 2005)

The key elements include:

■ Cost visibility – Brings costs out into the open and allows managers to ask if their department is as cost effective as it could be.

■ Activity cost profile – This is a way of presenting data (like an overhead reporting statement) allowing the asking of questions like why has the cost of quality control risen.

■ Identifying value added – Allows differentiation between costs which add value and those which don't. This can be used for further development into three categories core, support and discretionary costs. This enables better cost management by reducing resources on non-core activities.

■ Cost behaviour patterns – It is not always clear how and why cost behave as they do. An ABC-based cost hierarchy can identify how costs are driven and again focus on cost reduction.

8.4.2.1 ABC simple example

A hotel stores department issues out drink stock to other departments as follows:

	Restaurant	Bar	Room service	Lounge	Totals
Stock value	£12,000	£8,000	£1,000	£3,000	£24,000

Running the stores for a week costs £600 and this cost needs to be covered by the stock.

A traditional absorption costing approach would be to share this equally across the stock value:

£600/£24,000 = £0.025

		Restaurant	Bar	Room service	Lounge	Totals
Stock value		£12,000	£8,000	£1,000	£3,000	£24,000
Absorption rate per £ of stock	£0.025	£300	£200	£25	£75	£600

However, this doesn't allow for the stores 'activity', every time an issue from the stores is made a requisition process has to be followed and processed. The number of 'issues' by department vary considerably by department. Room service have little storage space so collect stock twice a day, the lounge once a day, the bar three times a week and the restaurant once a week.

		Restaurant	Bar	Room service	Lounge	Totals
Stock value		£12,000	£8,000	£1,000	£3,000	£24,000
Absorption rate per £	£0.025	£300	£200	£25	£75	£600
No. of issues per week		1	3	14	7	25

The 'driver' for this cost relates to the work the stores department undertake in issuing, the 'activity' of processing a stock requisition. ABC would share this cost based on usage of the activity.

ABC = £600/25 = £24 per stock issue

		Restaurant	Bar	Room service	Lounge	Totals
Stock value		£12,000	£8,000	£1,000	£3,000	£24,000
Absorption rate per £	£0.025	£300	£200	£25	£75	£600
No. of issues per week		1	3	14	7	25
ABC rate	£24	£24	£72	£336	£168	£600

The above example highlights that in both costing methods £600 of stores department costs have been apportioned, but the amount charged to different departments has changed considerably. Look at the restaurant as an example, under total absorption costing they were charged £300 as they requisitioned £12,000 of stock. However, the restaurant only placed one requisition, so when activity-based costing (ABC) is applied the proportion charged to the restaurant was only £24, not £300.

Another key finding when using ABC is that it highlights a significant cost for room service (including in room mini-bars). They account for 14 out of the 24 requisitions, so their £1,000 of stock costs £336 in requisition costs. This information can aid managers in decision making, changing the current process, may be adjusting room service selling prices and will lead to adjusting department operational profits.

8.4.3 ABC uses

ABC looks at 'cause and effect' relationships between costs and activity. This is seen as having a better fit with service operations than traditional absorption costing. It avoids arbitrary allocation of costs to products and services. Using ABC can aid managers in a number of ways:

- If can aid managers in identifying services, products, departments and activities that are profitable or those making a loss.
- It can aid operational level financial control.
- It can identify unnecessary costs for management action; and
- It can be used in cost-plus pricing (see pricing chapter).

ABC can give managers a better understanding of costs, this information can then be used in operational and strategic decision making.

8.4.4 ABC limitations

Identifying the correct activity drivers for costs and ABC allocation is more complex than traditional absorption costing, although ABC software does exist to support this. It can be viewed as costly and the cost of producing the information has to be outweighed by its benefits, otherwise it adds costs to a business.

8.5 Activity-based management (ABM)

ABM is the extension of ABC, going beyond costing to the management operational and strategic use of the information. The Chartered Institute of Management Accountants (CIMA 2008) define ABM as:

> **Operational ABM**: *Actions, based on activity driver analysis, that increase efficiency, lower costs and/or improve asset utilisation.*
>
> (CIMA Official Terminology, 2005)

Strategic ABM: *Actions, based on activity based cost analysis, that aim to change the demand for activities so as to improve profitability.*

(CIMA Official Terminology, 2005)

8.6   Customer profitability analysis (CPA)

Traditionally the difference in revenues between market segments (market segment analysis) has been conducted, but either only at this revenue level or with apportioning costs by products and services used to review operating profits. CPA uses the ABC approach to costing to track costs by activities associated with customers, not individual products and services. This chapter started by making the statement that it is customers, not products and services that make profits. A simple illustrated example of this is used to explain this.

8.6.1   Example: 'Customers, not products and services generate profits'

You are a producer and supplier of soft drink products and offer a free delivery service to your customers. You sell your lemonade at a price of £0.80 per bottle and the costs (excluding delivery) are £0.40. Delivery (lorry, driver, fuel, etc.) cost you £2.50 a mile. In this example two customers will be considered – see Table 8.3:

Customer A is a large events company and orders 10,000 bottles of lemonade for resale at a major annual sporting event. They want the 10,000 bottles delivered to one location 100 miles from your factory.

Customer B is a hotel company and orders 10,000 bottles of lemonade for resale in its chain of 20 hotels (500 per hotel) and needs delivery direct to each hotel, average 50 miles drive per hotel (20 hotels * 50 miles = 1,000 miles).

Table 8.3

Lemonade supply	Customer A	Customer B
Volume	10,000	10,000
Price	£0.80	£0.80
Cost price	£0.40	£0.40
Sales	£8,000	£8,000
Costs	£4,000	£4,000
Contribution, before delivery costs	£4,000	£4,000
Delivery cost	£250	£2,500
Profit	£3,750	£1,500
Profit %	47%	19%

In this example an identical product is sold to two customers, selling to one customer generates a 47% profit, whilst selling to the other customer only 19%. This difference in returns is due to difference in the customers' delivery requirements, not the product. At a basic level, this is customer profitability.

8.6.2 Customer profitability analysis in action

The simple example was the purchase of a single product and even then just delivery made the difference between customer profitability. Within hospitality, tourism and events this is rarely the case. Customers buy bundled products, or purchase multiple products and services (Figure 8.1).

Sector	'Bundled' products/services – bought as combined package	Products/services – bought individually
Tourism	The packaged tour, including in one price: Plane travel, transfers, accommodation, and all meals.	Plane travel, transfers, accommodation, meals, travel insurance, currency exchange, day trips, drinks, upgrades, car hirer.
Events	VIP package, including in one price: Event ticket, programme, hospitality food and drink package.	Event ticket, programme, food, drink, merchandising, travel.
Hospitality	Full board – room, breakfast, lunch and dinner	Room, breakfast, lunch, dinner, bar sales, in-room entertainment, spa treatments, golf green fees, merchandising.

Figure 8.1: Bundled and multiple products

At one time, accounting and costing treatments follow traditional departments, so in a hotel the key operating departments are rooms, food and beverages so they are the base for distributing costs. However, this doesn't fit well with customer behaviour, where the product and/or service they buy tends to go across these 'traditional' departmental boundaries. Customer profitability analysis uses ABC in order to track costs, therefore profits, by customer in place of the traditional individual product/service base for cost allocation.

As can be seen in Figure 8.2, CPA uses ABC, so indirect costs are associated with activities with which customers engage. Direct costs, such as food costs are easy to allocate to sales. Indirect costs are allocated by activities and there has to be a 'driver' for each activity, such as:

- Check in/check out – driver – customers/rooms
- Room cleaning – driver – room cleaning time (suites more time?)
- Bar service – driver – per item sold
- Meals service – driver – per meal

An example of how this may work in practice is demonstrated with the use of two customers: the corporate guest; and the leisure guest (see Table 8.4).

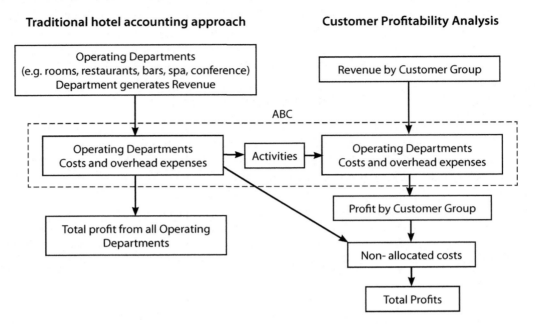

Figure 8.2: Traditional accounting and CPA. (Adapted from Harris, 2011)

Table 8.4: CPA in practice

			CORPORATE		LEISURE	
Activities	Activity drivers	ABC rate	No. of activity	Cost	No. of activity	Cost
Check in/out	No. of rooms/customers	£38.10	1	£38.10	1	£38.10
Room cleaning	No. of days/time per day	£36.79	3	£110.37	3	£110.37
Room service	No. of calls	£32.43	3	£97.29	0	£0.00
Breakfast service	No. of breakfasts	£10.75	3	£32.25	3	£32.25
Meal service	No. of meals	£15.88	3	£47.64	1	£15.88
Bar service	No. of items sold	£3.14	9	**£28.26**	2	**£6.28**
	Total customer activity costs			£353.91		£202.88
	Direct costs			£113.80		£55.67
	Total costs (direct and indirect)			£467.71		£258.55
	Total revenues			**£508.38**		**£232.92**
	Profit margin			**£40.67**		**–£25.62**
	Relative profitability			8%		–11%

From Table 8.4 it is clear that the corporate customer was more profitable, they paid more for their room, had breakfast and an evening meal every day and made use of room service and the bar. The leisure guest had a discounted room with breakfast, used the bar for two drinks and ate in once in the evening. This is not an uncommon pattern between such customer groups.

8.6.3   How can CPA aid managers' decision making?

This has been practically tested and applied in international hotel companies (Krakhmal and Harris, 2008). It can aid managers by:

- Explicitly identifying which customer groups (segments) generate the most profit can aid the targeting of resources and marketing efforts to these groups
- Providing information that can aid cost reduction, by highlighting costs by activities gives managers the chance to review the need of activities or how their costs can be reduced
- Assisting pricing of products, particularly packages and discounting for certain customer groups
- Allowing markets to be segmented on profitability, not just revenues
- Aiding a differentiation strategy; and
- Providing information for making more informed decisions.

It is a complex and technical process that takes time to set up the appropriate cost system, however organisations that have used it have reported managers having a better understanding of how costs follow customers. This has impacted on control and decision making internally and evidence of an increase in profitability.

8.7   Profit sensitivity analysis (PSA)

Profit sensitivity analysis is another tool to aid managers in understanding their business in more detail. As the name suggests, PSA concerns understanding how sensitivity profits are to changes, these could be changes in revenues, or changes in specific costs. An example would be:

What is the impact on profits if an individual variable (volume, selling price, or a cost element) changes by 10%?

By doing this, 'profit multipliers' (PMs) can be prepared for the business. These show the variation in profits due to a 10% change in the variable. A worked example of this is shown in the next subsection.

$$\text{Profit multiplier} = \frac{\%\text{ change in profit}}{\%\text{ change in key factor}}$$

8.7.1   Example PSA in a visitor attraction

Cotswold Animal Park is an attraction for visitors to the Cotswolds, UK. The planned data for restaurant sales is shown in Table 8.5.

Table 8.5: Profit sensitivity analysis (PSA), Cotswold Animal Park

	Predicted data
Average spend (selling price)	£8.00
Volume of sales	10,000
Variable food costs	£2.50
Fixed labour costs	£16,000
Other fixed costs	£30,000
Contribution statement	
Sales revenue	£80,000
Variable costs	£25,000
Contribution margin	£55,000
Fixed labour costs	£16,000
Other fixed costs	£30,000
Profit/loss	£9,000

If each element is taken in turn, assuming all else remains equal, what is the impact on profits? If customers spend less, so the average spend goes down by 10%, it reduces from £8.00 to £7.20. Given all else remains the same, the data would be as shown in Table 8.6.

Table 8.6: Profit sensitivity analysis, Cotswold Animal Park, lower average spend

	Predicted data	Average spend down 10%
Average spend (selling price)	£8.00	£7.20
Volume of sales	10,000	10,000
Variable food costs	£2.50	£2.50
Fixed labour costs	£16,000	£16,000
Other fixed costs	£30,000	£30,000
Contribution statement		
Sales revenue	£80,000	£72,000
Variable costs	£25,000	£25,000
Contribution margin	£55,000	£47,000
Fixed labour costs	£16,000	£16,000
Other fixed costs	£30,000	£30,000
Profit/loss	£9,000	£1,000

A decrease of 10% in average spend reduces profits from £9,000 to only £1,000. The percentage change is calculated as follows:

Revised profit – Original expected profit * 100
Original expected profit

$$\frac{£1,000 - £9,000}{£9000} * 100$$

$$= \frac{-£8,000}{£9,000} * 100 = -89\%$$

$$\text{Profit multiplier} = \frac{\% \text{ change in profit}}{\% \text{ change in key factor}}$$

$$= \frac{-89\%}{10\%} = -8.9$$

From this it can be seen that the one change of the average selling price (spend) per customer of 10% reduces the profit by 89%, which is a profit multiplier factor of –8.9. If it is asked: 'What would be the impact if the average spend increased by 10%?' The calculations would be revised and the answer would be a profit multiplier of 8.9, i.e. the same figure, put positive, as opposed negative. Given this, the sign can be ignored when ranking profit multiplier by size. Those that have the biggest negative impact are also those that can have the biggest positive impact – either up or down is showing profit sensitivity, either positively or negatively. This shows that every 1% change in this key factor has a corresponding impact on profits of 8.9.

Table 8.7: Profit sensitivity analysis, Cotswold Animal Park, with all the key factors considered

	Predicted data	Average spend		Volume of sales	Variable food costs	Fixed labour	Fixed other costs
		–10%	+10%	–10%	+10%	+10%	+10%
Average spend (selling price)	£8.00	£7.20	£8.80	£8.00	£8.00	£8.00	£8.00
Volume of sales	10,000	10,000	10,000	9,000	10,000	10,000	10,000
Variable food costs	£2.50	£2.50	£2.50	£2.50	£2.75	£2.50	£2.50
Fixed labour costs	£16,000	£16,000	£16,000	£16,000	£16,000	£17,600	£16,000
Other fixed costs	£30,000	£30,000	£30,000	£30,000	£30,000	£30,000	£33,000
Contribution statement							
Sales revenue	£80,000	£72,000	£88,000	£72,000	£80,000	£80,000	£80,000
Variable costs	£25,000	£25,000	£25,000	£22,500	£27,500	£25,000	£25,000
Contribution margin	£55,000	£47,000	£63,000	£49,500	£52,500	£55,000	£55,000
Fixed labour costs	£16,000	£16,000	£16,000	£16,000	£16,000	£17,600	£16,000
Other fixed costs	£30,000	£30,000	£30,000	£30,000	£30,000	£30,000	£33,000
Profit/loss	£9,000	£1,000	£17,000	£3,500	£6,500	£7,400	£6,000
% change in profit		–89%	89%	–61%	–28%	–18%	–33%
Profit multiplier		–8.89	8.89	–6.11	–2.78	–1.78	–3.33

The profit multipliers can be ranked in order of size (ignoring the sign):

Average spend down	Volume of sales down	Other fixed costs up	Variable food costs up	Fixed labour costs up
8.89	6.11	3.33	2.78	1.78

What this shows is that profits are more sensitive to changes in the average spend (selling price) than other key factors. If the average spend goes up by 10% it has the biggest positive impact on profits, but if it goes down by 10% it has the biggest negative impact. The lowest profit multiplier is fixed labour costs, at 1.78, so if labour costs change by 10% up or down the profit changes by only 1.78% which is far less than changes in other key factors.

8.7.2   The use of PSA by managers

This information can give managers a better understanding of the orientation of the business and areas where they should focus their time and attention. In the example, PSA identifies that ensuring the average spend is at least maintained and ideally increased, will have a good impact on the business. The business has to be very careful to ensure the average spend does not reduce. A manager could monitor this key factor daily, but just review the labour costs weekly. As a fixed cost, the labour shouldn't change in the short term, and even if it does, changes to this have the lowest PM, so lowest impact on profits. Therefore, this is not an area where managers need to focus as much attention.

In this example, this information could be used to focus management reporting through report timings and contents. The control policy can be geared to the most sensitive key factors. Equally, operational and marketing efforts can be focused around this area. This could include 'up selling' by restaurant staff to increase the average spend (selling a cake with a coffee, crisps with a sandwich, a desert with a main course). Or changing the menu to bundle products to increase average spend, as customers may be attracted to 'meal deals'.

There are a couple of criticisms of PSA:

- It does not take into account the likelihood of key factors changing by, for example 10%. You may have a key factor that has a high PM, but data over the last five years show it is stable and has a history of limited variation. In the example used here the volume of sales has the second highest PM at 6.11, but if it has been static for some time it may not be something management want to focus on. In this situation restaurant usage relates directly to visitors to the attraction, so it may be that focusing on ticket sales is a better option than focusing on trying to increase sales volume just for this one department.

- The other limitation is whether looking at key factors in isolation, holding all other factors constant is realistic. For example, both price (average spend) and volume of sales can go hand-in-hand. An increase in price can reduce volume of sales and a reduction in price an increase in volume of sales. Whilst this is a valid criticism, before looking at factors in combination, isolating them using PSA gives management a sound understanding of the nature of individual factors and their impacts when there is a change.

Summary of key points

This chapter has considered the usefulness of activity-based costing (ABC) and its use in understanding customer profitability analysis (CPA). Within these sectors, customers seldom purchase one item (product or service) and generally show a pattern of 'primary' and 'secondary' spend on a range of concurrent purchases of products and services. The key points are:

- To maximise profits you need to focus on the most profitable customers, but need a mechanism to know who they are.

- The combined roles of marketing and the accounting function can do so much more than working independently.

- Activity-based costing is an alternative to traditional absorption costing and proves more useful in service situations.

- Customer profitability analysis allows managers to identify the profits associated with customers, as opposed to departments, products or services.

- In complex environments where customers buy multiple services and products it is customers not products that need to be tracked to maximise financial returns.

- Profit sensitivity analysis (PSA) aids managers in understanding the relationship between individual costs and their impact on profits.

References

CIMA (2008) 'Activity based costing', *Topic Gateway Series No. 1*, CIMA

Harris, P. (2011) *Profit Planning for Hospitality and Tourism*, 3rd edn, Oxford: Goodfellow Publishers.

Krakhmal, V. and Harris, P. (2008) *Recommended Practice Guide: Developing Customer Profitability Analysis for Hotels*, British Association of Hotel Accountants (BAHA). (Note: now called HOSPA.)

Phillips, P. and Halliday, S. (2008) 'Marketing/accounting synergy: a discussion of its potential and evidence in e-business planning', *Journal of Marketing Management*, **24** (7/8), 751–770.

Further reading

Harris, P. and Mongiello, M. (eds) (2006) *Accounting and Financial Management: Developments in the International Hospitality Industry*, Oxford: Butterworth-Heinemann.

The two key chapters are by Paolo Collini, which considers cost analysis and customer-focused AMC, and by Krakhmal, which details his research in hotels.

Krakhmal, V. and Harris, P. (2008) *Recommended Practice Guide: Developing Customer Profitability Analysis for Hotels*, British Association of Hotel Accountants (BAHA). (Note: now called HOSPA.)

This is a useful guide for those wanting to implement CPA.

Self-check student questions

1 How can marketing and finance departments working together improve profitability?

2 Explain the difference between total absorption costing and activity-based costing.

3 What are the key elements of ABC?

4 How does activity-based management (ABB) build on ABC?

5 Explain the difference between a traditional hotel accounting approach and that used in CPA.

6 Describe the term 'cost driver' in relation to ABC. Give an example of a cost driver in events, hospitality and tourism.

7 How can CPA aid management decision making?

8 Explain the principles of profit sensitivity analysis and how it can aid managers.

Further questions and problems

1 a) In a sector with which you are familiar, (events, hospitality or tourism) consider the primary and secondary spend potential from an individual customer – list all products and services they could purchase.

   b) Consider potential cost drivers in this sector that could be used in ABC.

2 Using the data in Table 8.8, calculate the profit multipliers and review your answers by producing a full profit sensitivity analysis report.

Table 8.8: The Country Kitchen, Profit sensitivity analysis (PSA), predicted data

Average spend (selling price)	£8.50
Volume of sales	4,000
Variable food costs	£3.00
Fixed labour costs	£10,000
Other fixed costs	£8,000
Contribution statement	
Sales revenue	£34,000
Variable costs	£12,000
Contribution margin	£22,000
Fixed labour costs	£10,000
Other fixed costs	£8,000
Profit/loss	£4,000

9 The Use of Budgets in Organisations

9.1 Introduction and objectives

Budgeting is a popular management accounting tool – often quoted as the most commonly used management accounting tool. However, that does not mean it is universally accepted in the 21st century and is not without its critics.

After studying this chapter you should be able to:

- Explore the development of budgeting
- Consider the role of budgets within organisations
- Develop budget preparation skills
- Consider the behavioural implications of budgeting
- Evaluate the use of budgets in contemporary business environments

Planning can be divided into two main phases, long-term strategic, corporate level planning and short-term planning (within one year). Detailed budgets normally assist in the short-term phase, as is illustrated in Figure 9.1.

It can be seen that using a budget fulfils many roles across the organisation. The first use of budgeting dates back over 100 years, and they were initially designed for use in a manufacturing environment. In this chapter the traditional role of budgets within service sectors, how they have developed and the future of budgets in the 21st century are all considered. As with any managerial accounting technique, there are advantages and disadvantages to budgeting which need to be explored. There is also much to discuss concerning the human behaviour aspects of budgeting, beyond just the calculation of the figures.

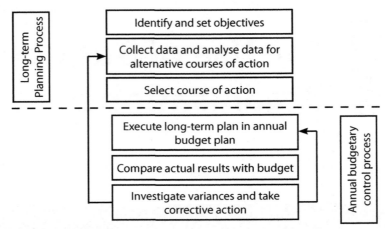

Figure 9.1: The relationship between long-term and short-term budgeting

9.2   The role of budgets

There can be many uses of budgets within an organisation. The key two that are mentioned in most academic literature on the subject are for planning and control. However, if a business is going to the effort of producing a budget, it would be sensible to know what other uses it could be put to. Work by Jones (2008a, 2008b) suggested hospitality organisations mainly used budgets for control and performance measurement, in addition to their role in planning.

They key to the success of a budget's success is whether they have been planned with much forethought and sensitivity – in these circumstances they can have many advantages:

■ They can aid **planning**, which gives a business direction. A budget takes the organisational plan (goal and objectives) and quantifies this into something tangible to aim for. Such forward planning aids anticipating future business conditions and helps avoid otherwise unforeseen problems.

■ Budgets have a role to play in **control** within an organisation. So it can be used to measure **performance** against the targets set in the budget. There are alternative performance measurement tools, as discussed in other chapters – whatever their merits the budget remains the mainstay of performance measurement in many organisations.

■ The budgeting process can encourage **communication** between departments/ employees and aid in the **coordination** of a firm's activities. The budget can be used to communicate financial plans throughout the different parts of the organisation – thus showing how the different parts fit together to form an integrated plan for the organisation as a whole.

■ There is also argued to be a **motivational** role for the budget – if set at the appropriate level. The argument being that the budget gives managers a target to strive towards. However there is also an argument that if set at an inappropriate level (too high or too low) it can have the reverse impact and can demotivate.

9.3   Master budget preparation

There are many approaches to preparing a budgetary plan, each having its merits. So the considerations before even looking at the figures and preparing the budget include:

- *Should the budget be prepared for a fixed financial year, or be a rolling budget?* The most commonly used approach to budgeting is for a fixed financial year for example 1st April 20X1 – 31st March 20X2. Typically 3–4 months before the start of the financial year the budget preparation starts and the budget for a full 12 months is completed and approved for use prior to the start of the year. This means the budgeting process takes place once a year, but the disadvantage can be in, for example January 20X1 you are trying to make predictions of what will be happening in March 20X2, so can the figures be realistic? An alternative is to have a rolling budget, where every month a budget is prepared for a further month as the current month 'rolls off' the budget – so in March 20X1 you write a budget for March 20X2. With a rolling budget, budgeting becomes a continuous process and you always have 12 months ahead. Whilst it can have benefits the annual budget is the most common approach, setting the budget for a whole financial year at a time. Some organisations argue this is what their external lenders (banks) require.

- *Is the best approach 'top-down', or 'bottom-up'?* In a hierarchical organisation it has to be agreed who is involved in writing the budgets. The traditional approach is 'top-down', where budgets are initiated and initially drafted at head office level in the organisation and then passed down the organisation for comment, negotiation and agreement. The alternative, despite the title, still starts at the top of the organisation – higher level management in the 'bottom-up' approach initially set key targets and direction and then managers at lower levels complete the first detailed draft of the budgets. Budgets then work up the organisation. The behavioural aspects of budgeting are dealt with later in this chapter in detail, but generally it is believed that the more managers have full involvement in preparing their own budgets the greater their commitment to achieving them.

- *Do we need a budget committee or a budget manual?* These are traditional tools to assist in the development and approval of budgets, however there is limited evidence of their use in industry these days. There is an argument that a budget manual takes a lot of time to prepare and can become out of date so it is far easier to just add guidance notes into budgetary spreadsheets – these are easily accessed and updated.

9

■ *Should we use a fixed or flexible budget?* These are further choices in the budgeting process. As discussed in earlier chapters, some costs (variable costs) vary with level of activity. With this in mind, if our sales budget is inaccurate it will have a knock-on effect on the variable costs. So a flexible budget 'flexes' to different levels of possible activity, whilst a fixed budget is written with one level of targeted activity (sales). The fixed approach is most commonly used as it is simpler and organisations do not feel the extra effort (cost) of producing a flexible budget gives the payback benefits.

■ *Should an incremental or zero-based approach be used?* An incremental approach is when the previous year's data is used as the base for the budget and adjustments are made from this base – it assumes minimal or predictable change year-on-year. However, there is a school that a better approach is to start from zero, i.e. to not make any assumptions about what is needed and start from scratch each year. It is considered this can give a more accurate budget, but the issue is it takes more time – this leads to a trade-off, does the extra cost of time outweigh the benefits of having more accuracy? Within industry sectors such as hospitality, tourism and events where there is a history of advanced bookings, often a year in advance; it is argued that incremental based budgets, using comparative date for advanced booking and adjustments for external factors negates the need for zero-based budgeting. Obviously with new product and service directions or for new companies there is limited comparable data for incremental budgeting, so zero-based budgeting has to be used.

9.3.1   Limiting factors

A limiting factor is a factor that is not unlimited, so can impede operations or growth. These could, for example, include customers, materials, physical capacity limitation (such as rooms, beds, seats, venue capacity, and plane capacity), labour or capital. As discussed in other chapters these could be a short-term restriction – new staff could be trained, more bedrooms built, alternative plane routes added in the longer term. It is important that when budgeting we recognise these limiting factors – if we use an incremental budget and decide to 'add 5%' to previous sales volumes we need to be aware when this might take us over 100% capacity.

9.3.1.1   Capacity

This is a particularly critical factor; 'absolute perishability' is a key factor for many services offered in this sector. An unsold hotel room, plane seat, theatre seat is a sale lost for ever. If the capacity is 400 rooms (or seats) that is the maximum we can sell on any given night/flight/performance, if they are not sold that opportunity is lost forever and we start the next day/flight/performance with the same 400 available. In manufacturing we could make 400 products each day, but can stockpile any not sold one day to sell another day, so selling 200 one day and selling 600 the next day is feasible when tangible products are being sold. So capacity utilisation and upper limits are critical when budgeting. Some types of capacity have a degree of flexibility, but this is still a limiting factor, for example in food and beverage areas adding extra tables to a restaurant or removing tables (more standing room) in bars can assist in peak periods, but a limit still applies.

9.3.1.2 Customers

This is a critical limiting factor – a budget can look fantastic on paper, but the actual results can only be achieved if a sufficient number of customers are attracted. Without a demand for services provided revenue will be limited and however tightly you control costs a profit will be hard to make. Market research and effective sales promotion can assist with managing demand.

9.3.1.3 Labour

Particularly in times of low unemployment, or for specific job roles where available worker are in short supply this can be an issue. This could relate to high-skilled roles – the demand for appropriately skilled and experienced staff, but equally could apply to mundane and laborious low-skilled jobs. This needs to be considered in budgeting as a limiting factor – if an issue, what can be done to overcome this? There is potential for training staff to develop skills levels if in short supply in the marketplace. Alternatively the service/product could be redesigned to require less skill to produce. Alternative multi-skilling human resource approaches may attract people to the less-skilled jobs if in short supply.

9.3.1.4 Management

Linked with labour more generally, the quality of management is a major factor. A good manager can ensure the impact of other limiting factors is minimised for the business – for example: pricing strategies that allow for peaks and troughs in demand; and staffing policies that understand the nature of the labour market. It is argued the success or failure of the business is ultimately in the hands of the managers, so their ability can be a limiting factor.

9.3.1.5 Capital

Having capital available to fund new projects or to extend existing activities is essential to long-term survival of a business. This could be long-term capital, or short-term funds to finance working capital. If a firm has growing demand it must adequately budget for the funds needed to support this. An example could be that restaurant sales are predicted to increase from 200 customers (covers) a day to 300 – this is a 50% increase in customers, so is likely to mean food costs will also increase in this proportion, so food costs (cost of sales) and inventory will also need to increase. If we do not adequately allow for the increased working capital funds needed to fund this extra inventory it may mean we run out of items and are not able to meet the needs of the potential additional customers, so sales are limited, thus capital becomes a limiting factor.

9.3.1.6 Other limiting factors

The limiting factors given here are examples; many others could exist for a specific business. It has been widely reported in newspapers that Glastonbury 2012 was cancelled due to a lack of police officers and Portaloos, caused by the increased demand from the 2012 London Olympics. Failure to get licences, lack of specific materials, demand for specific equipment, economic and political climates can all be factors to consider when budgeting. Obviously there are always events that are so rare they are not predictable (financial management literature refers to these as 'black swan' events) and cannot be predicted at the time of budgeting – this could include: the Gloucestershire, UK 2007 flooding that closed many venues, cancelled weddings and shut down businesses; the ash clouds of 2011 that shut down flights across much of Europe for an extended period of time; or terrorist threats. Across the hospitality, tourism and events sectors we have to be aware of the marketplace and what the specific limiting factors might be.

9.3.2 Classification of budgets

Figure 9.2 gives an overview of the master budget. All individual budgets can be separated into operating budgets and capital budgets. Operating budgets obviously deal with the operations side of the business – sales revenue, associated costs and operating profits, so aspects that together give you the income statement. Capital budgets relate to aspects you would find on a balance sheet (statement of financial position), so relate to assets and liabilities of the organisation.

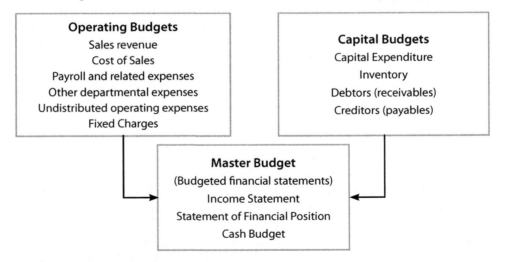

Figure 9.2: Classification of budgets

More detail of these identified budgets and cash budgets is discussed before an example of preparing budget is given.

Obviously the specific budgets shown above are just examples and will vary with industry sector. The importance of each budget will relate to the product/

services offered and their specific associated costs. Wherever feasible, physical quantities should be determined before calculating the revenue and cost values associated with them.

9.3.2.1 Sales revenue budget

For most commercial operations this is the key starting point and the most important budget as it sets the pattern for all other budgets. The total figure will be influenced by sales volume, sales mix and selling prices. So being able to predict these realistically is the key to producing a sound budgetary plan.

9.3.2.2 Maximising gross profit/contribution margin

In many hospitality, tourism and events situations there is an element of 'product' as well as service, so there is a 'cost of sales' (raw materials). Sales revenue has to be related to its associated costs and the resulting gross profit after cost of sales. This is important when we look at different products and services in a sales mix – we are trying to maximise sales from products and services that attract the most return. So we may look at capacity (hotel rooms, seating, floor space), compare this to actual usage the previous year and plan to attract additional customers to fill spare capacity. Or we may want to alter the proportion of space usage, or customer profile to maximise contributions. Using the principles of customer profitability analysis is an effective approach here. Where there is demand, available capacity should be targeted at revenue which attracts higher gross profits.

9.3.2.3 Interdependence

Within these industry sectors the complex nature and interrelationships between products and services is also an important factor. For instance, in a hotel an increase in room sales may have a knock on effect within the bar, restaurant, or spa treatment bookings. A major event, wedding or banquet will increase the demand for accommodation if visitors are not local.

9.3.2.4 Sales forecasting considerations

In order to assist in the preparation of a sales budget the following factors should be considered:

- Past sales volume and mix – past patterns
- Advanced bookings – what we already know about the future – are booking up or down?
- Market research information – industry and economic predictions
- Capacity – maximum limits
- Pricing policy – any alterations/changes anticipated
- Relative product/service profitability – potential profits to best sales mix (yield maximisation)
- Sales personnel, sales training – the ability to actively encourage sales and maximise yields

- Sales promotions – any planned promotions (impact on volume and price)
- Competition – strategic position against competitors and potential new entrants to the market
- Seasonality – knowing the peaks and troughs for the business in the coming year
- Local activities/events – impact of local and wider events on the operation, boosting or reducing sales

9.3.2.5 Cost of sales budget

Due to the nature of the cost of sales this is usually determined as a percentage of revenue, not physical quantities. If organising events the wedding menu might change, or a restaurant may change its menu a few times within the budget period, but a percentage of food or beverage cost can be calculated, with merchandising/memorabilia (festivals, music events, tourist venues) it may be easier to more accurately calculate physical quantities.

9.3.2.6 Payroll and related expenses budget

This is usually a large and significant cost in a service industry. You may be able to actually calculate permanent staffing numbers and requirements against set events; however it is more likely to be calculated in a similar way to cost of sales.

9.3.2.7 Other departmental expenses budget

Again this can either be built up by estimating exact costs or estimated as a proportion of sales revenue.

9.3.2.8 Undistributed expenses budget

As a large proportion of these costs are normally permanent or predetermined costs then estimating is quite common for this budget.

9.3.2.9 Fixed charges budget

This could include management contract fees in a hotel. The predictions for interest charges, to a greater extent, can be determined by economic conditions, whereas the depreciation charge is a matter of management policy. These are not generally related to sales revenue as they relate more to the assets, financing and long-term aspects of the business.

9.3.3 Cash budgeting

Cash is the life blood of any organisation – an organisation is more likely to get into financial difficulties due to lack of cash than by not making a profit in the short term. Only when all operating and capital budgets have been calculated can a cash budget projection be made. It is sometimes confused how a cash budget differs from an income statement. As an income statement uses the principals of accrual accounting it records revenue and expenses as they accrue during a period, not at the point where cash comes in or goes out. A cash budget solely records cash income and expenditure when cash changes hands, not when it is incurred.

A cash budget gives a useful overview of the inflow and outflow of cash in the budgeted period. This can forewarn management as to when cash is short, when an overdraft needs to be arranged, etc. Equally, in times of plentiful cash, short-term investments might be considered to keep the cash working for the business.

In seasonal businesses, as are common in these sectors, cash budgeting can be critical to survival through the peaks and troughs of the business. If an events company focuses on weddings the peak period will be over the summer, similar to the peak tourism season, but whilst more cash comes in during this period expenditure on core business elements are year-long and cash is needed for these.

In some non-commercial organisations, government funded or smaller charities, for example, the cash budget can be the key recording tool for the operation.

9.3.4   Example of preparing a budget (existing business)

The following example uses a hotel with three key operating departments (rooms, food and beverages). The same process can be followed for any hospitality, tourism or events organisation and the number of operating departments can be increased or decreased as necessary in a specific situation. It also shows examples of operating departments with and without cost of sales, which is important when trying to apply in other similar contexts.

Pallas International Hotel uses incremental budgeting, so uses last year's data as a starting point for its budget. In this example the known trading facts are already approved and individual budgets are supplied. This example begins by showing the statement of financial position (Table 9.1), and then the planned changes are applied. Once this 'base data' is explained the three key components of the master budget (income statement, statement of financial position and cash budget) are prepared for the 3 months April–June XXX2.

Table 9.1: Statement of financial position Pallas International Hotels, as at 31st March XXX2. Budget information from the statement of financial position and notes to the accounts

Liabilities	€000	Assets	€000
Trade creditors	25,000	Cash at bank	3,000
Trade accrued expenses		Trade receivables	45,000
Heat and power	5,000	Food inventory	2,000
Loan interest	25,000	Beverage inventory	30,000
Long-term loan	400,000		
Owners' capital	1,600,000	Non-current assets	2,420,000
Retained profit	445,000		
	2,500,000		2,500,000

This information is broken down into more detail than on the external statement of financial position, for example on the external statement 'trade payables' would include trade creditors and accrued expenses, whereas they are detailed separately here for budgeting purposes.

9.3.4.1 Agreed operating budgets

The budgets in Tables 9.2–9.4 were agreed for April–June XXX2.

Table 9.2: Budgeted operating departments revenue and expenses

	Sales revenue			Cost of sales		Payroll and related expenses			Other expenses		
	Rooms	Food	Bev.	Food	Bev.	Rooms	Food	Bev.	Rooms	Food	Bev.
	€000	€000	€000	€000	€000	€000	€000	€000	€000	€000	€000
April	100,000	40,000	20,000	16,000	10,000	12,000	10,000	5,000	9,000	4,000	3,000
May	150,000	60,000	30,000	24,000	15,000	20,000	15,000	8,000	11,000	5,000	3,000
June	250,000	100,000	50,000	40,000	25,000	35,000	25,000	12,000	16,000	11,000	5,000

Table 9.3: Budgeted undistributed operating expenses

	Administration		Marketing		Maintenance		Heat and power	
	Payroll	Other	Payroll	Other	Payroll	Other	Payroll	Other
	€000	€000	€000	€000	€000	€000	€000	€000
April	2,000	1,000	1,000	1,000	2,000	1,000	1,000	2,000
May	2,000	1,000	1,000	1,000	2,000	2,000	2,000	3,000
June	2,000	1,000	1,000	1,000	3,000	2,000	3,000	4,000

Table 9.4: Fixed charges per quarter

	€000
Rates and insurance	16,000
Loan interest (15% per annum)	15,000
Depreciation of non-current assets	30,000

9.3.4.2 Additional information for budget preparation

The following additional information is required for budgeting purposes:

a) Half of the sales revenue is received in cash. The remaining sales revenue is on credit and is received in the month after the sale takes place.

b) All food and beverage purchases are made on credit and are paid for one month after purchase.

c) The gross profit on sales revenue is: rooms 100%; food 60%, beverages 50%.

d) 'Payroll and related expenses' and 'other expenses' are paid in the month in which they are incurred.

e) 'Undistributed operating expenses' are paid in the month they are incurred, except 'heat and power' which is paid a month in arrears.

f) Rates and insurance are paid annually in advance on 1st April.

g) Loan interest is paid half-yearly in arrears on 1st May and 1st November.

h) Expenditure on the purchase of new hotels is planned to take place in May and will be 145,000 (€000).

i) Depreciation of non-current assets for the 3 months will amount to €30,000.

j) Note: '€000' assumed in written sections here, to be consistent with data presented above.

9.3.4.3 Cash budget

As discussed earlier in this chapter and in Chapter 2, there is a distinct difference between cash and profit. Also note there is a difference between a cash budget and a cash flow forecast, the latter is presented in Chapter 12. When preparing a cash budget, items are recorded in the month in which cash changes hands. For Pallas International Hotels a few examples of this are used to illustrate recording items on a cash budget.

Monthly sales revenue

In April the total sales for all three operating departments is (in €000):

€100,000 + €40,000 + €20,000 = €160,000

Note (a) of the additional information states half of this is paid in cash in the month of the sale and half in the month afterwards:

€160,000/2 = €80,000

For a cash budget this means in April €80,000 comes in and the other €80,000 will be recorded when it is paid in May. Does any other sales revenue come in during April? What about the credit sales from March? The assets section of the statement of financial position as at 31st March XXX2 states there are 'trade receivables' of €45,000 at the end of March, so this is the additional cash due to come in from sales revenue to be recorded in April.

Purchase and payment of inventory

In this example it is noted that the closing inventory remains constant – see note (j). Given this it is clear that purchases must be equal to the value of cost of sales. In April the cost of sales is €26,000 (€16,000 + €10,000). Note (b) states that all purchases are on credit and paid for one month after purchase. For cash purposes this means April's €26,000 is cash expenditure in May. Are there any trade creditors to pay in April? The statement of financial position shows a liability of €25,000 for trade creditors – this will be cash going out in April to pay the suppliers.

Following these cash budget example calculations and the information given for Pallas Hotels International, including the notes section, a full monthly cash budget can be calculated (Table 9.5).

Table 9.5: Pallas International Hotels, Cash budget for quarter ending 30th June XXX2

	April	May	June
Receipts:	€000	€000	€000
Revenue from credit sales	80,000	120,000	200,000
Revenue from cash sales	45,000	80,000	120,000
	125,000	**200,000**	**320,000**
Payments:			
Trade creditors (purchases)	25,000	26,000	39,000
Payroll and related expenses	27,000	43,000	72,000
Other expenses	16,000	19,000	32,000
Admin. and general expenses	3,000	3,000	3,000
Marketing	2,000	2,000	2,000
Repairs and maintenance	3,000	4,000	5,000
Heat and power	5,000	3,000	5,000
Rates and insurance	64,000		
Loan interest		30,000	
Purchase of hotels		145,000	
	145,000	**275,000**	**158,000**
Monthly surplus/deficit	(20,000)	(75,000)	162,000
Opening balance	3,000	(17,000)	(92,000)
Closing balance	**(17,000)**	**(92,000)**	**70,000**

The cash budget opening balance for April is the closing balance from March that is in the statement of financial position listed as cash at bank. Each month:

Receipts – Payments = Monthly surplus/deficit

Monthly surplus/deficit + Opening balance = Closing balance

9.3.4.4 Budgeted income statement

Unlike the cash budget, the income statement records income and expenditure when it is incurred (Table 9.6), not when it turns to cash (accrual accounting as previously discussed). For example the budgeted sales revenue from rooms for April is €500,000, so in the income statement that is what is reported. The same is true for expenses, what is incurred in a month is reported, not what was paid out in cash.

As you can see from Table 9.6, the 'net profit' and 'closing cash' positions are very different.

Table 9.6: Income statement for quarter ending 30th June XXX2

Operating departments	Sales revenue	Cost of sales	Payroll and related expenses	Other expenses	Profit (loss)
	€000	€000	€000	€000	€000
Rooms	500,000		67,000	36,000	397,000
Food	200,000	80,000	50,000	20,000	50,000
Beverages	100,000	50,000	25,000	11,000	14,000
TOTAL	800,000	130,000	142,000	67,000	461,000
Less: undistributed operating expenses					
Admin. and general expenses			6,000	3,000	9,000
Marketing			3,000	3,000	6,000
Repairs and maintenance			7,000	5,000	12,000
Heat and power			6,000	9,000	15,000
TOTAL			22,000	20,000	42,000
Total profit before fixed charges					419,000
Less:					
Rates and insurance					16,000
Loan interest					15,000
Depreciation of non-current assets					30,000
TOTAL					61,000
NET PROFIT					358,000

9.3.4.5 Statement of financial position

Using the same format as at the start of this example the financial position at the end of the three-month period can be calculated (Table 9.7).

Table 9.7: Pallas International Hotel, as at 31st June XXX2, Budget information from the statement of financial position and notes to the accounts

Liabilities	€000	Assets	€000
Trade creditors	65,000	Cash at bank	70,000
Trade accrued expenses		Trade receivables	200,000
Heat and power	7,000	Food stock	2,000
Loan interest	10,000	Beverage stock	30,000
Long-term loan	400,000	Pre-paid rates and interest	48,000
Owners' capital	1,600,000		
Retained profit	803,000	Non-current assets*	2,535,000
	2,885,000		2,885,000

* In calculating the non-current assets this is the previous figure, plus the new expenditure, less the depreciation.

Non-current assets = €2,420,000 + €145,000 − €30,000 = €2,535,000

Where do these figures come from? In the liabilities for example 'trade creditors' is the amount you still owe at 30th June, which is the value of June's purchases. On the assets side the 'cash at bank' figure is the June closing balance calculated in the cash budget.

As already discussed, once budgets are set they need to be used as a working document. Budgetary control is the important follow-up, where budgetary plans are compared to actual results.

9.4 Budgetary control

Once departmental budgets have been prepared and a full master budget has been confirmed it should not be filed away and ignored. Producing a budget can give many advantages, but it has to be a working document and utilised within the operation routinely to have a control function. So the budget should focus management's attention on financial targets for the year. Monitoring operating and financial progress needs to be at least month-by-month, but in larger operations could be weekly, or daily as it shows managers how they are doing in relation to the set targets. Most importantly it gives information to where operational issues might exist to aid management in operational control of the business.

At the simplest level this involves a comparison of budget to actual data to identify variances. It is important to note when doing this that a budget is an estimate, so it is unlikely that the actual figures will be a direct match to those budgeted. As a manager it is important to understand which variances are in the boundary of being acceptable and where a 'significant variance' exists. It is only significant variances that are of concern when we are evaluating performance or controlling variances.

Variances are always discussed in relation to their impact on profit. All else being equal, does the variance have an adverse (A) or favourable (F) impact on profit?

Variance:	Impact on profit:
Revenue up	Favourable
Revenue down	Adverse
Specific cost up	Adverse
Specific cost down	Favourable

9.4.1   Significant variances

What makes a variance significant? If our bar sales revenue for a week was predicted to be £50,000, but was £48,000 instead is this significant? How would we know? In reality an organisation will set a benchmark in advance, a threshold that if passed would highlight the variance is significant.

A variance could be set in £x, or x%, or a repeat of an adverse variance, or a combination of these could be utilised. In this example we might have a significant variance set at 5%.

> £50,000 * 5% = £2,500, so unless our variance is at least £2,500 we do not think it is worth investigating.

> Budgeted sales revenue = £50,000, Actual = £48,000, therefore the variance = £2,000.

The variance is not over our benchmark of £2,500 so at this point we do not believe it is worth investigating as it is within our accepted 5%.

What if the next month it is also down, £2,000 and in the third month it is down £2,200? Do we carry on not worrying about it? It is at this point the results may trigger another benchmark, 'a repeat of an adverse variance'. So being £2,000 down one week we think is not significant enough to waste management time investigating as it was 4% (£48,000). We would hope that next week it could just as easily be over by 4% (£52,000). When the results continue to be lower than expected, (£2,000 one week, another £2,000 the next week and a further £2,200 the week after) management should be more concerned and should investigate as this is a 'repeat of an adverse variance'.

The important part of this is that when a 'significant variance' is identified that it is investigated as to why and where possible action is taken to rectify the situation so the organisations improves in the future to maximise its returns (or if a not-for-profit organisations, minimises costs, maximises surplus).

The following is some basic data to illustrate the problems of understanding the reason for a variance occurring.

Sid's Spit Roast is a small event catering company which operates at local summer festivals and events, Sid just sells his pig roast in a bread bap with apple sauce and stuffing (the Pig Bap). He likes to keep it simple so he just sells the one product at a set price.

Here are his figures for June:

	Budget (£)	Actual (£)	Variance
Sales Revenue	13,500	12,000	1,500 A
Food costs	4,500	4,200	300 F
Gross profit	9,000	7,800	1,200 A

From these figures Sid knows his sales income was less than he budgeted for, but on the good side his costs were favourable as they were lower than he had expected, but the net impact is his gross profit is lower than expected. This basic level of detail only allows for limited analysis and will not help Sid to pinpoint the exact issues he has encountered. Adding some percentage data might help him.

Here are his figures for June, including percentages:

	Budget	%	Actual	%	Variance	%
Sales revenue	£13,500	100%	£12,000	100%	£1,500 A	11%
Food costs	£4,500	33%	£4,200	35%	£300 F	7%
Gross profit	£9,000	67%	£7,800	65%	£1,200 A	13%

This information helps him a bit more, but there are still many issues he would be unable to answer from this data:

■ Why has the sales revenue gone down? – difference in sales volume, selling price, or both?

■ Why has the food cost gone down? – as a variable cost, is it still the same per unit, but we sold less? – is it the quantity of ingredients used (portion size)? – or the price per kg that has changed?

Clearly it is these questions that need to be answered, but to do this we need more information and to use a 'flexed budget' to assist.

9.4.2   Flexed budgets

From studying the nature of costs in previous chapters we know that variable costs should, 'vary in direct proportion to level of activity'. So if Sid sold less volume we would automatically expect his total food costs to go down in direct proportion with the volume of activity – we use a flexed budget to aid budgetary control in this situation.

Sid had originally planned to sell his pork baps at £4.50 each and calculated his food costs at £1.50 each when he did his budget. In a flexed budget we take these 'standard costs' per unit and use these to write a budget 'flexed' to the actual level of activity. This shows us, at the actual volume of sales what the budget would have been. So given the actual volume of sales what sales revenue, food cost, and gross profit would we have expected. Sid in his original budget planned to sell 3,000 units (3,000*£4.50 = £13,500), in reality he only sold 2,500 individual units – with this additional information a flexed budget can be used to give us far more information to analyse the situation.

Sid's Spit Roast – Flexed budget for June:

	Per unit	Original budget 3,000	Flexed budget 2,500	Actual 2,500	Flexed to actual variance
Sales Revenue	£4.50	£13,500	£11,250	£12,000	£750 (F)
Food costs	£1.50	£4,500	£3,750	£3,800	£50 (A)
Gross profit	£3.00	£9,000	£7,500	£8,200	£700 (F)

The flexed budget shows that whilst there was an issue with volume (Sid sold 500 less than expected), he actually made more sales revenue than we would expect at this level, his costs per unit were up, however overall his gross profit was favourable for what was expected in the flexed budget.

9.4.2.1   Sales volume variance

If we look at the difference between the original budget and the flexed budget we can see the impact on the gross profit is purely down to the volume of sales. Both these sets of data are calculated using the budgeted figures per unit, so the difference shown in the gross profit can only be due to the volume of sales. The statement can be made: due to the volume reducing from the expected 3,000 units sold to 2,500 we would expect Sid's gross profit to reduce by £1,500 (£9,000 – £7,500 = £1,500). So the variance due to sales volume would be £1,500 adverse. The difference between the original budgeted profit and the flexed profit gives us the sales volume variance.

9.4.2.2   Selling price variance

If we look at the difference in the sales revenue between the flexed budget (£11,250) and the actual (£12,000) the variance is £750 favourable. Both the actual and flexed budgets are calculated for 2,500 units being sold so the difference in the totals can only be due to price, so tells us the price variance. What was the actual selling price? Revenue/number of units = selling price.

£12,000/2,500 = £4.80. So Sid charged £4.80 per unit, not the planned £4.50 in the budget. Charging an additional 30p per unit gave him an extra £750 profit (2,500*£0.30). So is it the increase in price that led to the reduction in sales volume? Has the impact in one outweighed the impact of the other? Would he have been better at keeping the price at £4.50 and selling more volume? This line of questioning relates to issues of cost-volume-profit analysis, as detailed in Chapter 4.

9.4.2.3   Food volume and price variances

We can see from the flexed budget, compared to actual data that food costs were £50 adverse at this level of activity – why is this?* The reasons can be split into two, just like sales revenue – is it due to the volume of food used being more (an extra slice of pork in the roll), or may be the cost per kg of buying the pork was higher than expected, or a combination of both?

First, the food volume variance will isolate the volume issue for Sid. Of his planned £1.50 food cost per unit sold £0.60 related to the cost of the roll, apple sauce and stuffing – there was no variation in this element whatsoever so the variance is with the pork.

Flexed Budgeted pork usage/price was as follows:

500kg * £4.50 per kg = £2,250 (plus other ingredient @ £1,500) = £3,750 food cost

Actual pork usage/price was as follows:

550.24kg * £4.18 per kg = £2,300 (plus other ingredient @ £1,500) = £3,800 food cost

The figures show a variance due to usage and due to price paid per kg. The impact of these is shown below:

Food cost variance   = flexed food cost – actual food cost

= £3,750 – £3,800 = **£50 (A)**

Food price variance   = difference in price * actual volume

= (£4.18 – £4.50) * 500kg

= –£0.32 * 500kg = **–£176 (F)**

Food volume variance =difference in volume * budgeted price

= (550.24kg – 500kg) * £4.50

= 50.24kg *£4.50 = **£226 (A)**

What does this tell us?

It is telling Sid that whilst the net impact on food costs is adverse by £50, when he splits this into how the usage of pork and the price he paid for the pork led to this result he has two major differences. First, his price variance is £176 favourable, so buying the meat at £0.32 cheaper than in his budget would give him £176 more profit. Unfortunately, he seems to have been over generous on his portion sizes, using 50.24kg more pork than he should have done – this had an adverse impact on his profits of £226.

It looks like, as Sid got his meat a bit cheaper, he thought he would add more pork to his rolls and charges extra for this, so put his prices up to £4.80. However, the higher price reduced the volume of sales and the amount of extra meat used cost him more than his saving on the price per kg for the pork.

This can be summarised in a profit reconciliation statement:

Sid's Spit Roast profit reconciliation statement for June

Original budgeted gross profit		£9,000
Sales variances		
Sales volume variance	£1,500 (A)	
Selling price variance	£ 750 (F)	£ 750 (A)
Food cost variances		
Food price variance	£ 176 (F)	
Food volume variance	£ 226 (A)	£ 50 (A)
Actual gross profit		£8,200

This statement gives far more detail than the basic information at the start of this example and summaries all the variance calculations. The answers can always be double-checked as the original budgeted profit adjusted by all the variance calculations should always equal the actual profit.

Note: in this example we have looked at food cost, but the principles are the same for looking at other variances. For example, the total staff cost could be broken down into time used and rate of pay to give us a price and quantity variance in the same way as calculating food price and usage variances.

9.4.3   Sales mix and flexed budgets

Not many organisations just sell one product, equally different products and services may generate different percentage operating profits due to different costs associated with them. Let's look at the example of wedding packages.

Tropical Dreams is a tour company that specialises in offering wedding packages abroad and offer 3 packages:

- **Option 1** – Essential tropics, this includes all the local wedding fees and certification, a wedding coordinator, and choice of wedding locations. This package allows you to make many choices yourself and not be tied in to elements you do not want.
- **Option 2** – The classic, this package includes all the elements of the basic package and additionally a wedding cake, bride's makeup and hair on the day, bridal bouquet and groom's buttonhole, and celebration canapés and wine.
- **Option 3** – Luxury package, included are all the elements of the essential and classic packages, plus pre-wedding spa treatments for bride and groom, post-wedding 4-course meal, and 50 photos in a luxury photo album.

Past experience shows the classic package is the most popular (50%), with those opting for the other two packages at 25% each. The budget is written on this basis, but Tropical Dreams see a change in the sales mix (Table 9.8), with more people opting for the cheaper options – how might this impact on the gross profit?

Table 9.8: Table Dreams sales mix

Package	Budgeted mix	Value	Gross profit %	Gross profit	Actual mix	Value	Gross profit %	Gross profit
Option 1	25%	£200,000	50%	£100,000	40%	£320,000	50%	£160,000
Option 2	50%	£500,000	55%	£275,000	45%	£450,000	55%	£247,500
Option 3	25%	£400,000	65%	£260,000	15%	£240,000	65%	£156,000
	100%	£1,100,000	58%	£635,000	100%	£1,010,000	56%	£563,500

What do the figures in Table 9.8 show? The company is selling the same number of packages and hasn't changed its selling prices – the only difference is which package customers have booked, with more booking the cheaper packages. The impact of this change in sales mix is twofold: first, as they are booking the cheaper packages the total sales revenue has gone down (£1,100,000 to £1,010,000); and second, as the balance moves to the packages with a lower GP% the overall achieved GP% has moved from 58% to 56%.

The difference between these two gross profit figures (£563,500 − £635,000 = £71,500), given equal quantity of sales, represents a 'sales margin mix variance' of £71,500 (A). It is equally possible to have both a 'sales margin quantity variance' and a sales margin mix variance if both total sales numbers and the mix changes.

9.5   Behavioural aspects of budgeting

A budgetary plan and variance analysis for control can provide useful financial data. However there are a lot of human influences on the budget at every stage and this has to be recognised through our use of budgets in an organisation. Budgets can be manipulated and budgetary gamesmanship, where managers' manipulate budgets to personal advantage is all part of the human aspects of budgeting. Any system of budgetary control relies heavily on individuals in the organisation, the attitude and use of budgets by top management can be a major influence on the behaviour of individuals and their attitude towards the budget. A few years ago, after a hotel chain takeover, the new owners wanted more profits so arbitrarily increased all sales budgets by 10%. For the managers lower down the organisation there was no involvement in the decision, no chance to discuss whether this was a realistic new target. As you can imagine motivation to achieve the revised target was low and gamesmanship to manipulate the budget becomes high in such situations.

9.5.1   Responsibility accounting

The concept of responsibility accounting can be used well alongside a system of budgetary control. Responsibility accounting links the accounting system with an individual manager's span of control. An individual manager should only be held accountable for those things which they can actually control, thus they can only be held accountable for financial performance for items they directly have control over. This means responsibility accounting matches responsibility with accountability for individuals in an organisation. Chapter 2 identified responsibility accounting reporting formats related to use of the USALI. Responsibility accounting separates costs into their 'direct' and 'indirect' components; these are discussed within Chapter 3.

An individual manager's responsibilities fall into one of four types of 'responsibility centres':

- Cost centre
- Revenue centre
- Profit centre
- Investment centre

9.5.1.1 Cost centre

A cost centre is a part of an organisation where individuals are held accountable for costs under their control. Examples would include support departments, security, housekeeping, administration and operations departments responsible for production, but not sales. The budget provides the target for these managers to work towards, so provides a guideline to work to. The budget can impact on the spending – if it is too generous then these managers could be encouraged to spend more than is necessary as they spend up to the allowance in the budget. A 'loose' budget of this nature is not effective for control. If the budget is too tight a manager may give up as they feel the budget is unrealistic and not achievable. For budgets to work effectively, from a behavioural point of view, the person held accountable needs to be motivated – the art of budgeting is to draw organisation and personal goals together (goal congruence) and to ensure the budget is set 'just right', tight, but achievable.

9.5.1.2 Revenue centre

In a revenue centre the manager is only held accountable for generating revenue, but not the costs associated with it. In a reservations or sales unit it is likely there is a target for sales revenue, yet the associated costs for this are outside that manager's responsibility. This has to be managed carefully so meeting their own personal targets is not achieved to the detriment of the organisation as a whole. For example, a conference booking is being negotiated – if this manager is only held accountable for revenue maximisation and not the costs or profits generated they may not negotiate a deal that is best for the organisation, but what meets their own targets. The concepts of revenue management and the impact of sales mix on the organisation helps in understanding the consequences in this situation.

9.5.1.3 Profit centre

Where a manager has responsibility for sales and the associated costs they can be held accountable for their departmental (or divisional) operating profit. The advantages claimed for profit centres is the encouragement it gives to managers to perform well by maximising revenues whilst also minimising costs to maximise profit returns. Profit responsibility can encourage a more positive attitude to financial aspects of operations management. Quite simply, if you are in control of a profit centre there isn't the 'not my problem' attitude that can be an issue in cost or revenue centres.

9.5.1.4 Investment centre

An investment centre gives the highest level of responsibility, in addition to revenue, costs and profits, these managers are responsible (accountable) for investment decisions within their span of control. Within a large organisation there are likely to be different divisions. Where a divisional manager has full control over the centre they will make longer-term investment decisions, so have a significant role in the future development and capital investment within their division. For it to be an investment centre there has to be central delegation to the divisional manager for decision making and operational authority over the division. If investment decisions are controlled by head office, then it would be a profit centre. From a behavioural viewpoint an investment centre can have advantages:

- Managers are more motivated to perform well because of the greater authority they enjoy
- The autonomy of divisional managers reduces communication problems; and
- In a decentralised structure, top management has more time to focus on strategic matters.

9.5.1.5 Transfer pricing

Whilst there are benefits in control to responsibility accounting it raises the issue of transfers between different centres, all trying to maximise their financial performance. Goods and services transferred between divisions have to be priced so that the supplying division gets the credit; this then becomes a cost to the receiving division. A transfer price may be set at cost, or include some form of profit – examples include a transfer price at variable cost, full cost, cost plus profit, market price, or a negotiated price. Transfer pricing can provide some conflicts as it is required to:

- Encourage good decision making which will be best for the division and for the company (goal congruence)
- Enable divisional performance to be fairly measured; and
- Provide a vehicle for achieving divisional autonomy.

A single transfer pricing method rarely satisfies all these objectives and so compromise is the norm. Resolving such a conflict is not easy and a negotiated transfer system can help. Of course outsourcing is always an option but there is a danger if the transfer price is set too high (market price) a division may go outside instead of using an internal transfer – this may, or may not maximise returns for the organisation as a whole.

Transfer pricing is utilised in manufacturing, a similar scenario with these sectors is that of separating out sales revenue 'fairly' when a packaged or bundles product is sold. A simple example would be a hotel selling a 24-hour spa package. This is sold for a combined price of £220 and includes a 1 hour spa treatment, 1 night's accommodation, breakfast, spa lunch and dinner (Table 9.9).

Table 9.9: Package pricing

Spa package components	Full rate
Hotel room	£160
Meals in restaurant	Breakfast £14, Dinner £30
Spa treatment	£60
Spa lunch	£16
Total purchased individually	£280

The packaged cost is £220, whilst buying the elements individually costs £280, So the packaged cost is £60 less. Therefore there has to be a mechanism for 'sharing' the £220 between departments, much the same as transfer pricing. In some hotels it is always the room that gets discounted, as it is considered to have no variable costs. This would allocate £100 to the rooms department as the £60 lost revenue would come from the room rate. However under responsibility accounting this is unfair to the rooms division and favours the other departments' operating profit. A fairer way, as recommended in the USALI, is to apportion evenly.

£220/£280 * 100 = 79%

This shows the package price is 79% of the full cost, so each element of the package should be allocated 79% of the 'normal' full cost, for example:

Room usually £160 * 79% = £126.40

This alternative allocation will take sales income away from the other departments, but increase the room divisions allocation from £100 to £126.40, which better reflects their 'fair share' of the income.

9.6   Beyond Budgeting/Better Budgeting

A number of academics and organisations have questioned the role of budgets in modern businesses. The arguments are around the fact that the origins of budgets can be traced back over 100 years, with their roots in the industrial revolution and manufacturing. The argument that 'traditional budgeting' is not 'fit for purpose' in modern business revolve around a number of factors:

- The change of pace in business – can we any longer produce a fixed budget for a year ahead, given rapid changes in the world we need to react to?
- Budgets restrict entrepreneurial risk-taking – this could have a negative impact on long-term business growth.
- Budgetary control can be inward looking – the external issues in the market and comparative analysis of competitors are seen as vital in modern business.
- Traditional budgeting can lead to 'budgetary gamesmanship' – this can lead to managers actions that are not in the best long-term interest of the firm as a whole.
- Budgets are time-consuming to produce – on a cost versus benefit basis are they valuable?
- Departmental barriers can be encouraged in budgets, often with competing targets – does this maximise the returns for the business as a whole?

These criticisms led to two different alternative schools of thought: 'beyond budgeting' and 'better budgeting'. Both these movements identified similar issues with traditional budgeting, but addressed these in very different ways. As might be suggested from the names, beyond budgeting believed firms should move 'beyond budgets' and look for alternative ways of planning and control in organisations. The better budgeting view was that budgets could be adapted to meet the needs of modern industry.

9.6.1   Beyond Budgeting

A group called the Better Budgeting Round Table (BBRT) have led this movement. They have written books and articles and have a website (www.bbrt.org) where examples of companies following their adaptive, relative performance approach can be found. Having first raised concerns around budgets this soon led to questioning traditional hierarchical organisation structures and many other aspects of managing organisations. Their 'adaptive and empowered' organisations include a number in the service sector – they name Southwest Airlines as a member of this group. Their twelve core principles are shown in Figure 9.3.

Figure 9.3: 12 Beyond Budgeting Principles (2011) (Data from BBRT)

Governance and transparency	
1. Values	Bind people to a common cause; *not a central plan*
2. Governance	Govern through shared values and sound judgement; *not detailed rules and regulations*
3. Transparency	Make information open and transparent; *don't restrict and control it*
Accountable teams	
4. Teams	Organize around a seamless network of accountable teams; *not centralized functions*
5. Trust	Trust teams to regulate their performance; *don't micro-manage them*
6. Accountability	Base accountability on holistic criteria and peer reviews; *not on hierarchical relationships*
Goals and rewards	
7. Goals	Set ambitious medium-term goals; *not short-term fixed targets*
8. Rewards	Base rewards on relative performance; *not on meeting fixed targets*
Planning and controls	
9. Planning	Make planning a continuous and inclusive process; *not a top-down annual event*
10. Coordination	Coordinate interactions dynamically; *not through annual budgets*
11. Resources	Make resources available just-in-time; *not just-in-case*
12. Controls	Base controls on fast, frequent feedback; *not budget variances*

Their approach is a complete new way of looking at many aspects of organisations, not just getting rid of budgets.

9.6.2 Better Budgeting

In the CIMA report (2004) Dugdale and Lyne reported both financial and non-financial managers still viewed budgets of being of value and having a role to play in businesses. The general feeling was that whilst there could be some issues raised with budgets they still proved a useful tool for management planning and control. Using them to assist and provide guidance, with a bottom-up approach (involving managers at a lower level in the organisation in writing the budgets), alongside non-financial performance measures was seen as the way forward. Another issue is the external one related to financial backers, banks making business loans to organisations. There is evidence that banks require budgets to be lodged with them as a condition of providing loans, so this is an external influence that also supports the need for budgets in organisations.

Early within the chapter it was noted that budgeting has a long history, dating back to the 19th century. Whilst the vast majority of organisation still use budgets the way in which they are used and the changes highlighted in the better budgeting versus beyond budgeting debate highlight how much things have changed in the 21st century. There have been a number of studies into budgeting practice within hotels since the 1980s.

Hospitality applied budgeting research has taken place for over 30 years. In the 1980s and 1990s research was predominantly USA-based. Since then research has taken place more widely around the world to include USA, the UK, Turkey, Australia and the Far East. This research has covered a number of aspects of budgeting, such as operational budgeting and forecasting, better budgeting, participation in budgeting, and the impact of environmental uncertainty. Whilst the aspects of budgeting research varies, so too does the theoretical stand point, research into budgeting shows a contribution from economic, psychological and sociological perspectives. Whilst the research already undertaken addresses some questions there is still much work that could be undertaken to fully understand budgeting in the hospitality and even more so related to tourism and events management.

Research has clearly shown budgeting is still alive and well in industry and whilst it has been adapting to meet modern market situations it is not 'dead and buried' as some were predicting a few years ago.

9

Summary of key points

There are many aspects to budgeting including: preparation, use in control, behavioural implications and more recent discussion regarding their usefulness. They are the most commonly used management accounting tool in organisations and have a key role in most organisations.

The key learning points from the chapter are:

- Budgets have existed for over a century within organisations.
- Budgets have many roles, including aiding; planning, control, performance measurement, communication, coordination, and motivation.
- There are a number of limiting factors when budgeting such as: physical capacity, customer demand, labour availability, management ability or capital available.
- A master budget combines all individual operating and capital budgets.
- Cash is the life blood of an organisation, so the cash budget is as important as the income statement and statement of financial position.
- Being able to identify 'significant' variances is an important aspect of budgetary control.
- Flexed budgets aid control when the sales volume is not as predicted in the original budget.
- Responsibility accounting aids the ability to match financial statements to the individual elements a specific manager is responsible for and has the ability to influence/control.
- Beyond budgeting and better budgeting are alternative ways of overcoming weaknesses with traditional budgeting.
- Beyond budgeting is not a method of budgeting, it is an alternative that does not use a budget.

References

BBRT (2012) Better Budgeting Round Table website, www.bbrt.org

CIMA (2004) *Better Budgeting: A Report on the Better Budgeting Forum from CIMA and ICAEW*, CIMA.

Jones, T.A. (2008a) 'Changes in hotel industry budgetary practice', *International Journal of Contemporary Hospitality Management*, 20 (4), 428–444.

Jones, T.A. (2008b) 'Improving hotel budgetary practice – a positive theory model', *International Journal of Hospitality Management*, 27 (4), 529–540.

Further reading

Proctor, R. (2009) *Managerial Accounting for Business Decisions*, 3rd edn, FT Prentice Hall.

This textbook includes three chapters related to budgeting, however the industry examples tend to be based around manufacturing.

Jones, T.A. (1998) 'UK hotel operators use of budgetary procedures', *International Journal of Contemporary Hospitality Management*, 10 (3), 96–100.

This gives details of earlier survey research related to budgeting, for those wanting to view the changes over a period of time.

Self-check student questions

1 Budgets have many uses; discuss the roles budgets can have in an organisation.

2 There are a number of limiting factors identify these and discuss them using illustrative examples related to hospitality, tourism or events.

3 Detail the components of the master budget and the individual budgets that will need to be prepared before the master budget can be completed.

4 Why is it important to have a detailed monthly cash budget? What financial issues might an organisation face without a cash budget?

5 Explain how a flexed budget could be used within a hospitality, tourism or events business with which you are familiar.

6 Explain what the advantages of responsibility accounting are and explain the various 'responsibility centres' that exist.

7 Explain the terms 'beyond budgeting' and 'better budget', how do these two concepts differ?

8 A music festival is offering a 'ticket-plus' package for £250. It includes a festival ticket, car parking, festival programme, and a souvenir tee shirt. Using the full prices below, how much revenue should be allocated to each element in the package?

Festival 'Ticket-Plus'	Individual price
Festival ticket	£230
Car parking for weekend	£20
Festival programme	£10
Souvenir tee shirt	£20
Total at full price	£280

9

Further questions and problems

1   Write a report for the manager of either a hotel, conference centre, or a museum explaining how budgets can be utilised as a performance tool and their limitations.

2   Prepare a cash budget, income statement and a statement of financial position using the data in Table 9.10.

Table 9.10: Sea Views Hotel, as at 31st March XXX2, Budget information from the statement of financial position and notes to the accounts .

Liabilities	£	Assets	€000
Trade creditors	35,000	Cash at bank	4,000
Trade accrued expenses		Trade receivables	55,000
Heat and power	6,000	Food inventory	3,000
Loan interest	30,000	Beverage inventory	35,000
Long-term loan	300,000		
Owners' capital	1,900,000	Non-current assets	2,629,000
Retained profit	455,000		
	2,726,000		2,726,000

The budgets in Tables 9.11–9.13 were agreed for April–June XXX2.

Table 9.11: Budgeted operating departments revenue and expenses

Month	Sales revenue			Cost of sales		Payroll and related expenses			Other expenses		
	Rooms	Food	Bev.	Food	Bev.	Rooms	Food	Bev.	Rooms	Food	Bev.
	£	£	£	£	£	£	£	£	£	£	£
April	110,000	50,000	30,000	18,000	10,000	14,000	12,000	8,000	11,000	1,000	3,500
May	160,000	70,000	40,000	26,000	16,000	25,000	18,000	10,000	13,000	6,000	4,000
June	280,000	110,000	60,000	43,000	28,000	40,000	28,000	15,000	18,000	12,000	5,500

Table 9.12: Budgeted undistributed operating expenses

Month	Administration		Marketing		Maintenance		Heat and power	
	Payroll	Other	Payroll	Other	Payroll	Other	Payroll	Other
	£	£	£	£	£	£	£	£
April	2,500	1,500	1,000	1,000	3,000	1,000	1,500	2,500
May	2,500	1,500	1,000	1,000	3,000	2,000	2,500	3,500
June	3,000	1,500	1,000	1,000	4,000	2,000	3,500	4,500

Table 9.13: Fixed charges per quarter

	€000
Rates and insurance	16,000
Loan interest (10% per annum)	7,500
Depreciation of non-current assets	20,000

Additional information for budget preparation

The following additional information is required for budgeting purposes:

a) Half of the sales revenue is received in cash. The remaining sales revenue is on credit and is paid the month after the sale took place.

b) All food and beverage purchases are made on credit and paid the month after purchase.

c) 'Payroll and related expenses' and 'other expenses' are paid in the month in which they are incurred.

d) 'Undistributed operating expenses' are paid in the month they are incurred, except 'heat and power' which is paid a month in arrears.

e) Rates and insurance are paid annually in advance on 1st April.

f) Loan interest is paid half-yearly in arrears on 1st June and 1st December.

g) Expenditure (£40,000) in the purchase of new equipment is planned to take place in April.

h) Food and beverage closing inventory for 30th June XXX2 are expected to remain unchanged from those reported on 31st March XXX2.

9

10 Event and Function Management Acounting Techniques

10.1 Introduction and objectives

This chapter focuses on a particular type of decision making that is associated with bespoke, 'one-off' events and functions. These can be associated with events in any sector and still have value to hospitality and tourism managers who often are involved in, or are impacted by such events locally, nationally and internationally. The chapter focuses on the specific nature of these decisions, as opposed to routine decision making or the running of 'standard' events follow a predetermined package that has been used many times before.

After studying this chapter you should be able to:

■ Gain a working knowledge of how the nature of events impacts on the management accounting tools useful in the decision making process

■ Develop a working knowledge of management accounting tools that aid event planning, operation, control and performance measurement; and

■ Understand the usefulness of management accounting in the events sector for management decision making.

10.2 Features of the events and function sector

Whether it is running a: wedding in a hotel banqueting suite, charity fun run, food and drink festival, weekend music festival, major international sporting event, an air show, major annual conference, literature festival, vintage steam fair, corporate event, product launch, or concert, all events have a common feature and that is they are not continuous. An 'event' is just that, it is an 'occurrence', 'activity', 'happening', 'gathering', 'activity', so whether it is bespoke, 'one-off' event, or one of a series events (concert tour, annual conference, annual charity ball) each individual event is usually discrete. If this is compared to a hotel, which is operating 24/7, 365 days of the year, they are quite different. This has implications for management accounting, the best techniques to use and the 'unit' of analysis.

In a hotel, customers arrive and depart all the time, it never stops. There is never a point where you are without customers, some will be arriving, some will be departing and other will be in the middle of their stay. In an event, whilst individuals may not all arrive at exactly the same time, by nature, an individual event has a beginning, middle and an end point predetermined. For example, for a local food and drink festival, stall holders may set up on the Thursday, it is open to the public set hours Friday–Sunday, and then the event is closed. The implications of this provide particular benefits, but also higher financial risks if management accounting information is not used effectively by event managers.

The risk is associated with the relative number of 'events' taking place. If the event company only runs 2–3 major national/international events a year financial failure of one event could represent a third of the year's the trading opportunity. In a hotel, if one night is a financial problem you still have 364 other nights trading in the year to rely on. With outside summer events external uncontrollable factors such as the weather could cause a significant impact on the event. It is therefore critical that event managers look at all potential scenarios and are able to financially model the 'What if?' implications at the planning stage, looking at worst case as well as expected scenarios.

The management accounting opportunity available to an event is related to its discreet nature. Financial planning and control can be at the level of 'the event'. In a continuous operation, such as a hotel, planning and control is best at the level of the individual customer/unit, or over a time period (day, week, a month, for example). Management accounting at the level of 'the event' is the equivalent of using 'job costing' within manufacturing. A separate financial plan can be set up for the event and controlled at that level throughout the planning, operation and review process. In this chapter sections will focus around how management accounting aids managers' planning, during and post-event. This has two purposes: one to ensure the individual event is financially as successful as possible; and second, that the financial data becomes a point for review and evaluation to aid planning further events in the future.

10.3 Event planning phase management accounting tools

There are many strategic and practical event planning tasks that can be aided by management accounting. The diagram in Figure 10.1 highlights some of the financial considerations and these are then discussed in relation to how management accounting tools can assist event managers.

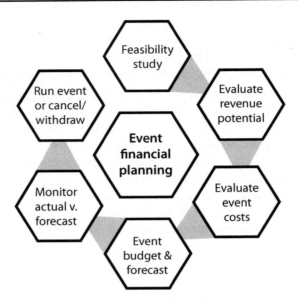

Figure 10.1: Management accounting in event planning

10.3.1 Feasibility study

Depending on the event type, it may be the event company is: being asked for a quote to run an event for another organisation; is the promoter/operator of their own event; or responding to an open public tendering process. However, in all circumstances a feasibility study is required before committing to the event. The feasibility study may include:

- Does the company have the required skills and expertise (or could acquire them) needed to run the event?
- Does the event fit with the strategic direction of the company?
- Is there time availability in the diary needed for the event (clashes with planning and running other events)?
- Can the event provide a financial return for the company?

It would make no sense to accept an event contract and after signing contracts realising it will be a loss-making event. Being able to consider the financial potential at an early stage in the planning process is critical to making the right decision.

10.3.2 Evaluate revenue potential

Depending on the type of event, it may be an all-inclusive fee for managing the event, selling tickets to the public, selling trader space, merchandising, bars, food and drink, additional workshops, VIP packages, etc. Operationally, it is about estimating the potential volumes and prices for each potential revenue source.

From a management accounting perspective, these estimates need to be based on as much financial data as possible:

- If the event, or a similar event, has been run before what guide does that provide? It may be you can identify spend per person on average spent on merchandising, etc.

    Example: past experience shows £8 is spent on merchandising per person. If ticket sales are predicted at 3,000 the merchandising income can be estimated.

    £8 * 3,000 = £24,000 estimated merchandising sales

- Pricing approaches identified in Chapter 6 can be utilised in setting a price in events sectors: positioning the price in the market (market-based pricing); ensuring costs will be covered (cost-plus pricing); or using target costing, working towards a set selling price can all be of use.

    Example: The HSE (1999) *Purple Book* makes a practical health and safety point related to pricing. If there will be 'cash sales' on the day, HSE advise the use of round numbers as a crowd/queue control measure. In Chapter 6, psychological pricing suggested using £19.99, as opposed £20, as better but for an event, with cash sales and likely queues, HSE advice would need to be followed. This identifies the complex nature of decision making and thinking through financial and operational consequences of decisions made at the same time.

10

10.3.3 Evaluate event costs

Depending on the type of event there are a number of approaches to this:

Cost Example A: If the situation is that the client knows exactly what they want and you need to quote them an event price, costing can be 'bottom-up'. What costs will be incurred to meet the client's requirements?

Cost Example B: A client states they have £60,000 to spend on a corporate event and expect 1,500 people and want to know what you can offer them. In this situation, a target costing approach may be better. Your required event operating profit is 40% (after event costs, not total costs)

If event operating profit is 40% and sales revenue = £60,000

Event operating profit = £60,000 * 40% = £24,000

Target costs = Sales − Profit

Target costs = £60,000 − £24,000 = £36,000

In this example (Figure 10.2), to make the required profit you would need the costs to be a maximum of £36,000. With this situation the 'must have' cost elements of the event should be ascertained first: venue hirer, food and drink, equipment, licences and any specific insurance. Once the 'must have' elements have been covered then the 'desirable' elements can be added within the amount of money left to cover costs. This is illustrated as a cone, the maximum is £36,000, cover all the essentials first.

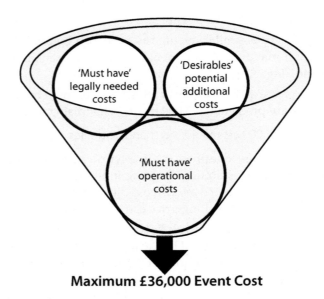

Figure 10.2: Evaluating event costs

At this point it may be that what is wanted from the client for the cost simply doesn't add up financially. Having used the financial data to reach this conclusion there are two options: decline the event; go back to the client and detail an event you could provide for their fixed fee; or how much they would have to pay for what they want. Until you have the financial data it is difficult to make an informed evidence-based decision.

It may be they want a celebrity as an after-dinner speaker, a full cost-benefit analysis would need to be completed to see if the additional cost was outweighed by the benefits to justify this cost.

10.3.4 Event budgeting and forecasting

The principles of budgeting in the last chapter can equally be applied to preparing a budget for a specific event, just as easily as for a department. Forecasting is more operational and relates to a shorter term. Depending on the type of event both or just a forecast might be needed. A number of major events are planned from years in advance (for example: Olympic events, world level football competitions, rugby tournament, trade exhibitions). From the starting point, a budget is essential to keeping control and managing cash flow and should be developed prior to a financial commitment to run an event. Operational sales and cost data are discussed in the previous sections. Cash budgeting is also important and the budget will highlight peaks and troughs in the demands for cash and the timing of cash coming in from sales.

Example: A forecast is a more short-term operational document. A year before a public food and drink festival is due to take place a budget for the event is put together which includes financial estimates. The same company has run this annual event for 5 years. Evaluating previous years' financial data it is clear usually 30% of attendees book tickets at least 1 month in advance of the event and 80% of trade stands are booked at least 1 month in advance.

For ticket sales the original budget was for 4,000 people to buy tickets for the event. Based on this fact and 30% usually booking at least 1 month in advance, to achieve the original budget 1 month before the event it would be expected 1,200 tickets would be booked.

Budgeted expected ticket sales 1 month in advance = 4,000 * 30% = **1,200** tickets

One month before the event actual ticket sales data shows only 800 tickets have been sold, not the budgeted 1,200 at this stage before the event. Given the known booking pattern a forecast can be undertaken. If 800 tickets have been sold a month before the event and that usually represents 30% of final ticket sales a revised forecast can be made.

$$\frac{800 * 100}{30} = \textbf{2,667} \text{ forecast total ticket sales}$$

The above calculations and similar details for the trade stand sales are summarised in Table 10.1.

10

Table 10.1: Ticket and trade stands sales

	Previous data % booked by 1 month in advance	Budgeted sales volume	Based on data, no to be booked 1 month in advance	Actual sales 1 month in advance	Based on actual bookings, forecasted sales
Ticket sales	30%	4,000	**1,200**	800	**2,667**
Trade stand sales	80%	100	80	60	75

The financial short-term forecast gives the events managers useful data for decision making and reviewing the event, and identifies to the event managers a possible issue. This is further explored in section 10.3.6.

10.3.5 Monitor actual v. forecast

Regular monitoring of actual data against forecasts (sales and costs) is critical to sound financial control, including cash forecasting. If the event company can identify that costs are too high three months before the event, or tickets sales have increased so more food will be needed on the day this is valuable data to ensure the event is revised and accurate forecasts are used for decision making about the event. Using financial data is not all about highlighting negative problems. It may be you predicted 4,000, but re-forecasting shows the numbers are likely to be 6,000. If you have the capacity for 6,000 this is positive news, but knowing this in advance means further temporary toilets and staffing can be arranged in plenty of time and make the event run more smoothly on the day.

In monitoring cash it is important to consider payment schedules and cancellation fees you have set in your terms with the customer. It may be a 50% deposit was required at the time of booking, but the balance is required in advance of the event. Making sure reminders for payments are sent and full payment is received in advance is an important element in working capital control.

10.3.6 Run event or cancel/withdraw

Setting out a budget and reviewing progress against targets regularly could highlight issues with an event. In the food and drink festival example advanced ticket sales and trade stand numbers are both down.

Table 10.2: Run or cancel?

	Budgeted sales volume	Based on actual bookings, forecasted sales
Ticket sales	4,000	2,667
Trade stand sales	100	75

Given this information what could the events company do?

Option A – Despite being a smaller event, it may still be financially viable so go ahead.

Option B – Having reviewed the 'relevant costs' it may be a better financial option to cancel the event; or

Option C – Spend more on advertising and promotion in the hope of attracting more public and trade sales.

The financial modelling, 'What if?' analysis, from earlier chapters would assist in making such decisions, using relevant costs.

10.4 Management accounting tools for use during the event

Control and contingency planning are important at an event. As far as possible, managers need to be proactive and consider potential scenarios and financial risks in advance so they can quickly implement the plans if needed. At the same time there will be situations where managers have to be reactive to unanticipated situations. In such situations management accounting information can aid the decision making process. At times health and safety (H&S) issues may mean a financial loss cannot be avoided as H&S takes precedence.

As an example, a number of years ago a charity battle re-enactment event was running on a bank holiday weekend. Over 2,000 people were camping and members of the public were parked in a field to watch the afternoon's event. Being late summer the field was dry and the weather was warm, though windy. As part of the event a replica cannon was fired, something that had been done at many events before. Within seconds the field was alight and being fanned by the wind and spread to the public car park. The event was stopped, the next day cancelled and the campsite cleared of thousands of campers. In such a scenario H&S takes priority and the decision to cancel is not a financial one. Incidents of flooded event sites, once the event has started, are similar situations. However, if looking at the alternatives to a flood site prior to an event starting a more proactive cost–benefit analysis can be used.

Figure 10.3: Management accounting during the event

10.4.1 Revenue control

Revenue control is not just a consideration in the planning phase. If you have 2,000 event tee shirts to sell as merchandising that are printed with the event name and date and artists they are worthless after the event. If sales are slow you might need to promote them, advertise on the stage between acts, or reduce the price to encourage sales at the end of the event. Proactively monitoring and reviewing revenue decisions during the event are important to maximising the financial returns.

Another example may be where through monitoring revenue you know sales are higher than you had estimated. If halfway through the event you have sold 80% of your predicted ice cream sales and the weather is still hot and sunny you might want to review stock levels and get more ice cream onsite – if you run out it is a sales opportunity lost forever. This equally applies to bar stock, where monitoring of stock and sales is important during the event taking place.

From a financial perspective you are trying to maximise revenue and a number of events will have considered this in the ticket terms and conditions. An example would be not allowing people to bring their own alcoholic beverages onto the festival site. This is set in the planning phase, before ticket sales take place, but needs to be monitored physically during the festival. Another example would be the refunds policy, for example no refunds unless the event is cancelled. In horseracing events it is common for the return policy to be:

- No racing = full refund;
- Racing abandoned after over 50% of races have taken place = no refund; and
- Racing abandoned after at least one race, but less than 50% of races = 50% refund.

If there are seven races planned the difference between stopping the races after 3 races, as opposed 4, has a significant impact on sales revenue. After 3 races, all customers get a 50% refund so your ticket revenue is halved, but after 4 races no refunds are issued. Abandonment is likely to be a H&S issue concerning the track surface or levels of light so it may not be possible to consider the financial impact in the decision. Where possible, delaying the decision may be the best financial alternative if there is any possibility of holding a fourth race during the day.

During the event taking place the focus is on monitoring, maximising and protecting revenue as much as possible.

10.4.2 Cost control

Ensuring the costs for the event stays within the budget or forecast set in the planning phase is important. This becomes a practical issue of physical management of key costs. Where there are a lot of temporary event staff, tight staffing controls are needed. It may be you have staff working different hours, with, for example, 2 staff running a coffee bar all day, but an additional member of staff covering the peak period. If you are paying staff on an hourly basis physical control of time sheets on the day, ensuring payment is only made for agreed hours on time sheets signed and confirmed by supervisors is a key financial control on staffing costs.

Another cost area is cost of sales. Stock management, can be a particular issue in a green field event where stock is in marquees and stock security can be key to meeting cost of sales targets. Equally the usage needs to be managed, particularly with temporary staff. Portion sizes of food, wastage and spoilage all need tight control on the day to stay within budgeted figures. Monitoring throughout the event and not just waiting until post-event financial analysis allows corrective action to be taken sooner and allows the profits to be maximised.

10.4.3 Cash control

Events can involve extensive amounts of cash changing hands, with thousands of pounds going through tills. Staff training and cash security is important; again the emphasis needs to be on constant control throughout the event and not discovering a problem too late. Not allowing staff to take bags or their own money into their work areas, checking till totals against physical cash and emptying tills on a regular basis are all measures event managers can take during the event. The important financial aspect is where issues are identified action is taken at that point in time so it does not continue for the whole event.

10.4.4 Constant review

The key point during the event is constant measurement and review of both physical items and review against the financial plan. Knowing there is a financial variance is only part of the picture, the key to maximising financial returns is to take corrective action as soon as possible. Being vigilant, maintaining tight controls and responding to changing situations are key to the financial success of the event.

10.4.5 Future event plans

Whilst the point has been made that a single event is a discrete unit for analysis purposes, its relationship to other events when the organisation is trying to max-imise financial returns in the long term should not be underestimated.

An example of this is the Wychwood Festival, each year at the event the dates for the next event are already set. This allows them to promote the next year's festival to those attending the current festival. They also allow discounted tickets to be booked for the following year; tickets are not usually available to the general public until later in the year. From the customer perspective they get a discount, from the organisers' perspective they get an indication of future sales and cash flow benefits. Where an event is part of a series of events, whether annual, the next monthly comedy night, or the next horserace, maximising revenue for the future can be achieved by utilising promotion and sales opportunities during the current event.

10.5 Post-event performance review management accounting tools

The end of the event is not the end of the event management process. First, there will still be a lot financially to complete with potential revenue cash still coming in and costs to pay. Second, a full financial review of the event needs to be under-taken, using management accounting data for the evaluation (Figure 10.4). The importance of the review is to learn from the event and to improve future decision making – strategically should we run such events in the future? If so, what can we learn from this event to perform better in the future?

Figure 10.4: Post-event management accounting review tools

10.5.1 Revenue review

A detailed breakdown of revenues by category, selling price and volumes can provide much detail for financial analysis purposes. It is important that clear records are kept of the detailed breakdown by specific sales points to aid detailed analysis. Knowing far more merchandising was sold by the unit when located next to the stage, as opposed to near food stands is important to know. Such information could lead to changing the location of the second merchandising point at the next event.

10.5.2 Cost review

As with revenue review, the importance is to have a detailed breakdown of all cost elements, by individual sales points so a detailed analysis can be undertaken. Post-event there may also be additional unpredicted costs, such as payment for site damage, fines for noise levels, or allowing the music to play beyond the licence curfew time. The basic calculation of sales revenue – costs = profits is important to remember here. If sales remain the same, every time costs go up, profits go down. For maximising financial returns in the long term, controlling costs and learning from each event to improve the next is critical.

10.5.3 Profit (surplus) review

For a commercial event the financial outcome is to maximise profits, for a charity fund raiser it will be to maximise the surplus, for other events the focus may be on breaking even, or staying within an allocated cost allocation.

10.5.4 Financial performance review – internal benchmarks

With any financial data having one set of data, in the case the actual data for a single event, it is difficult to judge success or failure without comparative data. Internally this can be the event forecast, event budget, or comparison to previous events (either the same event in previous years, or a similar event). Further details related to this are discussed in Chapter 16 on performance measurement.

The importance with review is not just to note variances, but to identify those that are financially significant and to learn from them for the future.

10.5.5 Financial performance review – external benchmarks

When reviewing financial performance it is important that the focus is not only on internal data. The weather, the general economy, and competing events may also have an impact. External information may help answer why performance doesn't compare well to previous events internally, it may be an external issue in the marketplace. In a buoyant market an organisation may look internally and be pleased in their growth, but looking externally the whole market may have grown and competitors are also doing better.

10.5.6 Learn for future events

Advanced financial planning is critical to maximising financial returns from an event. Constantly monitoring revenue and costs during the event can maximise the returns from an individual event. Management accounting and strategic management accounting are about using this review of previous data to aid future decision making. Identifying financial strengths and weaknesses of an individual event feeds back into the financial information for planning future events, which in turn feeds into the future event and provides more data to be analysed and turned into financial information for further future events. The three phases of the event fit together like cogs, perpetually working together to maximise the potential financial returns for an individual event and for events into the future (Figure 10.5).

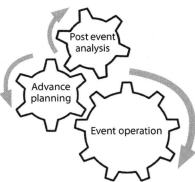

Figure 10.5

Summary of key points

Events and functions have specific characteristics that require specific consideration from a management accounting perspective. This chapter has followed the events planning, running and review phases and highlighted where and how management accounting can assist managers in running events.

■ Events can be considered as 'activities' for planning and control purposes.

■ In the event planning phase it is important to fully evaluate potential revenue alongside the associated costs to produce an event budget.

■ During an event it is important to closely monitor all aspects that could impact on its financial returns and not wait for post-event analysis.

■ Review post-event is essential to learn from the event to plan ahead for future events.

Reference

HSE (1999) *The Event Safety Guide: A Guide to Health, Safety and Welfare at Music and Similar Events*, 2nd edn, Health and Safety Executive (HSE) Books.

Further reading

A number of events operational textbooks container a chapter related to the financial aspects of events, these are usually brief and lack specific details found within this text, but may be useful to give a broad overview.

Bodwin, G., Allen, J., O'Toole, W., Harris, R. and McDonnell, I. (2010) *Events Management*, 3rd edn, London: Butterworth-Heinemann.

Chapter 9 in particular looks at the financial aspects of events management.

Conway, D.G. (2009) *The Event Manager's Bible: The Complete guide to Planning and Organising a Voluntary or Public Event*, How To Books.

As this book focuses on the not-for-profit sector it is useful in giving specific information concerning this events sector.

Vogel, H. (2010) *Entertainment Industry Economics: A Guide for Financial Analysis*, 8th edn, Cambridge: Cambridge University Press.

This book is quite broad in that it covers all entertainment industries from cinema, casinos, music, performance arts, sports and theme parks, but provides a very detailed guide to financing in the entertainment field, with some interest towards management accounting from a management perspective.

Self-check student questions

1 What makes an event unique in relation to the use of management accounting?

2 What is the purpose of having a detailed event budget?

3 Past experience shows for every event ticket sold, £24 is spent at the bar. If ticket sales are estimated at 6,000, what is the budgeted bar sales revenue?

4 Why is it important to monitor actual versus forecast data in the run up to an event?

5 Explain the relationship between Health and Safety guidance and event management accounting decisions.

6 What management accounting considerations should be made by managers whilst an event is taking place?

7 How can management accounting assist in the review of financial performance after an event?

8 How can past event information be utilised in planning future events?

10.10 Further questions and problems

1 An event is planned with budgeted ticket sales of 8,000 and is predicted to have sold 2,000 tickets (25%) 2 months before the event. However, 2 months before the event ticket sales are at 2,500. Recalculate the budgeted data to provide an updated forecast for the event.

2 Using information available online from their website (www.wychwood.com) consider how the management accounting considerations for events in this chapter could be applied to this specific event.

10

11 Financial Analysis of Performance

11.1 Introduction and objectives

It is important for managers to understand how to analyse and evaluate financial information and to be able to utilise a range of techniques to understand financial performance of organisations. Managers use financial information in their daily work, but rarely see the whole picture of the performance of the firm, this chapter provides a comprehensive set of tools to analyse the performance of a business, providing a comprehensive guide for managers of both generic approaches and industry specific measures. Financial information can be complex and detailed so it is very useful for managers to be able to confidently and systematically analyse that information to support their decision making. This chapter will build on early chapters, which explained financial statements and the principles underpinning them (Chapter 2) and will provide a foundation for the understanding of later chapters, such as 'Working capital management' (Chapter 12), 'Performance measurement' (Chapter 15) and 'Critical success factors and management information needs' (Chapter 17).

After studying this chapter you should be able to:

- Understand the main techniques for analysing financial information

- Use common-sized and comparative data

- Calculate a range of ratios and understand their limitations

- Evaluate ratios relating to profitability, liquidity, assets and debt

- Interpret operational ratios from a range of sectors.

11.2 Methods of analysis

There are several different ways to approach the analysis of financial statements, these include scanning, trend and time series analysis, common-sized statements and ratio analysis, these are summarised in Table 11.1.

Table 11.1: Analysis techniques

Technique	Summary and benefits
Scanning	Simple common-sense approach to analysing financial results, mainly useful for spotting exceptional or unusual factors, which stand out, such as losses or to direct more systematic analysis.
Trend analysis	Useful when figures are available for two years or more, can reveal changes in key figures or metrics over time. Involves identifying a base year and plotting changes in key figures from this point, can use index numbers or as percentage change. It is important to choose the base year carefully.
Common-sized statements	This approach facilitates the comparison of financial statements over time or between different companies. It involves expressing all items in the financial statements as percentages; in the income statement all line items are expressed as a percentage of sales; in the balance sheet all lines items are expressed as a percentage of the balance sheet totals. This technique emphasises the relative importance of items.
Ratio analysis	Express the relationship between two items with the aim of making them more expressive and revealing. Ratios facilitate comparison of different companies over different time frames and even different currencies.

The choice of technique depends on the perspective and purpose of the analysis, there are several different user groups who may be interested in financial reports, these include investors, shareholders, (both ordinary and preferences), lenders and banks, government (HMR&C), employees and management. (For a broader discussion on the users of financial information and their user needs see Berry and Jarvis 2011, Chapter 1.)

11.3 Scanning, trend analysis and time series

Scanning involves a systematic review of financial information to see what stands out, by looking at key items such as sales and cost of sales and other key expense items, it is possible to get a feel for what is happening; however it is more valuable to review performance of time. Trend analysis allows the comparison and evaluation of performance over time. The following example shows how trend analysis can reveal patterns over a period of time.

10

Simple example: a growing company using index numbers and percentage growth.

Growth figures (000s)	2009	2010	2011	2012	2013
Sales	4,750	5,938	7,030	8,550	9,025
Cost of sales	1,900	2,494	3,163	3,945	4,250

It is clear that this company is experiencing growth but how much growth? Index numbers show the growth of sales. (Index numbers are always calculated from the base year in this case 2009, so the index for 2010 is calculated by taking $100 \div 4,750 \times 5,938 = 125.01053$, index numbers are normally expressed as whole numbers, i.e. 125.) The choice of base year is important as different base years will result in different index numbers, if the base year is atypical (unusual or out of line with other figures), this can have an effect of distorting the numbers.

Growth figures (000s)	2009	2010	2011	2012	2013
Sales	4,750	5,938	7,030	8,550	9,025
Index numbers	100	125	148	180	190

These index numbers clearly show the sales volume is growing, but it is important to remember the effect of inflation when carrying out trend analysis, when inflation is high it is important to take into account how much of the growth is due to price inflation as opposed to increase in volume.

Index numbers are also useful to overcome the drawbacks of absolute or actual numbers, in this example, we can see that cost of sales is also rising, but without index numbers it is difficult to see if this is in proportion to the rise in volume. Calculating the index numbers reveals an interesting picture.

Growth figures (000s)	2009	2010	2011	2012	2013
Cost of sales	1,900	2,494	3,163	3,945	4,250
Index numbers	100	131	166	208	224

Index numbers now reveal that the cost of sales is increasing relatively faster than the sales, which will mean that performance, in terms of profit margins will be decreasing. So index numbers overcome the effect of absolute numbers and provide relative data, which can be directly compared. Another technique that facilitates this is percentage growth figures; look at the year on year change in figures so they are relative to the previous year not a base year. (Sales growth % 2011 is calculated as follows; $7,030 - 5,938 = 1,092$; expressed as a percentage of 5,938 the base year $- 1,092 \div 5,938 \times 100 = 18.39003$, simplified to 18%.)

% growth figures using the same data as above.

Growth figures (000s)	2009	2010	2011	2012	2013
Sales	4,750	5,938	7,030	8,550	9,025
Sales % growth		25%	18%	22%	6%
Cost of sales	1,900	2,494	3,163	3,945	4,250
COS % growth		31%	27%	25%	8%

In this case, it is clear that the cost of sales have increased at a higher rate every year (year on year), which means that the company is less efficient each year. This is contrary to what would be expected from economic theory, which states that as a firm grows it will experience economies of scale and can thus reduce costs. In this case it points to potential rising commodity prices and/or increasing inefficiency and lack of cost control by the firm.

It can be seen that with these simple techniques it is possible to start to identify areas for further investigation and start to build a picture of what is happening in a firm. Whichever method of presenting trend analysis is preferred, it is also clear from the above examples, that relative figures reveal more about a company than absolute figures. The difference between absolute and relative changes will be highlighted again later in the chapter, when common sized statements are considered. The next section will cover the basics of understanding ratios in general before looking at specific types of ratios.

11.3.1 Understanding ratios

Ratios are used to express the relationship between two values; they are useful because they enable you to compare companies of different sizes, different time periods and even financial results produced in different currencies. Ratios are generally expressed as percentages, but can also be expressed, as the number of times per annum or per month or as a measure of time e.g. years, months, or days, even hours. This chapter will introduce many different kinds of ratios, however it is important to remember that there is a lack of recognised definitions and that they are calculated from accounting information, so carry the same limitation identified in Chapter 2.

The same approaches can be applied to companies and their financial results, we see below two events companies of very different sizes – here ratios (in the form of percentages) enable us to compare their relative performance.

11.3.1.1 Using simple ratios to compare companies

Table 11.2: shows summary information from the income statement of two events companies, one is based on a single annual event (Company A), the other a large multinational events operator (Company B).

Table 11.2: summary information from the income statement of two events companies

Summary financial data from income Statement	Company A £	Company B £
Revenues	810,500	155,460,000
Cost of sales	372,830	80,839,200
Gross profit	437,670	74,620,800
Expenses	306,369	17,013,542
Net operating profit	131,301	18,804,442

The two companies have very different sizes, it is difficult to compare the results due to scale and complexity of the numbers, it can be seen that they are both making profit but which company is doing the best?

Table 11.3 includes percentage figures for both companies alongside the 'absolute' values from the income statement. These percentages are 'relative' figures which enable the comparison of these two companies, now it is easy to say which company is performing the best.

Table 11.3: Percentage figures and 'absolute' values from the income statement

Summary financial data from income statement	Company A £	Company B £	Company A %	Company B %
Revenues	810,500	155,460,000	100.0 %	100.0 %
Cost of sales	372,830	80,839,200	46.0 %	52.0 %
Gross profit	437,670	74,620,800	54.0 %	48.0 %
Expenses	306,369	17,013,542	37.8 %	22.8 %
Net operating profit	131,301	18,804,442	16.2 %	25.2 %

It is clear to see that Company A has a lower cost of sales than Company B, but its expenses are relatively higher, thus the performance of Company A in terms of net operating profit is worse than Company B.

Further detail is considered later regarding how to calculate various profit percentages and how to interpret them. The important aspect to understand at this point is the value or percentages and the different between absolute and relative figures. Although the ratios themselves are relatively straightforward to calculate, their interpretation requires a sound knowledge and understanding of the particular business under review.

Ratios can be used to compare different companies, but they can also be used to compare performance of the same company over time, for example, although Company A's performance is weaker than Company B, it is a stark improvement on the previous year's performance (see Table 11.4).

Table 11.4: Comparison within a company

Summary financial data from income statement	Company A 2012 £	Company A 2011 £	Company A 2012 %	Company A 2011 %
Revenues	810,500	598,544	100.0 %	100.0 %
Cost of sales	372,830	345,651	46.0 %	57.7 %
Gross profit	437,670	252,893	54.0 %	42.3 %
Expenses	306,369	212,731	37.8 %	35.5%
Net operating profit	131,301	40,162	16.2 %	6.7 %

So ratios help managers and analysts understand the top line performance of a business, but they can also be used to investigate performance and compare this over time at various levels of detail. The next example will show the usefulness of ratios and how they help managers understand the factors driving business performance.

Ratios can be used to analysis sales mix, City Hotel has seen an overall drop in profitability between period 3 and 4 despite an increase in overall revenue, analysis of sales mix helps reveal the explanation (Table 11.5).

Table 11.5: Analysing sales mix in a hotel context.

City Hotel	Period 3	%	Period 4	%
Rooms	34,200	50	37,757	48
Food and beverage	27,360	40	29,891	38
Conference and events	6,840	10	11,012	14
Total revenue per month	68,400	100	78,660	100

In City Hotel the rooms division is the most profitable followed by F&B and the least profitable is conference and events. Analysis of the sales mix reveals a shift from rooms and F&B, which have both reduced by 2% towards conference and events, which increased its share of revenue by 4%. So with relatively less revenue being generated in the more profitable departments or divisions, City Hotel has seen profit performance reduce even though it has generated more money overall. Managers need to see why this occurred and consider rebalancing the sales mix to maximise profit.

Finally it is worth noting that there are no real rules with ratios, thus terminology and formulae can vary, the most important thing to remember is that you must compare like with like, so when calculating ratios it is critical that the data is drawn from the same accounting period and that when comparing earnings or income the revenue or capital figures are for the same period and the same activity. For example, when calculating the return to shareholders, it is important to choose the correct figure of earnings available to shareholders and not the retained earnings or earnings after tax for example. You need to think carefully about what you are trying to understand and make sure the top half of the ratio matches the bottom half. The next section will present common-sized and comparative statements, which utilize these techniques to reveal insights into the performance of companies from their accounts.

11.4 Comparative and common-size statement analysis

This approach to analysis of financial statement helps to reduce complexity and turn large numbers into more digestible information. By converting absolute financial values, which could be in millions or thousands into percentages, this technique makes numbers more easy to comprehend, facilitates the comparison of companies of different sizes and the comparison of the same company over time. It does not compare one year to another, but focuses on the relative importance of different line items in the financial statements, to identify key costs or key assets and their relative importance. Example 11.1 will demonstrate how this technique can be used.

Example 11.1: Comparative statement analysis, The Restaurant Company income statement

Common-sized statements	Year 11	Year 12	Year 11	Year 12
Sales revenue	£	£	%	%
Food	1,183,000	1,462,500	66.42	75.00
Beverage	598,000	487,500	33.58	25.00
	1,781,000	1,950,000	100.00	100.00
Less cost of sales				
Food	412,100	552,825	23.14	28.35
Beverage	239,200	190,125	13.43	9.75
	651,300	742,950	36.57	38.10
Gross profit	**1,129,700**	**1,207,050**	**63.43**	**61.90**
Less expenses				
Payroll and related expenses	498,680	507,000	28.00	26.00
Other direct expenses	124,670	142,350	7.00	7.30
Administration	163,852	179,400	9.20	9.20
Marketing	44,525	54,600	2.50	2.80
Energy	60,554	59,800	3.40	3.07
Property management costs	58,773	60,970	3.30	3.13
Total expenses	**951,054**	**1,004,120**	**53.40**	**51.49**
Net operating profit	**178,646**	**202,930**	**10.03**	**10.41**

In Example 11.1, the income statement for The Restaurant Company is presented for year 11 and 12, followed by common sized statements for the same years. These are calculated by expressing each line item as percentage of the total revenue figure, for example food revenue in year 11 is 66.42% (calculated as follows, 1,183,000 ÷ 1,781,000 *100 = 66.42%). This shows that revenue from food sales contributes more than beverage sales, this is in fact nearly double beverage sales volume. It is also possible using this technique to clearly see the relative importance of different types of expenses, from this example we can see that payroll and related expenses are the most significant cost the company incurs. It is also possible to see the change in the relative importance of items from year to year; in year 12 the change in the balance of revenue from food versus beverages has changed with only a quarter of revenue being generated by beverage sales compared to a third in the previous year. Also it clearly shows that payroll costs have actually gone down relative to sales in year 12. So, common-sized statements can make numbers easier to understand, however another technique can reveal even more about the financial circumstances of firm, that is comparative statement analysis, which will be explained below.

Comparative statement analysis focuses on changes over time they can be used with monetary values or common-sized formats. In Example 11.2, the first column shows us the absolute difference between restaurant company's results in years 11 and 12 in monetary terms, the second column, shows the relative difference, that being the percentage change between the two years. These figures are calculated as follows:

Beverage cost of sales absolute difference = Current result (yr 12) 190,125 − Previous result or base (yr 11) 239,200 = £49,075; the % difference is 20.5% reduction in costs (calculated as 49,075 ÷ 239,200 (base year yr 11) * 100 = −20.5%.

Example 11.2: Comparative statement analysis for The Restaurant Company

	Year 11	Year 12	Absolute difference	Relative difference
Sales revenue	£	£	£	%
Food	1,183,000	1,462,500	279,500	23.6
Beverage	598,000	487,500	−110,500	−18.5
	1,781,000	1,950,000	169,000	9.5
Less cost of sales				
Food	412,100	552,825	140,725	34.1
Beverage	239,200	190,125	−49,075	−20.5
	651,300	742,950	91,650	14.1
Gross profit	**1,129,700**	**1,207,050**	**77,350**	**6.8**
Less expenses				
Payroll and related expenses	498,680	507,000	8,320	1.7
Other direct expenses	124,670	142,350	17,680	14.2
Administration	163,852	179,400	15,548	9.5
Marketing	44,525	54,600	10,075	22.6
Energy	60,554	60,450	−104	−0.2
Property management costs	58,773	62,400	3,627	6.2
Total expenses	**951,054**	**1,006,200**	**55,146**	**5.8**
Net operating profit	**178,646**	**200,850**	**22,204**	**12.4**

11

Observation of the income statement results shows that food revenue has increased by 23.6% and beverage revenue has decreased by 18.5%. The combined effect on total restaurant revenue is a rise of 9.5%. Thus, the overall revenue results have been constrained by the drop in beverage revenue. This should prompt management to raise questions about the promotion of beverages, the beverage pricing strategy and product range, whether staff are encouraging beverage sales or whether the clientele have changed.

Further review of the common-sized statements reveals that although gross profit has risen with the rising sales, it has only increased by 6.8% whereas the sales revenue has risen by 9.5%, this indicates a reduction in profitability. This reduction in profitability is due to the rising food cost of sales, which has risen more rapidly (34.1%) than the sales themselves (23.6), which is not offset by the relative reduction in beverage cost of sales. Thus management need to investigate whether food production has become less efficient, if purchasing costs have risen, or if commodity prices or food stocks and wastage have increased.

The final approach in comparative analysis is to compare the common-sized statements, this focuses even more precisely on change and the relative importance of different line items. Example 11.3 shows the % columns from the common-sized statements (from above) in columns 1 and 2 and shows the comparative analysis in columns 3 and 4. The comparative analysis figures are calculated as follows: food % value has decreased by 8.6 % points (75.0 – 66.4) shown in column 3, this constitutes nearly 13% increase (8.6 ÷ 66.4 = 12.9) shown in column 4. The calculation of the relative change is particularly useful as will be shown below.

Example 11.3: The restaurant company – common-sized statement comparative analysis.

	Common-sized statement		Comparative CSS	
	Year 11	Year 12	Difference	Difference
	%	%	Absolute %	Relative %
Sales revenue				
Food	66.4	75.0	8.6	12.9
Beverage	33.6	25.0	−8.6	−25.5
	100.0	100.0	0.0	0.0
Less cost of sales				
Food	23.1	28.4	5.2	22.5
Beverage	13.4	9.8	−3.7	−27.4
	36.6	38.1	1.5	4.2
Gross profit	**63.4**	**61.9**	**−1.5**	**−2.4**
less expenses				
Payroll and related expenses	28.0	26.0	−2.0	−7.1
Other direct expenses	7.0	7.3	0.3	4.3
Administration	9.2	9.2	0.0	0.0
Marketing	2.5	2.8	0.3	12.0
Energy	3.4	3.1	−0.3	−9.8
Property management costs	3.3	3.1	−0.2	−5.3
Total expenses	**53.4**	**51.5**	**−1.9**	**−3.6**
Net operating profit	**10.0**	**10.4**	**0.4**	**3.7**

This comparative common-sized statement really highlights the key areas of change; in this case the key aspect that now shows up is the increase of 12.9% in food sales with an increase in food cost of sales of 22.5% which is not commensurate. Focusing on this relative difference really helps explain the reduction in gross profit. The relative changes also show that the drop in beverage sales is not the main driver of reduction in gross profit because the beverage cost of sales also drops to a similar degree, thus not affecting the margins in the same way as food.

You should now understand the value of common-sized statements and the importance of recognising absolute and relative changes in the raw data and the percentage data to help explain changes in profit performance.

Example 11.4: Common-sized statement of financial position for The Restaurant Company.

	Year 11	Year 12	Year 11	Year 12
Assets	£	£	%	%
Non-current assets				
Land and buildings	1,170,000	1,170,000	64.2%	67.7%
Furniture and equipment	369,460	276,900	20.3%	16.0%
China and cutlery	166,400	158,600	9.1%	9.2%
	1,705,860	1,605,500	93.6%	92.9%
Current assets				
Cash at bank	7,020	13,000	0.4%	0.8%
Trade receivables (debtors)	65,520	58,500	3.6%	3.4%
Inventories	32,240	40,560	1.8%	2.3%
Prepaid expenses	12,220	10,920	0.7%	0.6%
	117,000	122,980	6.4%	7.1%
Total assets	1,822,860	1,728,480	100.0%	100.0%
Equity and liabilities				
Share capital	1,040,000	1,040,000	57.1%	60.2%
Retained profit	457,600	372,060	25.1%	21.5%
	1,497,600	1,412,060	82.2%	81.7%
Non-current liabilities				
Bank loans	240,500	224,120	13.2%	13.0%
Deferred tax liabilities	22,360	20,280	1.2%	1.2%
	262,860	244,400	14.4%	14.1%
Current liabilities				
Trade payables (creditors)	44,980	50,440	2.5%	2.9%
Accrued expenses	13,260	15,600	0.7%	0.9%
Advance deposits	4,160	5,980	0.2%	0.3%
	62,400	72,020	3.4%	4.2%
Total equity and liabilities	1,822,860	1,728,480	100.0%	100.0%

11

Common-sized statements can also be utilised to analyse a statement of financial position. Example 11.4 shows the statement of financial position (balance sheet) for The Restaurant Company for years 11 and 12. The figures are calculated as before for example, furniture and equipment in 2011 is £369,460 expressed as a percentage of the statement of financial position totals, i.e. 1,822,860 the calculation is (369,460÷ 1,822,860 x 100 = 20.268 = 20.3%).

Converting the statement of financial position to percentages reveals the relative importance of different categories of assets and liabilities within the company's overall financial position. We can see that overall The Restaurant Company is generally stable, but some elements of working capital are increasing, i.e. trade payables (creditors) and trade receivables (debtors), which could imply that the finance function is not working as effectively to keep these items in control. Alternatively it could be the result of increased trading activity associated with increased sales observed earlier.

So far this chapter has presented a range of techniques for analysing the financial results, including trend analysis, common-sized statements and comparative analysis, the next section will focus on the calculation and interpretation of a range of ratios which will help reveal areas for further investigation.

11.5 Types of ratios

The previous section demonstrated the power of ratios to reveal useful information; this chapter will now continue to present a range of different categories of ratios each with a different focus and each of which reveals different facets of organisational performance. The next section will be organised under the following common groupings as follows:

1 Financial ratios
   - Profitability and productivity (asset) ratios
   - Liquidity (including asset ratios)
   - Debt and investor ratios
2 Operating ratios
   - Sales mix
   - Productivity
   - Profitability

The following illustration (based on the fictitious restaurant company above) will be used to explain the various ratio types, how to calculate them and interpret them thus showing what they can reveal about the company performance.

11.6 Ratio analysis illustration

The ratio illustration utilises a fictitious hotel company based on real-life published data to provide a realistic rather than an over-simplified example. The income statement and the balance sheet are presented for 2012 and 2011 in Examples 11.5 and 11.6, then in the following section full explanation and workings will be show for all key ratios for 2012.

Example 11.5: The hotel company

Income statement	2012	2011
Sales revenue	£	£
Rooms	837,517	699,630
Food and beverage	636,700	536,340
Other income	253,700	284,390
	1,727,917	1,520,360
Les cost of sales		
Raw materials	136,180	112,580
Gross profit	**1,591,737**	**1,407,780**
Less operating expenses		
Payroll and related expenses	416,480	359,560
Licence fees	105,510	90, 390
Fuel, power and light	115,260	100,670
Depreciation and amortisation	108,460	104,140
Other expenditure	480,090	429,780
Total expenses	**1,225,800**	**1,084,540**
Earnings before interest and tax	365,937	323,240
Net interest	122,850	152,900
	243,087	170,340
Taxation	98,840	17,240
Profit after tax	144,247	153,100
Dividends	18,988	18,088
Profit retained	125,260	135,013

11

Example 11.6: The hotel company: Statement of financial position (balance sheet)

	2012	2011
Assets	£	£
Non-current assets		
Land and buildings	1,246,820	1,149,610
Furniture and equipment	1,322,350	1,230,970
Long-term deposits and investments	2,526,780	2,095,630
Intangible assets	36,010	27,740
	5,131,960	**4,503,950**
Current assets		
Cash at bank	95,310	447,120
Trade receivables (debtors)	103,960	121,620
Inventories food	16,430	14,100
Inventories beverage	15,400	17,150
Prepaid expenses	304,260	438,120
	535,360	1,038,110
Total assets	**5,667,320**	**5,542,060**
Equity and liabilities		
Share capital	75,950	72,350
Reserves and retained profit	2,152,960	1,716,870
	2,228,910	**1,789,220**
Non-current liabilities		
Bank loans	2,338,670	2,650,550
Deferred tax liabilities	40,540	4,100
	2,379,210	**2,654,650**
Current liabilities		
Trade payables (creditors)	240,320	244,320
Accrued expenses	163,270	148,570
Provisions	655,610	705,300
	1,059,200	**1,098,190**
Total equity and liabilities	**5,667,320**	**5,542,060**

11.7 Financial ratios

11.7.1 Profitability and productivity (asset) ratios

The first area for focus is on overall performance and profitability; however it is important to recognise the relationship between profitability and productivity.

Return of net assets (RONA) also called return of capital employed (ROCE) provides a measure of overall performance, relating profit earned from operations to the value of capital tied up in the business. Calculated as follows:

RONA/ROCE $\dfrac{\text{Earnings before interest and tax} \times 100}{\text{Total assets less current liabilities}}$

Illustration 2012 $\dfrac{365{,}937}{(5{,}667{,}320 - 1{,}059{,}200)}$ x 100   = 7.94%

Notice this ratio is calculated using profit before interest and tax, as these are deductions which are not affected by core operations but by financial and government policies, thus this is a measure of operational performance. This ratio can also be calculated using EBITDA (earnings before interest tax, depreciation and amortisation) if data is available; this also excludes the cost of writing off the cost of non-current assets (also called fixed assets) (see Chapter 2).

Net profit ratio (called net profit %, net margin or profit ratio) provides an important measure of performance, relating profit to revenue or sales. This shows how much profit is being generated from sales and how much excess revenue is available to cover finance costs and be retained to fund growth.

Net profit % $\dfrac{\text{Earnings before interest and tax}}{\text{Sales revenue}}$ x   100 = %

Illustration 2012 $\dfrac{365{,}937}{1{,}727{,}917}$ x 100   = 21.18%

Gross profit ratio is the core measure of profitability focusing down on service or product, excluding overheads and expenses, this ratio reveals the effectiveness of the pricing policy and control of costs of sales. Utilising gross profit, which is sales minus cost of sales, this ratio focuses on prime costs and core profitability.

Gross profit % $\dfrac{\text{Gross profit}}{\text{Sales}}$ x   100 = %

Illustration 2012 $\dfrac{1{,}591{,}737}{1{,}727{,}917}$ x 100   =   92.13%

Like the net profit margin, this ratio is related to sales and not assets. To investigate profitability and performance further calculating expenses as a percentage of sales can be useful and any expense item can be compared to sales to create a percentage figure, in essence this is what a common sized income statement achieves. (See common-sized statements above).

Asset utilisation (sometimes called asset turnover) provides a different view of the business focusing attention on productivity, in other words the efficiency with which the business is using its various assets, or put more simply, how hard assets are working. This ratio reveals how well a business is using its assets, by relating sales to net assets, but not as a percentage, rather as a ratio to one, showing how many sales, in monetary terms (£ or $ or €, etc.), are being generated from every £, $ or € invested in assets.

Asset utilisation $\dfrac{\text{Sales}}{\text{Net assets}}$: 1

Illustration 2012 $\dfrac{1,727,917}{4,608,120}$ = 0.375 : 1

This shows that 37.5p of sales are being generated from every £ of assets utilised by the business, normally the higher this figure the better, poor performance in this ratio may be reflected in low occupancy in hotels for example or poor control of working capital. This aspect of performance can be further investigated by calculating the fixed asset turnover or current asset turnover, which when compared over time can point to which aspect of the business is less efficient.

Fixed asset (also called non-current assets) turnover

$\dfrac{\text{Sales}}{\text{Total fixed assets}}$: 1

Illustration 2012 $\dfrac{1,727,917}{5,131,960}$ = 0.337 : 1

The primary ratio RONA /ROCE can be divided into two main elements of performance. First presented in the DuPont system (named after the American chemical company that first developed a systematic table of ratios in 1920s), this can be visualised as a triangle (Figure 11.1). Overall performance at the pinnacle supported, or delivered by, productivity at the base.

RONA/ROCE

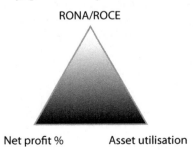

Net profit %   Asset utilisation

Figure 11.1: The RONA/ROCE concept

These ratios are conceptually and mathematically connected too, look back to see the calculations and figures above:

ROCE = $\dfrac{\text{EBIT}}{\text{Sales}}$ x $\dfrac{\text{Sales}}{\text{Net assets}}$

Illustration 2012   21.18% x   0.375   = 7.94 %

The top figure of the triangle can be easily calculated from financial reports and public domain data for PLCs or from management reports. It provides a useful overview at the start of any analysis. It should be noted that different companies will exhibit different levels of profitability and productivity depending on their business module. Business with high volume, low margin services/products like McDonalds will display a very different profile to a high-class brassiere such as the Savoy Grill, which has high margins but low volumes. However in real life, these differences can be masked by the complexity of different operational strategies, for example Virgin Atlantic (in Table 11.6) may lease more of its fleet, whereas easyJet may own its fleet and therefore have relatively more fixed assets leading to a lower asset utilisation, whereas easyJet is renowned for keeping its costs down and thus has a higher net profit ratio. In the events sector it is very difficult to compare companies as they have very different business models and in the case of these three examples are very different sized organisations.

11

Table 11.6: Comparison of real company performance. Data from published annual reports

Events companies	RONA	NP%	AU
Tarsus	15.5%	27.7%	0.56
Reed Exhibitions	9.3%	18.9%	0.49
Clarion Events	9.2%	3.1%	2.95
Airlines			
Virgin Atlantic	3.26%	1.8%	1.44
easyJet	3.73%	4.5%	0.83

We have seen how to evaluate the overall performance of companies and how this can start to lead to a range of questions about how to improve performance; this next section will focus down on cash management and liquidity.

11.7.2 Liquidity ratios (including asset ratios)

This area focuses on financial stability in the short term, as well as looking at the efficiency in managing and controlling key operational assets and liabilities. It also provides an important underpinning for the chapter on working capital management.

Current ratio is the main liquidity ratio relating the value of current assets and liabilities, it indicates the company's ability to pay debts which are about to become due. By relating short-term debts to the assets which are about to turn into cash (i.e. become liquid) this ratio provides an overview of the company's liquidity. Like other turnover ratios, it is expressed as a ratio to 1.

Current Ratio $\dfrac{\text{Current assets}}{\text{Current liabilities}}$: 1

Illustration 2012 $\dfrac{535,360}{1,059,200}$ = 0.505 : 1

If this ratio reveals cause for concern, or a worsening position, it is necessary to analyse further and breakdown the overview measure into its component parts, leading to the main working capital ratios. The key in this area is to understand the time it will take (on average) to turn assets into cash to pay debts when they become due, this is why these ratios are calculated to show the number of days.

The acid test ratio is a variant of the current ratio that excludes inventory from the equation, mainly used in manufacturing contexts on the grounds that it can take a long time to turn raw materials into sales and thus it is not a true indication of the ability to pay immediate debts.

Acid test ratio $\dfrac{\text{Current assets – Inventory}}{\text{Current liabilities}}$:   1

Illustration 2012 $\dfrac{(535,360 - 31,803)}{1,059,200}$ = 0.475 : 1

Inventory turnover the comparison is between the stock of goods for resale and the annual total of the cost of goods sold. The average inventory figure is used to try to reduce the effect of fluctuations in inventory levels at certain times of the year. In practice this is usually calculated by the addition of opening and closing inventory figures and then dividing by two.

Inventory turnover $\dfrac{\text{Average inventory}}{\text{Cost of sales}}$ x 365   = **Days**

Illustration 2012 $\dfrac{([31,830 + 31250] \div 2)}{136,180}$ x 365   = 84 Days

The number of days indicates how long between receiving and selling the inventory; in services where there is little inventory value, this ratio is less important, however in restaurants and other services where there is a significant element of materials, it is very useful.

Accounts receivable collection period (ARCP) shows the length of time it takes to collect money from a customer who has been allowed credit[1] that means they receive the services and then pay later, this is predominantly a business to business arrangement and not available for general consumers. When hotels, event

---

1   Credit sales should NOT be confused with paying by credit or debit card, these are cash equivalents, credit is where a customer (usually another business) arranges in advance to pay for services on a monthly basis as opposed to when services are received.

and travel companies allow credit it means there will be a delay receiving cash into the bank the ARCP is the average period of time this will take.

Accounts receivable collection period

$$\frac{\text{Accounts receivable} \times 365}{\text{Credit sales}} = \text{Days}$$

In the case of The Hotel Company 60% of sales are on credit.

Illustration 2012 $\dfrac{103,960 \times 365}{(1,727,917 \times 60\%)} = 36.6\text{ Days}$

Accounts payable collection period (ACCP) in a similar way to the ARCP this ratio shows how long the business takes to pay its own debts, or in other words how long it can delay paying out money.

Accounts payable collection period

$$\frac{\text{Accounts payable} \times 365}{\text{Credit purchases}} = \text{Days}$$

To calculate this ratio it is necessary to relate the accounts payable (creditors) to credit purchases, so normally the cost of sales or Cost of Goods Sold (COGS) figure must be adjusted for Inventory changes to work out the purchases figure (see web materials for more details here). In this case inventory values only change by a very small margin, so it is acceptable to use the COGS figure as a proxy for purchases.

The trade payables (creditors) figure is the balance sheet encompasses all creditors not only accounts payable relating to raw materials, to ensure we compare like with like we must isolate the specific accounts payable figure, or include a wide proxy for purchases. The figures for raw material accounts payable alone are £17,908 for 2012 and £16,039 for 2011.

Illustration 2012 $\dfrac{17,908 \times 365}{136,180} = 48\text{ Days}$

To gain a broader view of timing of cash payments required by the company, it would be necessary to broaden the figure used to encompass all trade payables and all key inputs to the business. For 2012 this would mean including expenses paid for under credit arrangements including licence fees, energy costs and other expenditure as a proxy for full purchases. This broader calculation would give a different figure to above.

Illustration 2012 $\dfrac{240,320 \times 365}{837,040} = 104.7 = 105\text{ Days}$

It is critical for companies to align the timing of receipts from cash sales and accounts payable with the payment of trade payables, to ensure they remain liquid, i.e. in a good financial position. Many businesses fail as a result of an inability to pay debts (lack of ready cash), rather than a lack of profitability. The final ratio in this section provides an indication of the cycle of cash, flowing through the business and can provide a collective view of liquidity. The cash operating cycle (COC) provides a measure of time that indicates how long a business must fund itself between paying out cash for purchases and receiving cash from sales. The longer the time of the COC and larger the business the more money will be tied up and need to be funded.

Cash operating cycle

$$\textbf{Inventory turnover plus ARCP minus APPP} \qquad = \textbf{days}$$

Illustration 2012 $84 + 37 - 48 = 73$ days

Or using the broader interpretation

$$84 + 37 - 105 = 17 \text{ days}$$

This case clearly demonstrates that it is important to use the correct numbers to calculate ratios and to understand precisely how they have been calculated to interpret them. These results will be discussed in the next section to show how to interpret them.

This section has focused on performance aspects relating to working capital, see Chapter 12 for a more detailed coverage of the elements of working capital and key issues of control of these important operational assets and liabilities.

11.7.3 Debt and investor ratios

The final set of ratios draws attention to the financial management of the business, the balance between long-term finance and the risk and returns to shareholders. Although this is arguably outside the remit of managerial accounting it is important for managers to understand the pressures and expectations of investors in the business. Investors and lenders need to receive a reward for the risk they face when providing funds to businesses, this group of ratios reveal these risks and rewards.

Return on equity (ROE) sometimes called return on investment (ROI although this can be used also in place of ROCE or RONA) shows what percentage return shareholders receive, this includes all profit attributable to shareholders regardless of whether this is paid out as dividends or retained in the business. It is presented as a percentage.

$$\textbf{Return on equity} \quad \frac{\textbf{Profit available to shareholders}}{\textbf{Equity}} \text{ x 100} \quad = \%$$

Illustration 2012 $\dfrac{144,247}{2,228,910}$ x 100 $= 6.47\%$

Profit available to shareholders is found lower down in the incomes statement after the deduction of all expenses, depreciation, interest and tax, plus after adjusting for minority interests. ROE is the main measure of return for shareholders and it should be viewed in the light of the risks of the business and the gearing ratio below.

Debt or gearing ratio provides a measure of financial risk by highlighting the balance of funding from equity sources or debt. In this context the term 'debt' refers to all fixed interest finance. The distinction between these different forms of finance is related to the payment of interest versus dividends. Dividends are a share of profits and are discretionary, that is if there is no profit they do not have to be paid, whereas interest must be paid, regardless of trading conditions and the health of the firm. It is thus considered more risky to have a relatively large amount of fixed interest debt relative to equity. The gearing ratio shows this relationship and is most commonly expressed as a percentage presenting debt as a percentage of total sources of finance, i.e. debt and equity added together, see below.

Gearing (or debt) ratio $\dfrac{\textbf{Debt}}{\textbf{(Debt + Equity)}}$ **x 100** **=** **%**

Illustration 2012 $\dfrac{2,379,210}{(4,608,120)}$ x 100 = 51.63 %

When calculated this way, the lower the percentage the better and the lower the financial risk. It should be noted that cumulative and preference shares, although a type of equity, are normally grouped with debt for the purposes of this ratios, as the company cannot avoid paying dividends to these shareholders. (For more information of these financial management topics see Head and Watson, 2009). The gearing ratio can also be shown as a ratio to 1. In the case of The Hotel Company this would be:

$\dfrac{\text{Debt}}{\text{Equity}}$ = :1

Illustration 2012 $\dfrac{2,379,210}{2,228,910}$ = 1.07:1

In addition to looking at the relative balance of debt and equity shareholders are interested in the company's ability to service their debt and pay dividends, (i.e. how much money is left over after expenses, to pay interest and how much money left over after interest and tax to pay dividends) the next two ratios show how many times available profit can cover these costs of finance.

Interest cover $\dfrac{\textbf{Earnings before interest and tax}}{\textbf{Interest}}$ = **No. times**

Illustration 2012 $\dfrac{365,937}{122,850}$ = 2.98 times

Dividend cover $\dfrac{\textbf{Earnings attributable to shareholders}}{\textbf{Dividend payable}}$ = **No. times**

11

Illustration 2012 $\dfrac{144,247}{18,988}$ =   7.60 times

This final group of ratios are considered the key investor ratios and are published in the annual report of a company; as a result, unlike most other ratios, the definitions are strictly determined.

Earnings per share (EPS) provide the figure of earnings per individual share, when more shares are issued this can be diluted and often results in the share price going down. Represented in pence or cents, this ratio is particularly affected when new shares are issued:

Earnings per Share $\dfrac{\textbf{Earnings attributable to shareholders}}{\textbf{Number of ordinary shares in issue}}$ = **£ or p**

Illustration 2012 $\dfrac{144,247}{75,950}$ = £ 1.90 or 190p

There are two other key ratios of interest to investors; these are earnings yield and the price earnings ratio. They relate the earnings per share to the market price of the shares, bearing in mind that shares are traded on the stock exchange, investors must pay market price for them (this is very different to their nominal value which is shown in the accounts). This ratio helps investors compare the investment benefits of one company and another. However these are outside the remit of this chapter to find out more about these ratios see McKenzie (2010, Chapter 12).

In this section, the focus has been on understanding the ratios and how to calculate them, the next section will focus on interpreting the results.

11.8 Interpretation of results

Having explained how to calculate the ratios and what they can reveal, this section will present ratios for the illustration case (The Hotel Company) with explanations of how they may be interpreted (Tables11.7–11.9). It is important to note that full interpretation must be undertaken with reference to the company history and the competitive and business environment (see Chapter 15, 'Performance management' for useful techniques). Figures are presented for 2012 and 2011, the calculations for 2012 were shown above, the full calculations for 2011 can be found on the companion website.

The interpretation in Table 11.7 clearly demonstrates that it is not possible to gain a definitive solution or answer when carrying out analysis of financial statement, but each ratio helps to build a picture and direct further investigations.

Table 11.7: Profitability and productivity (asset) ratios

Ratios	Presented as	2012	2011	Interpretation
RONA/ ROCE	%	7.94	7.27	Overall performance has deteriorated, by a small margin, despite sales increasing this means that either profitability is down, costs are up or productivity has decreased
Net profit %	%	21.18	21.50	The profit margin is down slightly, this could reflect that increased sales have been achieved by dropping prices, or that costs are up. Investigation of occupancy, or room rates, plus a common-sized income statement could reveal the reasons.
Gross profit %	%	92.12	92.60	This shows a slight decline, analysis of external factors could reveal increase in food prices or analysis of sales mix may reveal a shift in balance between rooms, F&B and other income. In addition this could be result of reduced prices, which would affect the margin.
Asset utilisation	: 1	0.375	0.342	This reveals an improvement with slightly higher utilisation of assets, this again could be as a result of increased occupancy and increased sales.
Fixed asset (FA) turnover	: 1	0.337	0.338	This ratio is more or less stable and shows that perhaps gains in productivity are due to changes in working capital not FA utilisation

Table 11.8: Liquidity ratios

Ratios	Presented as	2012	2011	Interpretation
Current ratio	: 1	0.505	0.945	The step change in this ratio can be explained mainly by the change in cash at bank balance, this has reduced significantly, whilst all other elements remain stable.
Acid test ratio	: 1	0.475	0.917	The difference between the current ratio and this ratio is very small showing that inventory is not a major item and thus this ratio has little relevance in service business interpretation.
Inventory turnover	Days	84	101	Inventory turnover has decreased, which is good, this means that The Hotel Company is not holding inventory for so long or holding as much. Improved inventory management may have been put in place or changes in sales mix could drive changes here.
Accounts receivable collection period	Days	37	48	There has been a marked improvement in this ratio, 11 days on average, this could be part of the explanation for improved asset utilisation and could reflect tighter credit control.
Accounts payable payment period	Days	48	52	This shows a small improvement, which may be facilitated by improved cash flow or better administration and prompt payment. It should be noted that paying suppliers earlier means the cash is not available to use for other purposes.
Cash operating cycle	Days	73	97	Overall cash operating cycle has reduced meaning the cash is flowing back into the business more quickly and there is a reduced need to fund working capital. Overall there is an improving picture for working capital.

The management of working capital is discussed in depth in Chapter 12.

11

Table 11.9: Debt and investment ratios

Ratios	Presented as	2012	2011	Interpretation
ROE	%	6.47	8.56	Return to shareholders has reduced, perhaps driven by reduced core profitability, however this may not be a cause for concern as the is also a commensurate reduction in risk (see gearing below)
Gearing	%	51.63	59.74	Gearing has reduced slightly from nearly 60% to just above 50%, this is reflected in a reduction in bank loans and an increase equity. This reduction in risk could offset the reduction in ROE.
Interest cover	No. of times (x)	2.98	2.11	Also shows an improving position with more profit available to cover interest, a review of the income statement reveals a drop in net interest paid due to the reduction in loans.
Dividend cover	No. of times (x)	7.60	8.46	Dividend cover has reduced; this is due to a decrease in the profit attributable to shareholders, rather than an increase in dividend.
EPS	£ or p	1.90	2.12	The amount of earnings per share reflects the same picture (as above) and shows how shareholders can be affected by reduced profitability.

The illustration and the interpretation in Tables 11.7–11.9, demonstrated how ratio analysis can reveal subtle changes in performance, when combined with common-sized statements and comparative statements. It is possible to identify areas where performance can be improved and where managers should prioritise their actions. The next section will focus down on operational ratios that are specific to different industries in the service sector.

11.9 Operating ratios

A range of operational ratios and statistics are used to help monitor and improve performance, this section will present and the most commonly-used ratios.

- Sales mix
- Productivity
- Profitability

11.9.1 Sales mix

Although not strictly a single ratio, the analysis of sales mix is a useful tool for understanding operational performance of a firm. The sales mix helps managers understand the composition of total sales and identify any trends in the proportion of revenue being generated in different departments or divisions of the business. Using data from The Hotel Company illustrative example, the sale mix analysis (in Example 11.7) shows that within the context of growth, the proportion of sales coming from the rooms division has decreased and 'Other income' has increased.

In hotels, rooms normally generates the highest gross margin or contribution so managers would want to reverse this change if it continued.

Example 11.7: Sales Mix for The Hotel Company

	2012	2011	2012	2011
Rooms	837,517	699,630	48.5%	46.0%
Food and beverage	636,700	536,340	36.8%	35.3%
Other income	253,700	284,390	14.7%	18.7%
	1,727,917	1,520,360	100.0%	100.0%

The Go Ahead Group provide a breakdown of their sales according to different revenue streams in their annual reports, plus they show profitability data against these headings, this reveals interesting information about the operational performance of this large transport company (Example 11.8).

Example 11.8: The Go Ahead Group Segmental Report. Source: Data extracted from Go Ahead Group plc Annual and Accounts Report 2011, p. 94.

	Revenue	Sales mix	Operating profit	Profit margin
	£m	%	£m	%
Deregulated bus	289.2	13.2%	27.2	9.4%
Regulated bus	361.7	16.5%	36.5	10.1%
Rail	1,537.8	70.3%	37.3	2.4%
	2,188.7	100.0%	101	

It is clear that 70% of their revenue comes from the operation of rail franchises, yet this part of the business only generates 37% of profits, this implies that the profit margins for the individual revenue streams are very different, as revealed in the final column. Such information can direct manager effort and set priorities, in this case, managers in Go Ahead Group will need to target more regulated bus services and prioritise cost control on the rail operations.

11.9.2 Productivity

Productivity is an important element of performance for service organisations due to the perishability of their products, as a result, hotels and airlines pay particular attention to occupancy and load factors, this next section focuses on the efficiency and productivity ratios utilised in various sectors.

11.9.3 Hotels

Rooms division and hotel performance, is monitored using a range of measures that isolate pricing, volume and capacity issues. Example 11.9 demonstrates how to calculate key ratios for hotels sector.

Example 11.9: Clarendon Country Hotel operational data year 2012

Rack rate per room	Single	£75
	Double	£90
Rooms available	Single	30
	Double	20
Rooms revenue		£800,000
Rooms sold		11,860
Number of guests		16,450
Total hotel revenue		£1,680,000

The major priority of any hotel manager i s to fill rooms, so one of the most important measures of performance is occupancy. This provides a percentage figure for the number of rooms sold as a proportion of total available rooms.

Occupancy rate $\quad \dfrac{\textbf{Rooms sold}}{\textbf{Rooms available}} \quad \textbf{x 100} \quad = \quad \textbf{\%}$

$$\frac{11,860}{18,250} \quad \text{x 100} = \ 0.6498 = 65\%$$

Managers will have targets to achieve for occupancy, which are based upon the time of year, day of the week and the location of the hotel and will be monitored against past hotel performance, rolling forecasts and external benchmarks. Occupancy will provide an indication of capacity utilisation, daily weekly, monthly and annually.

Double occupancy $\quad \dfrac{\textbf{Rooms double occupied}}{\textbf{Rooms sold}} \quad \textbf{x 100} \quad = \quad \textbf{\%}$

$$\frac{(\text{Number of guests} - \text{Rooms sold})}{\text{Rooms sold}} \quad \text{x 100} \quad = \quad \%$$

$$\frac{(16,450 - 11,860)}{11,860} \quad \text{x 100} \quad = 0.387 = 39\,\%$$

Double occupancy takes account of the number of sleepers, because extra revenue is generated from double occupancy, it gives an indication of bed capacity utilisation.

The next measures combine utilisation with pricing decisions to evaluate revenue and potential revenue generated.

Average room rate(ARR) $\quad \dfrac{\textbf{Rooms revenue}}{\textbf{Rooms sold}} \quad = \textbf{£}$

$$\frac{£800,000}{11,860} \quad = \quad £\,67.45$$

This is the most important and commonly monitored operating indicator in hotels, reflecting productivity and affecting profitability. In a market-orientated business with perishable products this indicator can be improved by increasing selling effort for higher-priced rooms and by improving the rate of double occupancy. The optimisation of revenue is a management discipline in its own right and the topic of yield management is covered in Chapter 7, 'Revenue and yield management'.

Yield $\dfrac{\text{Rooms revenue}}{\text{Maximum potential revenue}}$ x 100 = %

$\dfrac{£800,000}{[(30 \times £75) + (20 \times £90)] \times 365}$ x 100 =

$\dfrac{£800,000}{£1,478,250}$ x 100 = 0.54118 = 54%

This ratio also reflects occupancy achieved and prices charged and is discussed in more detail in Chapter 7 which focuses on revenue and yield management.

Revenue per available room, known as RevPAR, is one of the most monitored and yet contentious statistics utilized to monitor performance in hotels. It provides a measure of productivity linking total revenue to available room and reflects both the selling price (ARR) and the occupancy achieved.

Rev PAR $\dfrac{\text{Rooms revenue}}{\text{Rooms available}}$ = £

$\dfrac{£800,000}{18,250}$ = £ 43.84

This measure forms an important part of competitive benchmarking practice utilised in the hotel industry.

Total revenue per average room (TRevPAR) has been heralded as a much better measure of productivity that RevPAR because it takes into account the total revenue generated by a hotel, as has been discussed in Chapter 7, 'Revenue and yield management'.

TRevPAR $\dfrac{\text{Total revenue}}{\text{Rooms available}}$ = £

TRevPAR $\dfrac{£1,680,000}{18,250}$ = £ 92.05

TRevPAR figure will always be higher that RevPAR as it includes income from all other departments. Due to complex pricing strategies now adopted in hotels, room rates are set for different customer groups taking into account their total profitability it is sometimes worthwhile pricing rooms at a low rate to get certain customer groups into the hotel. It is for these reasons that it is argued that

TRevPAR is a more reliable metric that RevPAR.

Clarendon performance summary

Average room rate	£67.45
Occupancy rate	65%
Double occupancy	39%
Yield	54%
RevPAR	£43.84
TRevPAR	£92.05

This full set of operational ratios can give a picture of the performance of the hotel taking account of profitability, productivity and asset utilization and when combined into trend analysis can be used very effectively for external benchmarking. Example 11.10 shows typical example of the statistics produced by TRI Hospitality Consulting under their 'HotStats' trademark. For a deeper discussion about benchmarking see Chapter 15, 'Performance measurement'.

Example 11.10: European Chain Hotels Market Review – May 2012. Source: TRI Hospitality Consulting

	Occ%	ARR	RevPAR	TRevPAR	Payroll %	GOP PAR
Amsterdam	89.7	195.57	177.20	231.15	24.6	116.89
Berlin	79.5	131.16	104.29	155.33	25.4	62.12
Cologne	72.5	128.42	93.15	125.48	27.1	52.48
Dusseldorf	70.4	194.33	136.71	171.16	19.7	98.55
London	84.1	201.12	169.11	232.37	22.1	116.77
Milan	78.4	141.68	111.06	168.33	34.4	52.55
Munich	78.8	160.58	126.47	168.38	25.8	73.46
Paris	84.2	223.60	118.18	258.88	35.1	98.78
Prague	80.1	90.87	72.79	126.22	21.0	54.95
Warsaw	79.8	113.36	90.40	147.32	22.0	69.02

11.9.4 Restaurants and airlines

Restaurants tend to focus on three key performance indicators, these are; revenue per available seat hour (RevPASH), seat occupancy and average spend.

For example, a restaurant has 150 seats and makes £4,500 on Saturday between 6pm and 8pm. Its RevPASH for this time period is:

£4,500/150seats/2 hours= £15RevPASH.

RevPASH will vary between different months of the year, days of the week and different times of the day, this is because it is driven by the average spend and the seat occupancy which have large fluctuations, as discussed in Chapter 7. The key point with all ratios is to identify those factors that drive performance and take actions to improve these.

Airlines have developed similar ratios to monitor performance including revenue per kilometre (RPK) and the all-important, load factor, which similar to occupancy in hotels, focuses on productivity and the number of seats (or rooms) sold as a percentage of the full capacity. Lufthansa AG publish a range of operational ratios in their annual report each year, these include ratios discussed above such as return on sales (net profit %) and gearing. They also publish detailed efficiency statistics over a ten year period. Table 11.10 shows an extract of the last three years' traffic figures.

Table 11.10: Airline traffic data. Source: Lufthansa Annual Report and Accounts 2011, p. 228

Traffic figures, Lufthansa Group	Units	2011	2010	2009
Total available tonne-kilometres	(millions)	40,797.90	37,664.40	35,469.40
Total revenue tonne-kilometres	(millions)	29,906.10	28,274.30	24,942.70
Cargo load-factor	(%)	73.3	75.1	70.3
Available seat-kilometres	(millions)	258,262.60	234,376.60	208,225.70
Revenue seat-kilometres	(millions)	200,376.10	186,451.50	162,286.20
Passenger load factor	(%)	77.6	79.6	77.9
Passengers carried	(millions)	100.6	92.7	77.3
Revenue passenger tonne – km	(millions)	19,045.40	17,845.00	16,236.30

All sectors have specialised operational ratios to help managers monitor productivity, i.e. how well they are utilizing assets and whether the business is efficient as it could be. Profitability can also be evaluated at an operational level as will be shown in the next section.

11.9.5 Profitability

Generally operational profitability focuses on gross and net profit. We have already covered more generic profitability ratios. These additional ratios are commonly used in the hotel sector.

For these ratios we need some additional information to add to the Clarendon Hotel example shown in Example 11.10.

Clarendon Country Hotel Year 2012 – Additional information

Gross profit	£745,160
Payroll costs	£352,250

GOP PAR stands for gross operating profit per available room; this is a core measure of profitability, which takes account of productivity as well.

GOP PAR   **Gross operating profit**   = £
                  Rooms available

GOP PAR   £745,160   = £ 40.83
                ─────────
                  18,250

This ratio can be improved many ways, by increasing the number of rooms sold, improving the sales in associated departments and of course raising prices (or room rates). This is useful as it draw management attention to the core profitability before taking account of overheads, problems with performance in this ratio cuts to the heart of the core operations of the hotel.

Payroll % $\dfrac{\text{Payroll costs}}{\text{Total revenue}}$ x 100 = %

Payroll % $\dfrac{£352,800}{£1,680,000}$ x 100 = 21.0 %

This ratios shows how much the hotel is paying for labour in relation to total revenue, this means that for every £1 the hotel generates it is spending 21p on labour. The figure can be interpreted by comparing figures over time in trend analysis or by external benchmarking.

In the hotel industry these and other ratios form the basis of well-established benchmarking practices, which will be discussed in Chapter 15 alongside performance measurement. Similar ratios and measures can be utilised within other sectors. For example: revenue per available seat at an event, average spend per customer, labour (payroll) costs as a percentage of sales are not industry-specific and can be applied in many texts.

Summary of key points

This chapter has provided an overview of a range of techniques for analysing performance and has explained how to calculate and interpret a wide range of ratios. There has also been an explanation and discussion of sector operating ratios. Some key points to remember are:

- Scanning and trend analysis can use index numbers of percentages facilitated comparison over time.

- Common-sized statements can reduce the impact of size/scale and different currencies and facilitate comparison by highlighting relative rather than absolute data.

- Many different ratios can be calculated, but it is important to always compare like with like and understand the method of calculation when carrying out comparisons and analysis.

- Ratios can reveal performance in areas of profitability and productivity, liquidity and financial structure.

- Operational ratios are commonly used in various sectors to monitor efficiency/productivity and profitability and these can facilitate external benchmarking.

References

Berry, A. and Jarvis, R . (2011) *Accounting in a Business Context*, 5th edn, London: Thomson Learning.

Hotstats.Com, *TRI Hospitality Consulting*, London (www.hotstats.com)

Lufthansa AG (2011) *Annual Report and Accounts*. [Available online from http://investor-relations.lufthansa.com/en/]

McKenzie, W. (2010) *FT Guide to Using and Interpreting Company Accounts*, 4th edn, Harlow: Financial Times Prentice Hall.

Further reading

Head, A. and Watson, D. (2009) *Corporate Finance Principles and Practice*, 5th edn, Harlow: Financial Times/Prentice Hall.

Corporate finance is beyond the scope of this text, but details in this area for further study can be found in this text.

Thomas, A. and Ward, A.M. (2012) *Introduction to Financial Accounting*, 7th edn. McGraw Hill.

Self-check student questions

1 What are the four main techniques for analysing financial information?

2 When calculating index numbers, what is the 'base year' and why is its selection important?

3 What are the main benefits of common-sized statements and ratios?

4 Trade payables and trade receivables are also referred to as what?

5 Which two key ratios contribute to the return on capital employed (ROCE)? For each, explain what they reveal.

6 If asset utilisation was getting worse, which ratios would you calculate to try and explain the reasons.

7 What is the cash operating cycle and how is it calculated?

8 Which operational ratios are most commonly used in the hotel industry for external benchmarking?

11

Further questions and problems

1   a) Calculate the absolute difference and relative difference from this data.

(7 marks)

	Year 1	Year 2	Absolute difference	Relative difference
	£	£	£	%
Sales				
Food	678,950	787,582		
Beverage	378,450	280,053		
Total	1,057,400	1,067,635		

b) Using the above example, explain why it is important to consider both the absolute and relative difference in such comparative statements.

(6 marks)

c) Identify and explain the usefulness of six industry specific ratios that could be used in evaluating a hotel's rooms division performance.

(12 marks)

BAHA Stage Three – Strategic Management Accounting Exam Paper July 2010

2   From the extracts of data provided below for Easy Events, calculate the ratios the following ratios and explain what they reveal.

a)   ROCE

b)   Asset utilisation

c)   Net profit percentage

d)   Gross profit

e)   Fixed asset turnover

Company data extracts for Year 13	€
Sales/turnover	1,473,913
Cost of sales	402,674
Staff costs	313,609
Total expenses	923,027
Non-current assets (fixed assets)	3,233,135
Current assets	456,662
Current liabilities	691,658

12 Working Capital Management

12.1 Introduction and objectives

Capital is a scarce resource in any business and enormous attention is given to ensuring the right sources of finance are found and properly utilised with respect to the long-term non-current asset requirements of an organisation. However any business will require capital for short-term needs as well as long-term and this is known as working capital.

After studying this chapter you should be able to:

- Understand the importance of working capital to the business

- Evaluate the different working capital policies that can be adopted by a firm

- Understand what the key components of working capital are

- Consider the working capital requirements of a firm with respect to inventory, accounts receivable, cash and accounts payable

- Establish sound policies for the efficient management and control of the key component elements.

12.2 Understanding working capital

In the short term a business needs to ensure that it can pay its expenditure from its income, to generate income it must sell its products or services to customers. In doing this the business will often buy inventory – goods to sell on as a retailer, or raw materials with which to make a finished product such as a meal in a restaurant. The inventory then has to be sold to a customer (at a profit) and when the customer pays, cash flows back in to the business (Figure 12.1). The organisation must ensure it has enough capital invested to ensure that it can buy the required inventory and still pay bills while it waits for the inventory to be sold and the customers to pay. This in essence is the working capital requirement of the business.

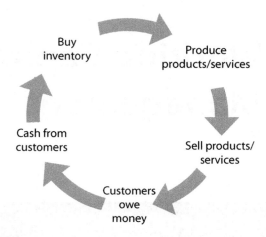

Figure 12.1: The trade cycle

The working capital of a business can be easily measured by looking at its statement of financial position. It reflects the current assets minus the current liabilities.

Money expected to flow in – Money expected to flow out

Working capital management is a matter of ensuring sufficient liquid resources (cash) are maintained this involves achieving a balance between the requirement to minimise the risk of insolvency (running out of cash) and the requirement to maximise the return on assets (be efficient with the cash). It is therefore important from two aspects, liquidity and profitability.

The working capital policy is a function of two decisions within the organisation:

The investment decision – what do I need to buy

The assets of the business can be categorised between non-current assets and current assets, it is generally expected that the non-current assets are financed by long-term sources of funds such as share capital or loans but should the current assets be financed in the same way?

Current assets can be categorised into two groups permanent and fluctuating.

■ Permanent current assets reflect that a business will always require a base level of investment into inventory and accounts receivable in order to continue to generate sales.

■ Fluctuating current assets reflect that the actual amount of investment required will change depending on a number of factors including seasonal demand, attempts to attract more customers and so on.

The finance decision – where can I access the money

The money can be accessed from long-term sources or from short-term sources, the choice to use long or short-term sources reflects the working capital policy of the organisation.

12.3 Working capital financing policy

Many organisations will use a *matching* policy so that non-current assets and permanent current assets are financed by long-term sources and the fluctuating current assets are financed by short-term sources (Figure 12.2). This is often also known as a moderate policy and will strike a balance between the need to have money available to meet demands but also ensures that money is not borrowed at high interest rates when it is not needed increasing efficiency and profitability.

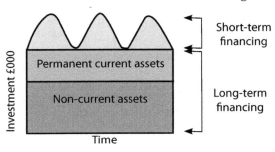

Figure 12.2: Matching policy for funding assets

There are two further policies a business can adopt depending on the managers' attitudes towards taking risks and the ability to clearly understand the organisation's working capital requirements.

The first is a non-risk taking approach known as a *conservative* policy, with this policy not only will all permanent assets be financed by long-term capital sources but some of the fluctuating current assets will also be financed in this way leaving only a small proportion of finance to be found short-term (Figure 12.3).

This tips the balance in favour of liquidity so the business will have fewer problems ensuring there is enough cash to meet needs but as a consequence it will be less efficient and less profitable as it is using more expensive long-term sources of finance even when they may not be required.

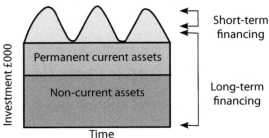

Figure 12.3: Conservative policy for funding assets

Finally the manager can take an *aggressive* policy which is a risk-taking policy (Figure 12.4). The manager will use short-term sources to finance fluctuating and some or all of the permanent current assets with the remainder of permanent current assets and non-current assets to be financed by long-term sources.

This sees the balance tip in favour of efficiency and profitability as finance is only being sought when needed and no excess cost is incurred however the firm is at more risk of insufficient cash if finance cannot be arranged in time to meet needs when they arise.

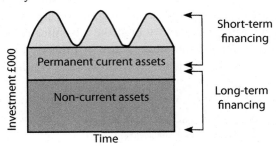

Figure 12.4: Aggressive policy for funding assets

The management of working capital provides a tension between operational imperatives and financial imperatives (Table 12.1). These have to be balanced and work together to the best interest of the organisation as a whole.

Table 12.1: Operational and financial perspectvies

Operational perspective	Financial perspective
The restaurant manager wants to ensure there is sufficient stock (inventory) in place to be able always offer the full menu and not run out of individual food items.	The accountant wants money 'tied up' in inventory to be kept to a minimum, so the resource is available to 'work' within the business.
In order to gain contracts for an event or conference the event's manager is willing to agree trade credit terms with the customer.	The accountant wants to ensure the customer is 'creditworthy' and if credit terms are allowed there is a high chance they will be able to pay in the future and on time.
The operations manager wants to have a good working relationship with their suppliers, so the suppliers will work with them when they need urgent extra supplies.	Financially, paying suppliers as late as possible (without incurring penalties) makes financial sense.

12.4 Working capital characteristics

Most businesses will have different working capital requirements because of three main areas:

- Holding inventory
- Time allowed for customers to pay
- Time taken to pay suppliers.

Businesses in service sectors tend to have very different characteristics to those in manufacturing sectors within the fields of hospitality, tourism and events the characteristics are broadly similar:

Inventory – Some inventories will be held for short periods of time such as foodstuffs but beverages are likely to be held for longer, particularly in fine dining with extensive wine lists. Inventory holding may be seasonal such as for an events company where most events take place during summer months.

Time allowed for customers to pay – In service industries many customers are required to pay in advance such as for some hotel bookings or flights or at the point of consumption such as a restaurant meal, or hotel extras during stay. Apart from organisations which have corporate clientele, the time allowed for customers to pay will be short, with many cash or advanced sales.

Time taken to pay suppliers – this will be in line with what is expected in any industry and will not differ significantly in the service sector. Buying power is a key factor, with major international companies able to 'require' their suppliers give them three months to pay for supplies, however smaller operators may only have one month's credit from their suppliers.

12.5 Working capital ratios

Example 12.1: The Hotel Company, Income statement

	2012	2011
	£	£
Sales revenue		
Rooms	837,517	699,630
Food and beverage	636,700	536,340
Other income	253,700	284,390
	1,727,917	1,520,360
Less cost of sales		
Raw materials	136,180	112,580
Gross profit	1,591,737	1,407,780
Less operating expenses		
Payroll and related expenses	416,480	359,560
Licence fees	105,510	90,390
Fuel, power and light	115,260	100,670
Depreciation and amortisation	108,460	104,140
Other expenditure	480,090	429,780
Total expenses	1,225,800	1,084,540
Earnings before interest and tax	365,937	323,240
Net interest	122,850	152,900
	243,087	170,340
Taxation	98,840	17,240
Profit after tax	144,247	153,100
Dividends	18,988	18,088
Profit retained	**125,260**	**135,013**

12

Example 12.2: The Hotel Company, Statement of financial position (balance sheet)

	2012	2011
Assets		
Non-current assets		
Land and buildings	1,246,820	1,149,610
Furniture and equipment	1,322,350	1,230,970
Long-term deposits and investments	2,526,780	2,095,630
Intangible assets	36,010	27,740
	5,131,960	4,503,950
Current assets		
Cash at bank	95,310	447,120
Trade receivables	103,960	121,620
Inventories food	16,430	14,100
Inventories beverage	15,400	17,150
Prepaid expenses	304,260	438,120
	535,360	1,038,110
Total assets	**5,667,320**	**5,542,060**
Equity and liabilities		
Share capital	75,950	72,350
Reserves and retained profit	2,152,960	1,716,870
	2,228,910	1,789,220
Non-current liabilities		
Bank loans	2,338,670	2,650,550
Deferred tax liabilities	40,540	4,100
	2,379,210	2,654,650
Current liabilities		
Trade payables	240,320	244,320
Accrued expenses	163,270	148,570
Provisions	655,610	705,300
	1,059,200	1,098,190
Total equity and liabilities	**5,667,320**	**5,542,060**

Working capital ratios were examined in Chapter 11 and can help to determine the requirements and provide a guide to the risk of cash flow problems and insolvency. By using the ratios, managers are better able to implement the correct measures to properly manage working capital.

An overall view of how well working capital is managed can be seen from the basic liquidity ratio, namely the current ratio and the acid test ratio.

Examples 12.1 and 12.2 the data used in Chapter 11 to calculate the ratios.

Table 12.2: The results of the calculations

Ratios	Format	2012	2011	Interpretation
Current	: 1	0.505	0.945	The step change in this ratio can be explained mainly by the change in cash at bank balance, this has reduced significantly, whilst all other elements remain stable.
Acid test	: 1	0.475	0.917	The difference between the current ratio and this ratio is very small showing that inventory is not a major item and thus this ratio has little relevance in service business interpretation

The data in Table 12.2 indicates that this business needs to investigate the reason for the change in the bank balance and employ techniques to ensure that cash is properly managed. It is perfectly acceptable for the current ratio to be less than one provided the flow of cash is adequate to meet demand.

12.5.1 The working capital/cash operating cycle

A business that wants to maintain liquidity but also wants to be profitable will aim to manage its working capital to reduce the length of the cycle (Table 12.3).

Table 12.3

Ratio	Format	2012	2011	Interpretation
Cash operating cycle	Days	73	97	Overall cash operating cycle has reduced meaning the cash is flowing back into the business more quickly and there is a reduced need to fund working capital. Overall there is an improving picture for working capital.

This ratio suggests that the management of working capital is improving in the organisation.

Two extremes can be reached if the organisation does not have a working capital policy and does not monitor its ratios:

12.5.2 Overcapitalisation

Overcapitalisation occurs if there is excessive working capital and can be identified where the current ratio is over 2:1, other symptoms are high inventory and accounts receivable periods and a further ratio which calculates sales over working capital also helps to display the lack of efficiency and profitability from the working capital. In this situation the working capital is not working as efficiently as it could be for the organisation.

12.5.3 Overtrading

Overtrading occurs when the business tries to do too much too quickly with too little long-term capital. It can be caused by:

- Increasing turnover without an adequate capital base
- Repaying a loan without replacing it with new finance

12

- The effects of inflation on retained profit increasing the need to use credit.

Overtrading can be spotted by:

- A rapid increase in turnover
- An increase in the volume of fixed and current assets
- A small increase in capital
- Significant changes to the working capital ratios.

Business failure has been the subject of a number of researchers including Altman (1968) who created a 'Z' score for organisations to show their likelihood of failure. Reducing sales or keeping tighter control over the level of inventory and outstanding debts can prevent overtrading. The most practical way however, is to ensure that sufficient additional capital is raised to finance any expansion.

12.6 Management of inventory

Since the inventory must be bought to generate sales it requires a significant investment of working capital which will not be recovered until the inventory is sold and then paid for by the customer. It has been suggested if the number of days inventory is held can be reduced the need for working capital reduces, however the management of inventory like working capital in general requires the need to balance the benefits of holding small amounts of inventory with those of holding high amounts of inventory.

Holding a high level of inventory will allow the firm to be flexible in supplying customers, there would be less chance of disruption to the production/service flow and satisfied customers will keep returning. However these must be weighed against the costs associated with holding inventory. Consider the effect on a restaurant of continuously being unable to offer dishes on its menu.

12.6.1 Classification of inventory costs

Inventory costs can be classified as:

- **Holding costs.** These are the most significant costs associated with holding high inventory as it has to be stored in the right conditions, using valuable space, all inventory held has to be managed and accounted for, it may perish, go out of date or even be damaged whilst in stores and therefore additionally requires insurance and security.
- **Procurement costs.** These are the costs of buying the inventory, if goods are bought in bulk then the costs of procurement go down but when a decision is made to hold less inventory it has to be purchased more often and this causes these costs to rise. So there has to be a balance and consideration of these combined.

- **Shortage costs.** Sometimes difficult to measure precisely these reflect the costs to the business of not having enough inventories to meet the needs of customers. If frequently a customer's first choice of menu item is unavailable it can impact on repeat custom. Some items are synonymous with certain events: strawberries with Wimbledon tennis, Guinness with the Cheltenham Gold Cup, or turkey at Christmas functions and 'running out' would have a negative impact on the business.
- **Cost of inventory.** This is simply the cost of the actual stock itself.

12.6.2 Inventory control policy

An inventory control policy should reflect the following four criteria (despite the fact that they usually operate against each other).

- Keep total costs down (ideally to a minimum).
- Provide satisfactory service levels to customers.
- Ensure smooth-running production systems.
- Be able to withstand fluctuations in business conditions, for example, changes in customer demand, prices, availability of raw materials, etc.

  Company policy will dictate which of these will take precedence.

  The use of the inventory turnover ratio can be used to evaluate the degree to which the inventory management policy is effective (Table 12.4).

Table 12.4: Evaluating inventory management

Ratio	Format	2012	2011	Interpretation
Inventory turnover	Days	84	101	Inventory turnover have decreased, which is good. It means that the Hotel Company is not holding stock for so long or holding as much. Improved stock management may have been put in place or changes sales mix could drive changes here.

12.6.3 Inventory control systems (inventory management systems)

Traditionally inventory control systems were paper-driven systems using cards and 'bins' where the movement of stock was physically recorded. Many organisations now make use of available technology and employ warehouse management systems (WMS) and barcode technology to keep track of stock. The large chain hotels use fully integrated systems which control purchasing, receiving, requisitioning, inventory control, operational control and even recipe management.

12.6.4 Inventory control levels

The objective of inventory control is to minimise the costs of carrying inventory. Two key questions must be asked:

- How much to order?
- When to order?

12.6.5 Inventory control formulae

Reorder level

Maximum usage x maximum lead time

Minimum level

reorder level – (average usage x average lead time)

Maximum level

reorder level + reorder quantity – (minimum usage x minimum lead time)

Average inventory

safety inventory + 1/2 reorder quantity

These calculations will generally be done by the computer package that the organisation chooses to employ for stock control.

12.6.6 Inventory models

There are several inventory models that seek to minimise the costs.

- **Stochastic models.** Where the demand for the product is unknown but can be predicted, inventory will be reordered according to the current level of inventory or when the level of inventory reaches a reorder specification.

- **Deterministic models.** The demand and other perimeters are known and a formula can be used to determine the quantity to be bought. The main model used is the economic order quantity (EOQ).

Economic order quantity (EOQ) formula

$$Q = \sqrt{\frac{2 \times C_0 \times D}{C_h}}$$

Where :
$$D \quad = \quad \text{demand}$$
$$C_0 \quad = \quad \text{cost of one order}$$
$$C_h \quad = \quad \text{holding cost per inventory unit per annum}$$
$$Q \quad = \quad \text{quantity to be ordered}$$

Total cost will be:

Hol ding Cost + Reordering Cost

$$\text{Holding} = \frac{Q \times C_h}{2} \qquad \text{Reordering} = \frac{D \times C_0}{Q}$$

Example

Perfecto Pasta uses tomato puree on a regular basis throughout the year. The annual demand of the puree is 5,400kg and the cost of holding 1kg in terms of shelf and fridge space is £0.75. Records show that it costs £2.50 to place and process an order.

$$\text{Using the EOQ formula} = \sqrt{\frac{2 \times 2.50 \times 5400}{0.75}} = 190\text{kg}$$

This means that the most economical order size when both the holding and ordering costs are taken into account is 190kg per order.

On this basis the company would make

$$\frac{5400\text{kg}}{190\text{kg}} = 28.42 \text{ orders}$$

Which is the equivalent of one order every 13 days.

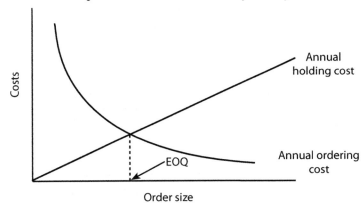

Figure 12.5: Graphing the EOQ

As well as the use of this formula the business should also hold a 'safety inventory' against uncertainties in lead time. This has a cost of:

No units safety inventory   x   holding cost per unit per annum

12.6.7 Discounts

The EOQ formula may need to be modified if bulk discounts are available. It is necessary to minimise the total of:

■ Total purchase costs

■ Ordering costs

■ Inventory holding costs

The total cost will be minimised at the pre-discount EOQ level so that the discount is not worthwhile or at the minimum order size necessary to earn the discount.

12

Example

Perfecto Pasta regularly buys prosecco from a local wholesaler. The cost of making an order has been estimated at £3.00 and the cost of holding a bottle in stock is £1.50, the annual purchase from the wholesaler has been 19,600 bottles at a price of £7 each. On this basis the economic order quantity for Perfecto has been 280 bottles per order. The wholesaler has now offered Perfecto a deal where if they order in batches 400 they can have a 1% discount per bottle.

Is it beneficial for Perfecto to take the order and hold a greater number of units? The annual cost of using the EOQ should be calculated first and then compared with the cost of the new offer.

There are three elements to the cost, shown in Table 12.5.

Table 12.5

		£
Purchase price	£7 x 19,600 bottles	137,200
Holding cost	280/2 x 1.50	210
Ordering cost	19,600/280 x 3	210
Total cost of ordering 280 bottles per order		**137,620**
New offer buy 400 bottles per order		
Purchase price	£7 x 0.99 x 19,600 bottles	~~135,828~~
Holding cost	400/2 x 1.50	300
Ordering cost	19,600/400 x 3	147
Total cost of ordering 400 bottles per order		**136,275**

In this case it is better for Perfecto to accept the offer from the ~~supplier~~ as the saving on the purchase price outweighs additional holding cost.

12.6.8 JIT (just in time)

This is a system whereby costs rather than inventory levels are minimised. Goods are obtained just in time to meet production or customer demand. In hotels and restaurants where advantage is taken of fresh local produce an effective just in time system is in place with regards to food; however it would be impractical to order beverages in this way. In an event scenario merchandise stock will need to be built up prior to an event and again the use of just in time would be impractical.

12.6.9 Special value items

In the hospitality, leisure and tourism industries it is important to consider the types of inventory that will be held and to look at individual stock turnovers as well as general figures. Food and beverage will form a large part of any inventory. Food is less likely to be of high value (meat usually representing a higher value than other items) but will be seasonal and will need to be turned over relatively quickly; therefore the levels of inventory will require constant monitoring to ensure menu items are available at customer request.

Generally, beverage stock will not turn over as quickly (exception being for specific events) but it will require secure storage some of which will need to meet certain ambient conditions. Fine wines for example will be considered high value items which will require additional control and security.

12.7 Managing accounts receivable

Businesses of most types need to allow credit to achieve satisfactory sales. Allowing credit however, results in:

- An interest cost of funds tied up in giving credit to customers
- Possibility of bad debts (this occurs when customers do not pay the amount they owe).

A balance has to be found between sales volume, credit allowed, interest costs and bad debts.

12.7.1 The credit cycle

The stages in the credit cycle are as follows:

1 Receipt of customer order
2 Credit screening and agreement of terms
3 Goods dispatched or service provided with delivery note
4 Invoice raised stating credit terms
5 Debt collection procedures
6 Receipt of cash.

The longer the credit cycle, the more cash there is locked into working capital. Reducing the length of the credit cycle will improve cash flow and thus improve the organisation's liquidity position.

The accounts receivable days give an indication of whether customers are being managed effectively (see Table 12.6).

Table 12.6

Ratio	Format	2012	2011	Interpretation
Trade receivables period	Days	37	48	There has been a marked improvement in this, 11 days on average, this could be part of the explanation for improved asset utilisation and could reflect tighter credit control.

NB. Whilst the trade receivables could include additional items such as prepayments it is assumed that in this example it only relates to accounts receivables.

The data in Table 12.6 suggests that the approach for managing receivables is effective in terms of reducing the number of days but the cost of reducing the number of days must also be investigated. It is possible that lost income from offering a quick payment discount is greater than the cost of extending credit for extra days. A hotel will carefully have to balance any discount to its room rate for advance payment with the payment of the full amount on arrival, but this would also link with its revenue management policy, see Chapter 7 for more details related to 'discounting' in this sector.

12.7.2 Credit control

This is the control exercised by a firm over its accounts receivable to ensure that customers pay their debts on time and to minimise the risk of bad debts.

Management when formulating a credit control policy must consider the following factors:

- Cost of managing accounts receivable
- Procedures for controlling credit
- Capital required to finance credit
- Credit terms and allowing discount for prompt payment
- Creditworthiness of customers.

Some of these items need to be considered in more detail.

12.7.3 Cost of managing accounts receivable

Accounts receivable management as previously mentioned is about balancing the benefit of extending credit against the costs. The costs to be considered are:

- The opportunity cost of capital
- Cost of bad debts
- Cost of extending settlement discounts
- Administration costs of managing the credit control function.

12.7.4 Assessing creditworthiness

- Gather references from at least two sources, one of which should be from the customer's bank
- Check credit ratings
- Set credit limits and payment terms and review them regularly
- Review the files of clients
- Use internal sources such as reports from salespeople
- Utilise external information, e.g. government, press
- Analyse their financial statements
- Visit the organisation.

12.7.5 Stages in debt collection

There is no optimal debt collection policy that will be applicable to all companies. Debt collection policies will differ according to the nature of the business and the level of competition.

An effective solution will require the following.

- Dedicated, well-trained credit control personnel
- Well-defined procedures for collection of overdue debts that take account of the potential costs of collecting an outstanding debt, and the need to maintain good relationships with customers
- Monitoring of overdue accounts
- Flexibility to allow for changing circumstances.

12.7.6 Collecting debts

There are two stages in collecting debts the first involves efficient and prompt procedures for dealing with paperwork:

- Customers must be fully aware of the credit terms
- Invoices should be sent out immediately after delivery
- Checks should be carried out to ensure that invoices are accurate
- The investigation of any queries or complaints should be carried out promptly
- Monthly statements should be sent out early enough for them to be included in the customer's monthly settlement of bills.

The second involves procedures for pursuing overdue debts:

- Reminders on final demands
- Chasing by telephone
- Making personal approaches
- Stopping credit
- Transfer of debt to specialist collection team
- Instituting legal action
- Transfer of debt to external debt collection agency.

12.7.7 Monitoring

The position should be regularly reviewed using techniques such as age analysis, ratios and statistical data.

12.7.7.1 Age analysis of accounts receivable

The accounts and payment histories of customers are analysed in order to establish those customers which require greater monitoring or where debt collection procedures need to be invoked. Consider the analysis for Homely Hotels in Table 12.7 and its corporate clients.

Table 12.7: Homely Hotels Ltd, Age analysis of accounts receivable as at 31 March 2012

Account number	Customer name	Balance	Up to 30 days	31–60 days	61–90 days	Over 90 days
C005	Coolerage Ltd	175.40	120.15	55.25	0.00	0.00
J002	Jenkins Ltd	679.30	486.00	0.00	193.30	0.00
M008	Maple Plc	243.90	243.90	0.00	0.00	0.00
S012	Stanton Ltd	1,346.70	0.00	0.00	419.40	927.30
T001	Trent Ltd	396.53	264.80	131.73	0.00	0.00
Totals		2,841.83	1,114.85	186.98	612.70	927.30
Percentage		100%	39.0%	6.6%	21.6%	32.6%

The age analysis of accounts receivable can be used to help decide what action should be taken about debts that have been outstanding for longer than the specified credit period. It can be seen from the table above that 32.6% of Homely Hotels outstanding accounts receivable balance is over 90 days old and is due to one client, Stanton Ltd. It may be that Stanton Ltd is experiencing financial difficulties. There may already have been some correspondence between the two companies about the outstanding debts. This breakdown gives far more information for management decision making. Within hotels, collection of payments may only be left with local financial controllers for up to three months, and then a central control department will manage the debt. The company is also likely to set targets, for example a maximum of 15% of debts to be over three months old.

12.7.8 External ways of managing accounts receivable

12.7.8.1 Credit insurance

This can be taken out against specific bad debts it is normally available for up to 75% of the potential loss. The company will have to give the insurance company the name and amount of credit for each customer it wants to insure against.

12.7.8.2 Factoring

This is an arrangement whereby debts are collected by a factor company who advance a proportion of the debt it is due to collect. Factors can actually provide a number of services:

- Administration of the client's invoicing, sales accounting and debt collection
- Credit protection (insurance) against the loss from bad debts
- Factor finance – this is where the factor will advance money to the client against the security of the customer
- Invoice discounting – the factor will purchase trade debts of the client at a discount. This can be done confidentially so the customer would only be aware of the arrangement if they failed to pay.

It is possible to numerically calculate the effect of using a factoring arrangement.

12.7.8.3 Invoice discounting

This is a method of raising finance against the security of receivables without using the administrative services of a factor. In this situation the customer will not be aware of any arrangement and will pay the seller as normal.

12.8 Managing accounts payable

The management of trade credit involves:

- Seeking satisfactory trade credit from suppliers
- Seeking credit extension during periods of cash shortage
- Maintaining good relations with suppliers.

Trade credit is seen as a free source of finance and therefore there is a tendency to try and extend the period. Remember that again it is a balancing act between liquidity and profitability and that if a discount is offered by a supplier for prompt payment then the credit is no longer free.

Example

A catering supplier of Wondrous Weddings events offers a discount of 2% if bills are settled within 15 days otherwise bills must be settled in full within 30 days. If Wondrous Weddings take the extra 15 days credit it effectively costs 2%.

12.9 Management of cash

This relates to two areas in many businesses:

- How much cash should be kept in the bank (profitability)
- How to deal with cash flow problems (liquidity).

The treasury manager must be skilled in managing the various accounts which the company has, switching money between them so as to maximise interest receivable and minimise interest payable.

For companies with physical cash onsite, particularly events companies, the management of cash must also consider the security of physical cash.

12.9.1 Cash security

On the day of an event a large amount of cash will be received it is important to consider how the cash will be handled and by whom and also how it is stored. All cash should be secured in cash boxes or sealable containers and not left unattended. Cash should be periodically deposited at a central cash office and should be stored securely. A main problem with events is the volume of cash and volume of people who may have transient access to it, including casual staff.

12.9.2 Cash flow forecast

This document is an essential one in any business; it records the expected inflows of cash and expected outflows, enabling a company to predict its cash requirements. Should additional finance be required the needs can be analysed and resources found efficiently and effectively in advance. Should surplus cash be available this can be invested in order to increase the profitability of the firm.

The accuracy of this document rests on the ability to make realistic predictions of the movement of cash, particularly the forecast sales. Some businesses will undertake risk analysis by producing best and worst case scenarios of the cash flow.

Computerisation and the use of spreadsheets have benefited the production of cash flow forecasts enormously, allowing adjustments to be made to the data with instant changes to the underlying cash flow. Whilst a cash flow forecast (budget) is an important tool for all hospitality sector businesses due to the need to predict seasonality, it is particularly important for events companies who may have to pay out significant expenses before income is received. Festival organisers for example have to pay acts well in advance of an event in order to be able to use their name on advertising literature to attract ticket sales.

12.9.3 Analysing the cash flow forecast

The following are a number of elements of the cash flow that may require attention:

Cash flow problems can arise in various ways:

- Making losses
- Inflation
- Growth
- Seasonal business
- One-off items of expenditure.

Methods of easing cash shortages:

- Postpone capital expenditure
- Accelerate cash inflows
- Sell off assets
- Reduce cash outflows
- Efficient use of cash budgets.

Example

Glastowood festival is a major event put on each year in August. The festival organisers produce a cash flow forecast each year on a quarterly basis to monitor the cash inflow and outflow associated with the festival.

Table 12.8: Cash flow forecast for the festival due to take place next August.

	Quarter 1 Jan–March £	Quarter 2 April–June £	Quarter 3 July–Sept £	Quarter 4 Oct–Dec £
Receipts				
Ticket sales	400,000	1,500,000	500,000	0
Franchise outlets			347,000	98,000
Merchandise		37,000	460,000	32,000
Total receipts	400,000	1,537,000	1,307,000	130,000
Payments				
Band bookings	85,000	378,000	124,000	0
Venue hire	60,000	0	0	2,000
Marquee hire	45,000	45,000	45,000	0
Staffing	200,000	200,000	400,000	200,000
Overheads	95,000	136,000	297,000	72,000
Food and beverage inventory	79,000	258,000	596,000	0
Total payments	564,000	1,017,000	1,462,000	274,000
Opening cash balance	5,000	−159,000	361,000	206,000
Net cash flow	−164,000	520,000	−155,000	−144,000
Closing cash balance	−159,000	361,000	206,000	62,000

The cash flow forecast in Table 12.8 clearly shows that the festival expenditure is way above income in the first quarter as a result of having to spend money to secure the venue and acts in particular. Ticket sales will not be received early unless a significant incentive is given such as a discount or knowing which acts will be headlining the festival.

The festival organisers will need to use the cash flow forecast to decide what action to now take in respect of the predicted cash flows. Table 12.9 is the cash flow which would be the new position if the organisers decided to offer a 10% discount for early purchase and half of those buying in quarter 2 take up the offer:

The cash flow position is now acceptable but the overall position is that the business will lose some of the revenue it would have made as a result of the discount.

Another potential solution to the cash flow problem may be to spend additional funds to secure a headline act early which would also encourage early sales. This would ensure that there is a positive cash balance at the end of quarter 1 and the same amount of overall cash would be made (Table 12.10).

12

Table 12.9: Cash flow forecast for Glastowood Festival, with early purchase discount

	Quarter 1	Quarter 2	Quarter 3	Quarter 4
	£	£	£	£
Receipts				
Ticket sales	1,110,000	750,000	500,000	0
Franchise outlets			347,000	98,000
Merchandise		37,000	460,000	32,000
Total receipts	1,110,000	787,000	1,307,000	130,000
Payments				
Band bookings	85,000	378,000	124,000	0
Venue hire	60,000	0	0	2,000
Marquee hire	45,000	45,000	45,000	0
Staffing	200,000	200,000	400,000	200,000
Overheads	95,000	136,000	297,000	72,000
Food and beverage inventory	79,000	258,000	596,000	0
Total payments	564,000	1,017,000	1,462,000	274,000
Opening cash balance	5,000	551,000	321,000	166,000
Net cash flow	546,000	−230,000	−155,000	−144,000
Closing cash balance	551,000	321,000	166,000	22,000

Table 12.10: Cash flow forecast for Glastowood Festival, with headline act

	Quarter 1	Quarter 2	Quarter 3	Quarter 4
	£	£	£	£
Receipts				
Ticket sales	900,000	1,000,000	500,000	0
Franchise outlets			347,000	98,000
Merchandise		37,000	460,000	32,000
Total receipts	900,000	1,037,000	1,307,000	130,000
Payments				
Band bookings	285,000	178,000	124,000	0
Venue hire	60,000	0	0	2,000
Marquee hire	45,000	45,000	45,000	0
Staffing	200,000	200,000	400,000	200,000
Overheads	95,000	136,000	297,000	72,000
Food and beverage inventory	79,000	258,000	596,000	0
Total payments	764,000	817,000	1,462,000	274,000
Opening cash balance	5,000	141,000	361,000	206,000
Net cash flow	136,000	220,000	−155,000	−144,000
Closing cash balance	141,000	361,000	206,000	62,000

Summary

Working capital management is an essential element of a business's success.

- Too little investment in the key elements of inventory and accounts receivable hinders the liquidity of the business.

- Too much investment hinders the profitability of the business.

- Each element of the business's current assets and current liabilities must be managed effectively to provide the correct balance for the business.

- Operational and financial perspectives need to be taken in working capital decisions.

Reference

Altman, E. (1968) 'Financial ratios, discriminant analysis and the prediction of corporate bankruptcy', *Journal of Finance*, **23**,(4) Sept., 589-609.

Further reading

Dopson, L.R. (2010) *Food and Beverage Cost Control: Study Guide*, John Wiley & Sons.

This book is a very practical guide specific to cost control of food and beverages. Those with stock being an important part of their working capital may find this practical guide to stock operations helpful.

Attril, P. (2011) *Financial Management for Decision Makers*, 6th edn, Pearson.

This book aimed at managers, covers all aspects of financial management including working capital management.

Self-check student questions

1 What are the key elements of working capital?
2 Name the three working capital policies a business can follow.
3 How can overtrading be spotted?
4 What are the main items of stock of a hotel?
5 Calculate the economic order quantity given the following data:
   Annual demand   7,000 units
   Ordering cost   £1.20 per order
   Annual holding cost   £1.68 per unit
6 What are the main factors to consider before giving credit to a customer?
7 What is the purpose of a cash flow forecast?

12

Further questions and problems

1   You are part of the financial management team of an events firm called Allegro Ltd. As part of your job you have carried out a benchmarking exercise with other firms in the industry to evaluate your firms' control of working capital. In particular you discover:

	Allegro Ltd	Others
Inventory holding	150 days stock	70–80 days stock
Accounts receivable days	100 days	55–65 days
Accounts payable days	70 days	50–70 days

Required:

Write a report to the financial director that discusses each of the three ratios and proposes appropriate policies for bringing the company into line with competitors.

2   a)   Explain what is meant by 'working capital cycle' and its importance to managers.

(5 marks)

b)   Given the data below, calculate the working capital requirements for next year compared to this year.

	Food £	Beverage £
Current year		
Sales	820,000	410,000
Cost of sales	246,000	102,500
Gross profit	574,000	307,500

For next year:

Food sales to be £895,000, beverage £485,000

Cost of sales % to remain unchanged

Accounts receivable to increase from 6% to 10% of total sales

Customers take 6 weeks to pay

Stock holding averages 1 week for food and 3 weeks for beverages

Suppliers give you 4 weeks' credit.

(15 marks)

c)   What are the implications of these results?   (5 marks)

(BAHA stage three – Strategic Management Accounting Paper July 2010)

13 Business Finance

13.1 Introduction and objectives

Management accounting decisions whether short-term or long-term cannot be made without some consideration of how they are to be financed. The financing decisions that an organisation makes will generally relate to the length of time the finance is required, the cost of capital and the capacity to borrow.

After studying this chapter you should be able to:

- Identify the main sources of short-term finance
- Identify the main sources of long-term finance
- Distinguish between the financing sources available to different sizes of organisation
- Understand the specific financing options available to hospitality, tourism and events organisations.

13.2 Short-term sources of finance

Short-term finance generally refers to sources of funding which will not be required for more than one year. The previous chapter showed that a sound working capital financing policy requires short-term assets to be generally financed by short-term liabilities. The most common sources of short-term finance are considered below.

13.2.1 Bank overdraft

One of the most important external sources of short-term finance, particularly for smaller businesses, is the overdraft. An overdraft facility allows the business to spend more money than is deposited in the bank account. The amount of the overdraft will rise and fall as funds are deposited and spent from the account. Features that make the overdraft popular are:

- The bank will agree to a maximum overdraft limit or facility. The borrower may not require the full facility immediately, but may draw funds up to the limit as and when required which promotes flexibiiity.

- Legal documentation is fairly minimal when arranging an overdraft. Key elements of the documentation will be to state the maximum overdraft limit, the interest payable and the security required.
- Interest is only paid on the amount borrowed, rather than on the full facility.

The drawbacks of overdraft finance are:

- The overdraft is legally repayable on demand, which means that the facility could be withdrawn at any time.
- Security may be required over the businesses assets.
- Interest costs vary with bank base rates.

13.2.2 Term loans

The retail banks offer term loans these are also a useful source of funds for smaller businesses due to their accessibility. A term loan is for a fixed amount with a fixed repayment schedule. Usually the interest rate applied is slightly less than for a bank overdraft. The lender will require security to cover the amount borrowed and an arrangement fee is payable dependent on the amount borrowed.

The advantages of term loans are:

- Easily and quickly negotiated
- Flexible payments may be offered
- Variable interest rates.

A term loan also has the following advantages over overdrafts:

- Both the customer and the bank know what the repayment schedule is which is important for planning cash flow and also the precise terms of the agreement.
- Peace of mind – no risk of immediate withdrawal of the loan.

13.2.3 Trade credit

Trade credit is an important source of finance for most businesses. Trade credit is the money owed to the suppliers of goods and services as a result of purchasing goods or services on one date, but paying for those goods on a later date. The management of trade credit was discussed in the previous chapter. The amount of trade credit available will vary depending on the nature of the industry, the product being supplied and the ability of the two parties to negotiate.

Advantages of trade credit:

- Convenient/informal/cheap
- Available to organisations of any size.

13.2.4 Deferred income

A key feature of service business such as events operators and tour operators is the advance payment of fees and ticket sales. In such businesses customers pay well in advance for the services they are going to use, such as fees for an exhibition stand or advance payment for a holiday. This is a vital source of finance for these businesses as they receive the cash up to 12 months ahead of delivering the service and can use this to fund their operations. It should be noted that if the company subsequently fails to deliver the service they will have to repay this money plus additional penalties.

Advantages of deferred income

- Convenient/informal/cheap
- Occurs naturally as part of business operations
- Available to organisations of any size
- Must be repaid if services not provided.

Example 13.1: the balance of short-term liabilities for ITE (international large events company). Extracted from ITE Annual Report 2011.

ITE short-term finance	%
Bank overdraft	13.5
Trade and other payable	19.2
Deferred income	65.9
Provisions and derivatives	1.4
	100.0

The clearly shows that deferred income is their major source of short-term finance.

13.3 Long-term sources of finance

Long-term sources of finance are required when the organisation requires funds for investment, which will take more than 12 months to mature. The capital investment decisions considered in the next chapter rely on the ability to raise finance from long-term sources. Long-term sources can usually be divided into two types:

- Equity
- Debt.

13.3.1 Equity

Equity refers to funds provided by the owners of the organisation. In a small business the initial capital is supplied by either an individual owner (known as a sole trader) or by several owners (known as a partnership).

13

In a company the owners are shareholders who each contribute a portion of the equity through the purchase of ordinary shares. A company has a greater capacity to raise funds through equity than a sole trader and a partnership as there is likely to be a large pool of potential investors.

As a company grows it is able to raise additional share capital by either issuing new shares or by conducting a rights issue (where shares are sold to existing shareholders on a pro rata basis). The key advantages associated with the use of equity finance are that the investment from the shareholder does not have to be repaid unless the company becomes insolvent and ceases trading. In addition there is no legal obligation to pay a dividend to ordinary shareholders, although companies normally establish clear patterns for dividend payment, which are rarely changed.

However, there are also several disadvantages to using equity finance in a company. The cost of raising the funds is expensive as share issues have to be marketed and a number of professional organisations have to be employed to assist with the share issue, a rights issue does not incur the same cost as a new issue but it is still administratively expensive.

Equity is also an expensive source of finance because the shareholders expect a return (that is their cost of capital). The return the shareholders expect is relatively high because they take the most risk out of all the suppliers of finance. The final disadvantage for a company is that any dividend that is paid to the shareholders is not classed as a running expense of the business and does not offset the tax the company has to pay.

13.3.2 Retained profit

As a business makes a profit any which is not distributed to pay expenses or returned to the owner is retained by the business. The retained profit adds to the equity capital of the business. The retained profit it is the best source of funds for any business as it is generated through business success and carries no issue cost or interest cost, however retained profit is also owned by the shareholders and if they are not receiving the profit in the form of a dividend but it is retained for use in the business they will expect the business to invest it wisely to give them a return from the investment so even this is not a free source of capital.

13.3.3 Preference shares

Preference shares are also available for a company to use as a source of long-term funds but even though they are shares they do not form part of the equity capital of the business. Preference shares have very different characteristics to ordinary shares, in particular they pay a fixed dividend whilst the dividend to the ordinary shareholders varies with the amount of profit retained and the company's dividend policy, and whilst the ordinary shareholders are able to vote the preference shares carry no voting rights. The final key difference is that most preference shares are cumulative which means any dividend due and not paid will be carried forward to the next period and when funds are available they will be paid. In corporate finance the preference shares are included with the debt finance in gearing calculations as their characteristics are more similar to debt than equity.

13.3.4 Debt

Debt finance represents funds which are loaned to the business by an external source. There are a number of different sources available depending on the size of the organisation. All debt finance shares some common features though:

- Interest is payable on the amount borrowed
- Interest will either be a fixed rate or variable rate
- A repayment schedule will be set
- Interest is tax deductible so will reduce the tax burden
- Security for the debt will be required.
- As the level of debt increases so does the gearing of the firm and the financial risk of the business.

The following are some of the more common types of debt finance.

13.3.5 Term loans

Term loans were considered under short-term sources of finance the features of a term loan are the same whether they are arranged for a short or long period of time. The amount of security required is likely to increase in line with the term of the loan and the riskiness of the project for which the funds are required.

13.3.6 Bonds

This type of finance is only available to companies. Bonds are sold on a unit basis (via the capital markets) so each lender only provides the amount of funds they each want to lend. Each bond will usually have a value of £100 in the UK so a lender who wants to provide £1000 to the company would buy 10 bonds.

There are a number of different types of bonds each having slightly different features which can be tailored to the borrowing requirements of the company. For example some bonds will carry a high level of security over the assets of the business (generally termed debentures) and some a low level of security or no security (termed loan stock); some bonds will carry a low interest rate (deep discount bonds) and some will pay no interest (zero coupon bonds) to compensate the lender for the low or zero interest payments the bonds will usually cost less than £100 each to buy but will still repay £100 on the redemption date.

As can be seen from the real life example in Example 13.2, typically companies use a range of sources at the same time to construct a portfolio of finance over time. We have not explained all sources of finance, but have covered the main

13

sources. For more in-depth information about financing businesses, please refer to Arnold (2007) *Essentials of Corporate Financial Management.*

Example 13.2: Lufthansa debt and equity 2011. Extracted from Annual Report 2011

	€ millions	%
Issued capital	1772	14.8
Capital reserve	857	7.1
Retained earnings	1541	12.8
Bonds	2107	17.6
Liabilities to banks	1007	8.4
Payables to affiliate companies	1713	14.3
Other liabilities	2999	25.0
	11996	100.0

13.4 The weighted average cost of capital (WACC)

Every source of capital that a business uses has its own cost of capital. The cost of capital is the minimum return that is acceptable to the provider of finance. As the ordinary shareholders take the most risk, they expect the highest return and their cost of capital is the highest. The providers of debt finance who have security over the assets of the business will expect a lower return as they take less risk and therefore their cost of capital will be lower. It is possible to calculate the exact cost of capital of each source of finance but this is a financial management technique which is outside the scope of this textbook.

If a company is to survive and grow it must ensure that the investments it makes achieve a return over that required by the providers of finance. Therefore it is necessary to calculate a target cost of capital which the company can use in investment decisions (see the next chapter for details).

One method to find the cost of capital is to calculate a weighted average cost of capital based on the amounts of each source of finance invested in the company.

Worked example

Spiritual Spas has two sources of finance: equity provided by the shareholders and bonds.

The cost of equity has been calculated at 14% and the cost of debt has been calculated at 6%. The capital structure of the company means that £750,000 has been provided by equity and £250,000 by bonds. The WACC can be calculated as follows:

Total capital invested is £750,000 + £250,000 = £1,000,000

The equity proportion is £750,000/£1,000,000 = 75%

Therefore the debt proportion = 25%

Weighted cost of equity =	14% x 0.75	= 10.5%
Weighted cost of debt =	6% x 0.25	= 1.5%
WACC		= 12.0%

Any investment that the company makes will need to earn a return over 12% in order to ensure the company remains successful.

The weighted average is affected by the relative costs and the amounts of each source of capital so in order to reduce this hurdle rate the company would need to fund more of its business from cheaper sources of finance, i.e. debt. If the above example is revised to show equal amounts of debt to equity the WACC will become:

Weighted cost of equity =	14% x 0.50	= 7%
Weighted cost of debt =	6% x 0.50	= 3%
WACC		= 10%

However the company cannot continue to use more and more debt without consequence as more debt means a greater chance that the company will become insolvent if it cannot afford to pay the growing interest payments associated with more debt (refer back to the gearing ratio calculation in Chapter 11) and this increases the risk that the ordinary shareholders take so eventually their cost of capital will rise and the WACC will no longer fall but will rise. In the above example if the amount of debt is raised to 75% of the capital structure the cost of equity will go up to 40% the WACC will become:

Weighted cost of equity =	40% x 0.25	= 10.0%
Weighted cost of debt =	6% x 0.75	= 4.5%
WACC		= 14.5%

This principle shows that the company must give consideration to the amount of capital it raises from each source of finance as there are significant consequences if the level of gearing rises too high.

13.5 SMEs and micro businesses

The smaller a business is, the more difficult it can be to raise the required capital to start up and continue to grow from internal (owner) sources and therefore the smaller organisations rely on being able to secure external funding in order to survive.

There has always been a 'funding gap' in the financial markets where insufficient funds are available for smaller business, the gap is both in terms of ability to raise equity due to expense and poor investor information and also the ability to raise debt finance due to their inability to provide sufficient security and no track record of credit risk. What is more, since the banking crisis the main high street banks have further restricted their funding of smaller businesses.

The UK government, like governments of all developed countries, provide a range of grants for small businesses; these are usually linked to the government priorities, the state of the national and global economy and can also change from year to year, government to government. The key areas where government funding is usually available are:

- Business start-ups
- Innovation research and development grants
- Regional regeneration grants.

The UK government also provides Small Firms Loan Guarantee (SFLG) scheme to encourage banks and other lenders to provide funds to small businesses, this and other government grant schemes can change at any time so no details are provided here, but can be found at the appropriate national government websites.

13.6 Sector-specific financing

Major projects can require significant funds for a business. P&O are reported to have invested £500 million in developing a new 'superliner' cruise ship, whilst Royal Caribbean's 'Oasis of the Seas' (at time of launch the world's largest cruise ship) is reported to have cost £800 million and they have already ordered a sister ship. In London estimated hotel building costs for a 5* hotel are believed to be around £250,000 per room, refurbishment approximately £20,000 per room, and a fitting out for operation (furniture, fittings, equipment, and operating supplies) being a further £30,000 per room. Multiply these figures by 300 rooms for example, and it is clear such investments and growth decisions need careful thought before even considering the funding options available.

These sums of money will not be financed fully from internal sources, or from a local bank, these are major investments that require careful consideration and need to be financed in a way that is affordable to the company.

Deferred income, discussed above, is a significant source of short-term finance for many (although not all) service businesses. Another feature of financing in this sector is associated with investment in long-term assets such as hotel premises, aircraft and cruise ships. Different mechanisms have evolved to finance these. Tour operators with airline operations often buy aircraft from the manufacturers and then immediately sell aircraft and lease them back (from finance companies), smaller cruise operators often charter vessels from independent (or related) shipping companies. These mechanisms reduce the amount of money tied up in non-current assets and release it for further growth, this used to be called 'off balance sheet' finance, but this is now disclosed in the notes to annual financial accounts. Budget hotels are often run in leased properties, sometimes extended to leasing the furniture and even the curtains inside the property.

In new markets in developing countries the use of foreign direct investment (FDI) is common in tourism development and the development of resort hotels.

The expansion of tourism globally leads to the need of FDI, not just for financial investment in developing countries, but also to provide the skills base needed for such developments in newly-opened markets.

Other ways of financing hospitality, tourism and events businesses include, franchising, most popular in the fast food sector; leasing and operating leases, used in travel agents and tour operators; and management contracts used along-side the other techniques in hotels.

13.6.1 Restaurant franchising

Within the restaurant sector franchising is a major source of business financing. From the corporate franchiser perspective it offers advantages of: expanding without investing their own capital at a relatively low cost; less unit level administrative costs; and purchasing discounts from suppliers. For an individual franchisees perspective they are offered: a proven brand name and concept; business assistance; and lower failure rates than non-franchised small businesses.

13.6.2 Hotel management contracts

The use of management contracts in hotels is significant. In this arrangement a hotel is owned by one company or party, often a tax-efficient real estate investment trust (REIT) and is operated by another, often a branded chain hotel operating company. The operator runs the hotel for a fee whilst the owner retains limited control over the operation of the assets and bears the risk. Management fees are made up of a base fee and an incentive fee (generally a percentage of gross operating profit). Contracts normally specify the term (length of contract), the fees (as mentioned above), any operator guarantees and performance measures that will be used, also agreement of how capital investment will be handled and how to terminate the contract. Chapter 2 discussed this in relation to USALI and standardising management accounting formats where management contracts are in use.

Management contracts have been the standard in USA for many decades, but this has become more widespread internationally in more recent times. The separation of hotel ownership from hotel operating used to be viewed purely as a US model (Atkinson and Jones, 2008). This increasing trend in the use of management contracts globally has been supported by firms such as HVS and PKF providing contract and valuation intermediary services to hotel companies and hotel investors. Hotels may be owned by banks and investment trusts, but also specialist hotel ownership companies and REITS. A number of global branded hotel chains, for example; Hilton, Marriott, Carlson Rezidor, use management contracts, whereas many smaller independent hotels still own their own property.

Research by Singh and Schmidgall (2000) applied the Delphi method and found optimism in the fact different sectors of hotels would find finance opportunities available to them. Upscale luxury hotels were found to be financed by life insurance companies, pension funds and investment banks. Mid-scale and budget hotels tended towards finance from local and community bankers and finance companies. They also found more recent interest in investing in hospitality related to gaming properties, such as in Las Vegas.

13.6.3 Entrepreneurial activity in hospitality, tourism and events

Whilst management contracts and REITs can aid larger operations it has to be considered that despite some large organisations, the vast majority of business in these sectors would still be considered SMEs, or even micro business. A bed and breakfast (B&B), an owner-run local events business, or a small tourist attraction will find it hard to attract such funding opportunities. The research of Brooker (2002) specifically looks at issues of financing small hotel enterprises and discusses this in relation to other tourism sectors. Ozer and Yamak's work (2000) in Turkey confirms small business in the sector being mainly funded through personal funds and retained earnings, with the use of debt financing being low.

There are additional funding opportunities for entrepreneurial activity in the form of local grant funding, or funding for the arts if developing performing arts-based events. Likewise, 'business angels' are a useful source of funding for new start-ups. For young entrepreneurs the Prince's Trust is a source of grants and advice in the UK that has funded a number of set-up businesses in these sectors.

Summary

There is a wide array of sources available to businesses. The sources chosen or available have a significant effect on the decisions that managers can make.

- Short-term finance should be used where finance is required for short-term projects and for working capital requirements.

- The two main types of long-term finance are equity and debt.

- The relationship between equity and debt is important to ascertain the WACC.

- A variety of bespoke financing methods are available in the hospitality, tourism and events sectors.

- The size of the operation will impact on the sources of finance available to an individual organisation.

References

Arnold, G. (2007) *Essentials of Corporate Financial Management*, Harlow: Pearson

Atkinson, H. and Jones, T. (2008) 'Financial management in the hospitality industry: themes and issues', in B. Brotherton and R. Woods (eds), *The Sage Handbook of Hospitality Management*, Sage Publications, Chapter 10.

Brooker, D. (2002) 'How to raise finance for a small hotel enterprise – a way forward', *Hospitality Review*, 4 (1), 13–20.

Ozer, B. and Yamak, S. (2000) 'Self-sustaining pattern of finance in small businesses evidence from Turkey', *International Journal of Hospitality Management*, **19** (3), 261–273.

Singh, A. and Schmidgall, R. (2000) 'Financing lodging properties', *Cornell Hotel and Restaurant Administration Quarterly*, **41** (4), 39–47.

Further reading

Attril, P. (2011) *Financial Management for Decision Makers*, 6th edn, Harlow: Pearson.

This book, aimed at managers, covers all aspects of financial management including sources of short-term and long-term finance.

Brotherton, B. and Woods, R. (eds) (2008) *The Sage Handbook of Hospitality Management*, Sage Publications.

In addition to Chapter 10 already mentioned in the reference section, Chapter 16 by Paul Beals specifically focuses on research into hotel real estate finance and investment, covering this topic in depth.

Visit the HVS website (www.hvs.com) and go the library section where you can download several complimentary guides on topics covering hotel management contracts and franchising.

ITE Group plc (2011) *Annual Report and Accounts 30 September 2011*. London. ITE Group plc.

Lufthansa (2011) *Annual Report*. Cologne. Deutsche Lufthansa AG.

13

Self-check questions

1   What are the advantages of using equity capital?

2   What are the main types of equity capital?

3   How do preference shares differ from ordinary shares?

4   What are the advantages of using debt finance?

5   Describe the features of bonds.

6   What method of financing are now most commonly used in hotels?

7   How can the size of operation impact on sources of finance available?

8   What does FDI stand for?

Further questions and problems

1   a) The owner of a successful privately-owned 60-bed hotel wishes to expand but requires more capital to do so.

Identify and evaluate the potential methods the business could use to raise such capital and indicate, with reasons, your preferred method.

(15 marks)

b) Using hospitality examples, explain what is meant by gearing and the importance of this in the hospitality industry.

(10 marks)

(BAHA Stage Three – Strategic Management Accounting, July 2010)

2   a) From the data shown below calculate the weighted average cost of capital.

(7 marks)

Source	Amount (in £000)	Cost/expected return %
Ordinary shareholders	15,000	18
Preference shareholders	5,000	9
Lender 1	10,000	8
Lender 2	20,000	12

b) There are various sources of finance available to hospitality organisations in the short, medium and long term. Identify 6 different sources if finance capital and for each of those identified discuss its merits and associated cost of capital.

(18 marks)

(BAHA Stage Three – Strategic Management Accounting, September 2009)

14 Capital Investment Appraisal

14.1 Introduction and objectives

Capital investment is a medium or long-term strategic decision that is often a multimillion pound investment and is difficult to change direction once started. Capital investment appraisal is sometimes referred to as capital budgeting, as it relates to the allocation of funding for capital expenditure. Due to these factors, making the wrong decision can be very costly so it is important that any organisation undertakes a thorough appraisal of their potential capital investment projects prior to committing to them. Whilst this chapter focuses on financial appraisal, some consideration is given to the wider appraisal of projects, including the match to organisational strategy and risk management.

After studying this chapter you should be able to:

- Understand the importance of capital investment appraisal (CIA)
- Develop a working knowledge of financial CIA techniques
- Appreciate the 'time value' of money in the CIA context; and
- Be able to consider the strategic implications of CIA decisions.

14.2 The value of investment appraisal

For a company to continue to grow it needs to continue to invest and develop, looking at exploiting new market opportunities, plus redevelopment and updating of existing assets in order to meet customers' constantly changing demands. Investment appraisal is a way of financially assessing the value of potential investments to ensure financial resources are utilised effectively by the organisation.

There are a number of different triggers for investment: keeping up with competitors; replacing old assets; expansion or to utilise newly developed technology. There are a number of alternative techniques that can be utilised in practice. Pike

(1996) has undertaken many surveys of industry practice, including longitudinal studies stretching from the 1970s to the 1980s. Back in the 1970s, most organisations used one or two methods, most commonly payback period (PBP) and accounting rate of return (ARR). As computer usage developed so did the ease of investment appraisal, by the 1990s, Pike was reporting companies generally using four methods, up from the previous one or two, with far higher use of 'sophisticated' discounting methods. So the traditional methods were not replaced by the newer methods, research still showed PBP as the most commonly-used method. Work related to small firms (SMEs) identifies less use of the more sophisticated CIA methods.

The most common methods are:

- Accounting rate of return
- Payback period
- Discounted payback period
- Net present value
- Internal rate of return
- Profitability index.

These are explained and demonstrated in this chapter and their advantages and disadvantages discussed.

14.3 Example data

The following data will be used in this chapter to illustrate the investment appraisal process, using a variety of different methods. A country house hotel has an old barn in the grounds and has decided they could utilise it as a wedding/event venue, if they refurbish. Another alternative suggestion for investment is updating the current spa facility within the hotel to be utilised as a day spa facility. The costing and predicted profit returns are as shown in Table 14.1.

Table 14.1: Costings and predicted returns

	Project A – Event venue	Project B – Spa facility
Project investment costs (year 0)	£1,500,000	£1,500,000
Expected profit returns		
Year 1	£30,000	£45,000
Year 2	£35,000	£50,000
Year 3	£45,000	£55,000
Year 4	£60,000	£60,000
Year 5	£80,000	£65,000
Year 6	£90,000	£65,000
Total profit returns	**£340,000**	**£340,000**

Given the normal advance booking time for weddings and having to build trade, the event venue will not be as profitable in earlier years, but as the reputation grows over time bookings will grow. For the spa facility, the use by guests is more instant, so trade starts earlier with guests using the facility and the day spa trade develops over time, but the facility is small and has a limited capacity. For both projects after six years they will be a need to incur further costs for refurbishment and updating, so these projects and their returns are for a six-year period. At the end of the six years the capital investment has no residual value and depreciation over the six years uses the straight-line method.

14.4 Accounting rate of return (ARR)

This approach calculates the average annual profit as a percentage of the average amount invested. It is the only CIA method that is based on profits; all other methods use cash flows (discussed later). It is calculated as follows:

Average Annual Profit * 100 = %ARR
Average Investment

An alternative formula is to use 'initial investment' instead of 'average investment'.

Average Annual Profit * 100 = %ARR
 Initial Investment

There is an argument that as the investment by the end of year 6 is £0, due to depreciation, the average invested in the project (half the original investment) is a more realistic figure to use. Either formula can be used; as long as the same formula is used consistently valid comparisons can be made between projects. Given projects A and B have the same initial investment, same total profit returns and same life in years the ARR calculations are the same for each project.

Average annual profits = total profits/number of year of project

$$= £340,000/6 = £56,667$$

Average investment = initial investment + residual value at the end of the project/2

$$= £1,500,000 + £0/2 = £750,000$$

ARR Projects A and B (using average investment)

$$\frac{£56,667}{£750,000} * 100 = 7.6\%$$

ARR Projects A and B (using initial investment)

$$\frac{£56,667}{£1,500,000} * 100 = 3.8\%$$

If using ARR there is no difference in these two projects, they both make the same financial returns over the six-year period. It is a method more widely used with projects with a shorter time period and has a number of failings:

14

- Using the average profit can disguises great variations in annual profits. In this example project B gives more profit returns in the earlier years compared to project A, but using ARR this is not recognised.
- It is based on profits, not cash flows. Profits are more open to variation, or even manipulation, due to accounting practices. For example, the depreciation method used will impact on annual profit levels. It is generally considered that cash flows are less open to accounting manipulation than profits so are a better measure of returns. Cash is a physical return that can be put in the bank or reused in further investments, whereas profit is a non-physical monetary value. Refer back to Chapter 2, section 3, for a detailed discussion of the difference between profit and cash.

14.5 Payback period (PBP)

As previously stated, this method has a high usage rate in industry. This is due to its ease of calculation and simplicity. As the name suggests, this considers how long it takes to get back in cash inflows what went out in the initial investment.

14.5.1 Turning annual profits into cash flows

The data given for projects A and B shows profit returns, in order to calculate the PBP (and other cash flow based methods) this needs to be turned into cash flows. To do this 'non-cash' expenses taken off in the income statement need to be added back to the profit – the main item generally is depreciation.

In this example (see Table 14.2), the capital invested was £1,500,000 and a straight-line method of depreciation was used. This means the depreciation was equally distributed over the six years of the project as follows:

Depreciation = £1,500,000/6 years = £250,000 depreciation per year.

£250,000 needs to be added back into the stated profit figures to give the cash flows, i.e. year 1 profit £30,000 + depreciation £250,000 = cash flow of £280,000.

Table 14.2: Total cash flows

	Project A – Event venue	Project B – Spa facility
Project investment costs Year 0 (cash outflow)	–£1,500,000	–£1,500,000
Expected cash inflows		
Year 1	£280,000	£295,000
Year 2	£285,000	£300,000
Year 3	£295,000	£305,000
Year 4	£310,000	£310,000
Year 5	£330,000	£315,000
Year 6	£340,000	£315,000
Total cash flows	**£340,000**	**£340,000**

To calculate the payback period you need to identify how long it takes for the cash inflows to match the initial cash outflow of the investment (see Table 14.3). In this case, how long does it take to recover the initial £1,500,000 invested in the project?

Table 14.3: Calculating the payback period

	Project A – Event venue	Cumulative cash flows	Project B – Spa facility	Cumulative cash flows
Project investment costs Year 0 (cash outflow)	−£1,500,000	−£1,500,000	−£1,500,000	−£1,500,000
Expected cash inflows				
Year 1	£280,000	−£1,220,000	£295,000	−£1,205,000
Year 2	£285,000	−£935,000	£300,000	−£905,000
Year 3	£295,000	−£640,000	£305,000	−£600,000
Year 4	£310,000	−£330,000	£310,000	−£290,000
Year 5	£330,000	£0	£315,000	£25,000
Year 6	£340,000	£340,000	£315,000	£340,000
Total cash flows	**£340,000**		**£340,000**	

For project A the cumulative cash flows clearly show that at the end of 5 years the initial investment has been returned in cash inflows.

Project A = 5 years

The data for project B needs a bit more calculation – the data shows that £0 point must between the fourth and fifth years, but a calculation is needed to state the exact time frame.

| Year 4 −£290,000 | ←————— Year 4+? = £0 —————→ | Year 5 £25,000 |

Within this year £315,000 cash inflow is generated, but at what point in the year has £290,000 come in – that is the point where cumulative cash inflows match the initial investment.

4 years + 290,000/315,000 = 4 years + 0.92 = 4.92 years

To understand this in months or days, as opposed a decimal fraction, a further calculation is needed.

4 years + (0.92 * 365) = 4 years, 336 days

4 years + (0.92 * 12) = 4 years, 11 months

Project A = 5 years and Project B = 4 years, 11 months

Using PBP the 'best' project is the one that returns the initial money the quickest, so in this example project B would be favoured. In this example both projects return the same amount over six years, but PBP ignores what happens after the initial payback period – even if an alternative project made twice as much cash flow, if the initial payback is longer it would still not be favoured.

14

An organisation with liquidity problems may favour such 'quick return' projects. It can also be seen as a sign of a dynamic management to favour short PDP projects. Predication of returns are harder over longer periods of time, changes in the environment such as new competition, changes in interest rates, recession can be an issue in the longer term, so there is an argument that getting the initial investment back as quickly as possible ensures that a business eliminates risk.

The main drawback as we could see from the above example is that it takes no account of what happens after payback, so the overall cash flows for a project are not considered. One project may only return the initial investment whilst another takes longer to initially payback, but then goes on generating cash inflows for a further four years. This method, in calculating fractions of a year, assumes the sales are evenly distributed throughout the year. Up to the payback point, the distribution of cash inflows is not considered. A second major consideration is the timing of the cash flows – two projects could have an identical PBP of 4 years, one of them has no cash flowing in until year four but the other project returns equal amounts of cash in each of the four years.

14.6 The time value of money

Methods that take account of the time value of money are often referred to as 'sophisticated' methods. To understand the time value of money, consider this question – If someone borrowed £100 from you, would you prefer to get it back in 6 months or 6 years? If you receive the money in 6 months you are then able to use that money for another purpose, such as investing it in the bank or spending it on some new clothes. If you choose to wait 6 years for your money you have not been able to utilise the money in the meantime. This issue is exacerbated by the influence of other factors such as inflation and risk.

Looking at projects A and B how are they to be financed? If the organisation has the cash available what else could they do with it? The £1,500,000 could be invested in a 'safe' long-term investment for 6 years that gives a fixed, guaranteed return of 5% for an example. Each year 5% is added to the total (compound interest). The £1.5m becomes just over £2m after 6 years (Table 14.4).

Table 14.4: Return on an investment of 5% over 6 years

Year	5% investment
0	£1,500,000
1	£1,575,000
2	£1,653,750
3	£1,736,438
4	£1,823,259
5	£1,914,422
6	£2,010,143

Alternatively, perhaps the £1.5m investment needs to be borrowed to make the investment and each year 7% interest has to be paid, alongside a repayment of the capital loan over the 6-year period. The investment in either project A or B now has to make as much money from the investment as could have been made from an alternative use or could have been saved from not borrowing the money. This is known as the opportunity cost of capital.

In order to see if a project is worthwhile, the cash inflows from the project are compared with the initial outlay by bringing them back to their present value, i.e. what would they have been worth in time 0 when the money is spent, using the opportunity cost of capital to do so. In large organisations where a number of sources of capital are used the weighted average cost of capital (WACC) can be calculated and can be used in CIA decisions. For further details on the WACC see Chapter 13.

These considerations come under the concept of the 'time value of money'. This involves the use of a 'discount' factor (which represents the cost of capital) being applied to future returns so the returns can be valued at 'today's value of money' (time 0). If for an example a 5% rate is considered for interest over a 5-year period, Table 14.5 shows how £1 will change over that time.

Table 14.5: Future value of money

Year	5% interest
0	£1.00
1	£1.05
2	£1.10
3	£1.16
4	£1.22
5	£1.28
6	£1.34

So a £1 invested at 5% today would be worth £1.34 in 6 years' time, how much is £1 received in 6 years' time worth at today's value of money? = £1/£1.34 = £0.7463, so receiving £1 in 6 years has the same 'value' as receiving 75p today, as illustrated in Table 14.6.

Table 14.6: Discounted value of money

Year	5% interest
0	£0.7463
1	£0.78
2	£0.82
3	£0.86
4	£0.91
5	£0.95
6	£1.00

This concept is known as discounting, discount tables exist to aid the process of discounting, but they can also be calculated. In the examples used in this chapter a discount rate of 4% is used by the organisation, this is the organisation's cost of capital. To calculate what £1 in future years is worth at today's value of money the value is discounted by this amount each year (see Table 14.7).

The formula to calculate the discount factors is:

$$\frac{1}{(1 + r)^n}$$

Where: r = the cost of capital and n = the number of years in the future

Table 14.7: Calculating a 4% discount factor. (Rounded data)

Year:	Calculation @ 4%:	4% Discount Factor
0	1	1
1	$1/1.04$	0.9615
2	$1/(1.04)^2$	0.9246
3	$1/(1.04)^4$	0.8890
4	$1/(1.04)^4$	0.8548
5	$1/(1.04)^5$	0.8219
6	$1/(1.04)^6$	0.7903

This identifies every £1 received today is worth £1, but £1 received in year 3 is worth £0.8890, at today's value of money, and so on. This concept is used in a number of CIA methods to show the value of returns at today's value of money.

14.7 Discounted payback period

This method is the same as the previous payback approach, but the cash inflows are discounted, using the agreed discount factor (4%) (see Table 14.8).

Table 14.8: Project A, discounted cash flows

Project A	4% discount factor	Project A – Event venue	Discounted cash flows	Cumulative cash flows
Project investment costs Year 0 (cash outflow)	1.00	–£1,500,000	–£1,500,000	–£1,500,000
Expected cash inflows				
Year 1	0.9615	£280,000	£269,220	–£1,230,780
Year 2	0.9246	£285,000	£263,511	–£967,269
Year 3	0.8890	£295,000	£262,255	–£705,014
Year 4	0.8548	£310,000	£264,988	–£440,026
Year 5	0.8219	£330,000	£271,227	–£168,799
Year 6	0.7903	£340,000	£268,702	£99,903
				£99,903

When the returns are discounted by a factor of 4% the discounted payback period for project A is between years 5 and 6 (see Table 14.9).

5 years + 168,799/268,702 = 5 years + 0.628 = 5.628 years,

or 5 years 229 days, 5 years 7½ months.

Table 14.9: Project A, discounted cash flows

Project B	4% discount factor	Project B – Spa facility	Discounted cash flows	Cumulative cash flows
Project investment costs Year 0 (cash outflow)	1.00	–£1,500,000	–£1,500,000	–£1,500,000
Expected cash inflows				
Year 1	0.9615	£295,000	£283,643	–£1,216,358
Year 2	0.9246	£300,000	£277,380	–£938,978
Year 3	0.8890	£305,000	£271,145	–£667,833
Year 4	0.8548	£310,000	£264,988	–£402,845
Year 5	0.8219	£315,000	£258,899	–£143,946
Year 6	0.7903	£315,000	£248,945	£104,999

When the returns are discounted by a factor of 4% the discounted payback period for project A is between years 5 and 6.

5 years + 143,946/248,945 = 5 years + 0.578 = 5.578 years,

or 5 years 211 days, 5 years 7 months.

When compared to the non-discounted payback period you can see a distinct difference and the longer time taken to payback the initial investment. This method does account for the time value of money, but still ignores what happens after payback, the continuation of cash inflows beyond payback.

14.8 Net present value (NPV)

The NPV approach allows for the time value of money, by using a set discount factor. Unlike the discounted payback period it also takes into account cash inflows over the full life of the project. Given the discount factor the rule is if the NPV value is above £0 the project is acceptable, any project with a negative NPV should be rejected. If funds are not available to fund all projects then the projects should be prioritised in the order of the maximum NPV first (see Table 14.10).

The steps in NPV calculations are:

1 Identify discount factor to be used
2 Calculate discount factor, or read off discount tables

14

3   Multiply all annual cash flows by the discount factor for that specific year (remember the initial investment is a negative, as it is a cash outflow, not inflow)

4   Total the discounted cash flows; and

5   If positive = accept project, if negative = reject project.

Table 14.10: Calculating the Net Present Value. (Data rounded)

	4% discount factor	Project A – Event venue	Discounted cash flows	Project B – Spa facility	Discounted cash flows
Project investment costs Year 0 (cash outflow)	1.00	–£1,500,000	–£1,500,000	–£1,500,000	–£1,500,000
Expected cash inflows					
Year 1	0.9615	£280,000	£269,220	£295,000	£283,643
Year 2	0.9246	£285,000	£263,511	£300,000	£277,380
Year 3	0.8890	£295,000	£262,255	£305,000	£271,145
Year 4	0.8548	£310,000	£264,988	£310,000	£264,988
Year 5	0.8219	£330,000	£271,227	£315,000	£258,899
Year 6	0.7903	£340,000	£268,702	£315,000	£248,945
Total cash flows			£99,903		£104,999

In this situation both project A and B are positive, so could be accepted. If there are not enough funds for both projects, project B gives the highest returns so should be prioritised. This approach overcomes issues identified in ARR, PBP, and DPBP. It gives a figure that is realistic in relation to trying to maximise shareholder wealth.

14.9 Internal rate of return (IRR)

An alternative to NPV, that still uses discounting is IRR. NPV sets a discount factor based on the cost of capital and then assesses if this gives a return above or below £0. IRR works in the opposite way be considering what discount rate (cost of capital) can be applied in order for the NPV to equal £0. From calculating NPV for projects A and B they both have a positive NPV using a 4% discount factor, this means a higher discount factor is needed before £0 will be reached. Manually IRR is a 'trial and error' calculation, to calculate it you need to have a positive and a negative NPV for each project. In this example 4% is positive, so try using a discount factor of 7% (Table 14.11).

With a 7% discount factor the values are negative, highlighting that a £0 NPV return will be when the discount factor is somewhere between these two values, so more than 4%, but less than 7%.

Table 14.11: IRR with a 7% discount factor. (Data rounded)

	7% discount factor	Project A – Event venue	Discounted cash flows	Project B – Spa facility	Discounted cash flows
Project investment costs Year 0 (cash outflow)	1	−1,500,000	−1,500,000	−1,500,000	−1,500,000
Expected cash inflows					
Year 1	0.9346	280,000	261,688	295,000	275,707
Year 2	0.8734	285,000	248,919	300,000	262,020
Year 3	0.8163	295,000	240,809	305,000	248,972
Year 4	0.7629	310,000	236,499	310,000	236,499
Year 5	0.7130	330,000	235,290	315,000	224,595
Year 6	0.6663	340,000	226,542	315,000	209,885
Total cash flows			−50,254		−42,323

Project A IRR calculation:

NPV 4% = £99,903, NPV 7% = −£50,254

Range of 3%

Rate	4%	?	7%
NPV	£99,903	£0	−£50,254

◄────── Range 99,915 + 50,241 = 150,157 ──────►

How to calculate the point where the NPV is 0 for project A is shown below:

The positive rate, in this case **4%**, plus the following calculation:

$$\frac{\text{Positive NPV value}}{\text{Range value}} * \% \text{ range} \quad = \quad \frac{£99,903}{£150,157} * 3\% = 1.996\%$$

Project A IRR = 4% + 1.996% = 6.0%

Project B IRR calculation:

NPV 4% = £104,999, NPV 7% = −£42,323

Range of 3%

Rate	4%	?	7%
NPV	£104,999	£0	−£42,323

◄────── Range 104,999 + 42,323 = 147,322 ──────►

How to calculate the point where the NPV is 0 for project B is shown below. The positive rate, in this case 4%, plus the following calculation:

$$\frac{\text{Positive NPV value}}{\text{Range value}} * \% \text{ range} \quad = \quad \frac{£104,999}{£147,322} * 3\% = 2.138\%$$

Project B IRR = 4% + 2.138% = 6.1%

14

In this circumstance there isn't much between the IRR for each project, project B is slightly better. This is telling you a discount factor of up to 6% can be applied to project A before the NPV reaches £0. In other words the cost of capital can go up to 6% before the project is not worthwhile. It is important to note with IRR calculation the number of decimal places used and the specific two values used will impact on the exact figure obtained – the closer to £0 the NPVs are, the more accurate the answer will be. In this case using discount factors of 5% and 7% will give a slightly different answer.

The results show there is little between the two projects. What it does show is that the cost of capital can be up to 2% higher than the company established cost of capital (6%–4%). However, at 6% this is still quite low, the higher the % the less financial risk in the project, if suddenly the banks increased their interest rate to 8%, then neither of these projects could cover the initial investment and the cost of borrowing the capital.

With IRR the projects would be ranked in order of highest discount factor % – the higher the better. It is considered easier to compare in % terms than when looking at NPVs with positive and negative monetary values, because this is a relative value and not affected by the size of the projects. This However is fine when projects are of similar size, but ultimately would you prefer 10% of £500,000 (£50,000), or 8% of £800,000 (£64,000)? It is the maximisation of pounds, not percentages that should be considered, so when comparing projects if NPV and IRR rank different projects in first place the general view is that NPV takes priority over IRR.

14.10 Profitability index

When ranking projects another alternative is to calculate their profitability index (PI). This is done by dividing the discounted inflows by the investment. At the required 4% NPV the answers would be as follows:

Discounted inflows

Initial investment

Project A = $\dfrac{£1,599,903}{£1,500,000}$ = 1.067

Project B = $\dfrac{£1,604,999}{£1,500,000}$ = 1.070

Using a PI, the rule is any figure over 1 is acceptable, rank highest PI project first. This is useful when multiple projects have a positive NPV, but capital is 'rationed', so not all projects can be funded.

14.11 Uncertainty in investment projects

There are no certainties on forecasts, sometimes attempts are made to lower such uncertainty to aid the decision-making process. Methods that can be employed are:

- Adjusting the basic cash flows.
- Adjusting the rate required. A higher rate may be required from projects with higher levels of risk.
- Use of three estimates – a high, medium and low estimated (best, expected and worse case scenarios). This gives the extreme potential results.
- Applying probability factors. This is a more sophisticated version of the three estimates approach, where the likelihood of each outcome is weighted into the estimates.
- Sensitivity analysis. This can involve looking at each aspect of the project (income and expenditure) and considering how sensitive each element is to change. For example; what if sales changed by 10%, or what if staff costs changed by 10%?

14.12 Integrated strategic approaches

Financial evaluation is just one consideration, when looking at potential projects other things need to be considered as well:

- Fit with strategic plan
- Chance of negative publicity
- Impact on current market position
- Environmental impact
- Level of risk
- Project feasibility studies
- Periodic review and cost comparison once projects are started; and
- Post-completion audit of project, lessons learned for the future.

Traditionally, financial appraisal, risk, environmental impact and strategic direction have all been considered individually, sometimes by different committees at different stages of the process. A number of authors have discussed the need for a strategic approach, where the strategic decision to invest is taken using one process that combines all these elements, as opposed to considering each one individually. A number of alternatives exist, one being that of Lefley. His approach contains three different aspects: the net present value profile model (NPVP); the project risk profile model (PRP); and the strategic index model (SI) in one integrative model to evaluate projects.

14

What also needs to be considered is the size of the project in relation to how sophisticated the appraisal needs to be. The example used in this chapter was a refurbishment of a facility for a project with returns over 6 years. In the pharmaceutical sector or in oil exploration investment decisions are being made on projects, where the return may not be until 10–20 years later. An example in the tourism sector has been the development of space tourism. Virgin Galactic is an example of such a 'provider' of suborbital space flights. This is a major investment in new technology, with many years of development before any financial returns will be seen on the investment – individuals have been reserving places since 2005. Such a project needs to be fully strategically considered, not just financially.

Summary of key points

Capital investment appraisal (CIA) is important to organisations, correcting 'wrong' decisions is very expensive and can have a major strategic impact on an organisation. Therefore it is important that a full appraisal is made before financial commitment is entered into. Key points in this chapter are:

- Accounting rate of return is the only method to be based on profits, all others use cash flows.

- Payback period is a simple method, but still commonly used in organisations.

- Discounted cash flow methods consider the time value of money.

- Where IRR and NPV rank projects differently, the NPV should be followed.

- A number of integrated strategic approaches exist that integrate financial considerations with aspects of risk and strategic imperatives.

References

Pike, R.H. (1996) 'A longitudinal survey on capital budgeting practices', *Journal of Business Finance and Accounting*, **23** (1) Spring, 79–92.

Further reading

Drury, C. (2012) *Management and Cost Accounting*, 8th edn, Cengage Learning EMEA. This is a detailed generic textbook that covers this subject from a management accountant's perspective.

Lefley, F. and Ryan, R. (2005) *The Financial Appraisal Profile (FAP) Model*, London: Palgrave Macmillan.

Self-check student questions

1   Why is capital investment appraisal strategically important to an organisation?

2   Name four CIA methods that can be utilised.

3   What are the disadvantages of using a profit-based approach?

4   Explain how discounted cash flow (DCF) aids capital investment appraisal.

5   Which and how many methods would you recommend using prior to committing to a £1m development project?

6   The hotel has a maximum of £800,000 available for capital investment.

	Project A	Project B	Project C	Project D	NPV table @ 5%	
Cash flows	£000s	£000s	£000s	£000s		
Year					Year	5%
0	−400,000	−400,000	−200,000	−200,000	0	1
1	200,000	4,000	106,000	5,000	1	0.9524
2	200,000	4,000	106,000	5,000	2	0.9070
3	10,000	320,000	6,000	105,000	3	0.8638
4	10,000	320,000	4,000	105,000	4	0.8227

Note: these figures are cash flows; depreciation is straight-line over 4 years.

a) Calculate the payback period, accounting rate of return and the net present value for each of these proposals   (18 marks)

b) From a financial perspective, recommend which project(s) the hotel should fund, with supporting justification for your answer, including method based discussion.   (7 marks)

(BAHA, Question 2, Strategic Management Accounting Paper January 2012)

7   Using the data from question 6, calculate the IRR. How does this impact on your decision making?

14

Further questions and problems

1 As the management accountant, the manager has asked you to explain the merits of the following capital investment appraisal techniques and make recommendations for a capital investment process to be utilised in your organisation.

- Payback period
- Accounting rate of return
- Net present value
- Internal rate of return
- Profitability index

Please illustrate your answer with hospitality, tourism or events industry examples.

(Adapted from HOSPA, formerly BAHA Strategic Management Accounting paper, July 2012)

2 The hotel can only fund one of these three projects.

Cash flows/year	1	2	3
0	–6,000	–3,000	–3,000
1	500	1,700	0
2	600	1,850	0
3	3,500	500	0
4	3,500	650	4,800
Total	2,100	1,700	1,800

Note: these figures are cash flows; depreciation is straight line.

NPV table @ 5% for calculating NPV only, PBP is not discounted

Year	5%
0	1
1	0.952
2	0.907
3	0.864
4	0.823

3 a) Calculate the payback period, accounting rate of return and the net present value (at 5%) for each of these proposals.   (12 marks)

b) From a financial perspective, recommend which project the hotel should fund, with supporting justification for your answer.   (8 marks)

c) What non-financial considerations might also need to be considered in making such a decision?   (5 marks)

(BAHA, Question 3, Strategic Management Accounting Paper January 2011)

15 Performance Measurement

15.1 Introduction and objectives

Performance measurement techniques evolved in response to the weaknesses of financial measures, this is not to say that financial measures do not have a place, but that reliance on these alone is insufficient to properly manage a business. A range of models have been developed which combine financial and non-financial measures to provide a more holistic view of the performance of organisations, these measures are termed multi-dimensional performance measures. This chapter will explain the development of these approaches, present the main models or frameworks and explain how they are used in the hospitality, tourism and events industries.

After studying this chapter you should be able to:

■ Understand the need for a range of measures to monitor businesses

■ Describe and critically evaluate the main performance measurement frameworks

■ Appreciate the developments in this area and understand the links to strategic management accounting

■ Understand the practice and value of benchmarking in specific industry sectors.

15.2 Performance measurement history and development

There has been increasing recognition that measuring performance requires more than a financial focus, increasingly businesses use a range of metrics to provide a broad view of business performance. The old saying that 'what get measured gets done' means that if there a sole focus on profitability, then decisions are likely to focus on short-term means of maximising profit, such decisions as cutting staffing to save costs or outsourcing key processes to save money can have long-term effects. Thus traditional performance measurement with its emphasis on financials has been criticised for being short-term, narrowly focused, internally-orientated and backward-looking (Eccles, 1991; Kaplan and Norton, 1992).

In addition, it is widely recognised that the influence of globalisation and developments in information technology have changed the way companies do business (Neely, 1999), with increasingly sophisticated and empowered consumers and increased importance of supply chains (Atkinson, 2006). As a result companies must be more flexible and agile, pay more attention to customer needs and the marketplace, which means that they must monitor more than just financial results. The traditional measures of performance, such as profit and return on investment, are also criticised for being lag measures, in that they monitor performance after the events have taken place. Fitzgerald et al. (1991) emphasised the need to identify lead measures, which are items such as customer satisfaction and market share, which are drivers of financial performance and competitive success (Atkinson, 2006). So modern performance measurement systems will track a range of performance metrics and managers will be held accountable for performance areas such as customer satisfaction, staff turnover and new product innovation, as well as operating profit and return on investment.

Performance management has developed encompassing the use of multidimensional performance measures and drawing on principles and practices from a range of management disciplines, primarily management accounting, but also strategy, operations management, human resources management and marketing. The key premise of performance management is in setting the strategy and managing the resources to ensure the measures are achieved.

The major framework that links performance measurement and performance management that is most widely recognised is the Balanced Scorecard, developed by Kaplan and Norton in 1992. This model has become a major brand, but has also become a generic term for multi-dimensional performance measurement/ management frameworks (in the same way that people call a vacuum cleaner, a Hoover, regardless of the manufacturer) so now many large companies from across the world will have some form of scorecard, it has also spread to public sector organisations from hospitals to higher education providers.

The scorecard notion developed by Kaplan and Norton has evolved through use such that the framework is much more than a collection of measures and has become a complete strategic management tool (Kaplan and Norton, 1996). A number of major organisations now have a scorecard, which is closely or loosely grounded in Kaplan and Norton's original ideas; these are integrated into sophisticated management control systems and are used to manage the business proactively.

15.3 Key frameworks and models

This section will present three of the major models that are utilised or have influenced performance measurement and management practice. These are the Results and Determinant model (Fitzgerald et al., 1991); the Balanced Scorecard (Kaplan and Norton, 1992) and the Performance Prism (Neely et al., 2002).

15.3.1 Results and determinant model

This model was developed from a CIMA (Chartered Institute of Management Accountants) funded multidisciplinary research project, which focused on service businesses in the UK. It recognises the distinctive nature of services; including intangibility, perishability, simultaneity and heterogeneity, and the implications this has for performance measurement. Grounded in operations management, service quality, marketing and accounting this model identifies six dimensions of performance, within two categories (see Figure 15.1).

	Performance dimensions	Types of measures
Results	Competitiveness Financial performance	Relative market share and position Sales growth Measures of the customer base Profitability Liquidity Capital structure Market ratios
Determinants	Quality of service Flexibility Resource utilisation Innovation	Reliability, responsiveness, aesthetics/ appearance, cleanliness/tidiness, comfort, friendliness, communication, courtesy, competence, access, availability, security Volume flexibility Delivery speed flexibility Specification flexibility Productivity Efficiency Performance of the innovation process Performance of individual innovators

Figure 15.1: Results and determinants model, (Adapted from Fitzgerald et al., 1991: 8)

The key feature of this framework is the overt emphasis on lead versus lag measures and the detailed linked to empirically grounded theory in operations management. This model has been tested and developed by Fitzgerald and Moon (1996) working with four service firms in the UK. This revealed the importance of implementation and the need not merely to identify key measures, but also to set clear standards and equitable rewards. Table 15.1 summarises their findings, in terms of questions for firms to ask themselves.

Table 15.1: Implementation questions, (Developed from Fitzgerald and Moon, 1996)

Aspect of system	Characteristics	Questions
Standards	Ownership	Do managers participate in setting targets, do they own them?
	Achievability	Are standards set at a reasonable level?
	Equity	Do standards allow for local circumstances and external influences?
Rewards	Clarity	Do managers understand what is trying to be achieved?
	Motivation	What are the benefits to managers for achieving targets?
	Controllability	Are rewards linked to those aspect managers can actually control?

In addition Fitzgerald and Moon advocated a clear link to strategy, adoption of a wide range of measures, the use of internal and external benchmarking of performance, regular reporting and engagement from top management.

The advantages of this model are that it is focused on service businesses and was tested with a range of UK service businesses. However, it can be criticised for including too many dimensions and not focusing management attention sufficiently on strategic priorities.

15.3.2 The Balanced Scorecard (BSC)

As already mentioned, the Balanced Scorecard was developed by Kaplan and Norton (1992, 1996), combining financial control measures with non-financial control measures. It is fundamentally a performance measurement tool aimed at aligning key performance areas of a business with its strategy (see Figure 15.2). It provides a framework across four dimensions that can be easily adapted to any industrial or service setting and implemented at different levels within an organisation linking strategy and operations.

Figure 15.2: The Balanced Scorecard, (adapted from Kaplan and Norton, 1996)

The four dimensions represent a causally related set of generic components that can deliver, it is argued, long-term organisational performance and success.

- **Financial perspective** – emphasising shareholder satisfaction this dimension includes measures such as profitability, return on capital, share price, market share, sales growth, cash flow.

- **Customer perspective** – focuses on customer satisfaction and key issues such as quality, performance (adherence to brand standards) services provided and cost.

- **Internal business perspective** – addresses internal processes that must be excellent to deliver continued customer satisfaction, such as key competences and critical skills, internal processes, productivity and technologies valued be the customer.

- **Innovation and learning perspective** – draws attention to company's ability to change and develop proactively in the face of changing customer and competitive demands, such issues as product/service design and innovation, culture and creativity, knowledge sharing and empowerment.

These dimensions and strategic priorities can be broken down into goals and measures with which success can be evaluated. The technique is flexible allowing it to be used both at corporate level but also at a business unit level or even department level, thus integrating every level of the organisation. Scorecards created at each level of the organisation, will emphasis different targets but will be aligned to the corporate goals.

For example, the corporate strategy of a meetings, incentives, conferences, and exhibitions (MICE) company is to increase brand awareness and market penetration, the conference and banqueting department scorecard could look contain the information shown in Table 15.2.

Table 15.2: Departmental scorecard for conference and events

Dimension	Objectives	Areas to be monitored
Financial	Increase sales volumes	Like for like sales growth Enquiry conversion rates
Customer	Customer satisfaction Increase customer retention rates	Increase satisfaction rating to 90% score on satisfaction survey Repeat business % total business
Internal business	Sales training for departmental staff	No of staff completed training
Innovation and learning	Adopt new booking system	Number of clients utilising new booking system as percentage of total bookings

It can be seen that lower down the hierarchy of the scorecard measures become very specific and relate directly to agreed initiatives and objectives.

The measures in the BSC are mutually consistent and reinforcing and are designed to be more than a collection of disparate financial and non-financial indicators. The scorecard method monitors a set of cause-and-effect relationships that lead to better financial returns. This is accomplished by ensuring that a vertical vector runs through the four BSC perspectives, as demonstrated in Figure 15.3.

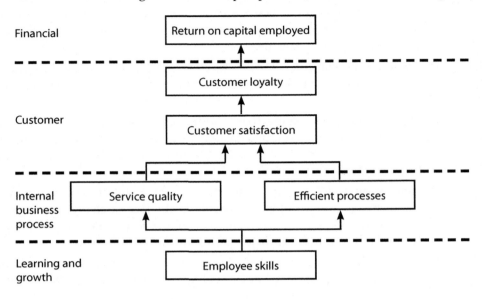

Figure 15.3: Causal links in the Balanced Scorecard, adapted from Kaplan and Norton (1996, p31)

The vertical vector relationship between balanced scorecard measures presented by Kaplan and Norton, emphasises these links, it should be noted that the mapping of causal relationships is a vital part of scorecard design and implementation.

The main benefits attributed to the balanced scorecard are:

- Avoids management reliance on financially-based measures
- Allows an external as well as internal focus
- Can link the corporate strategy to divisions and functions
- Can assist stakeholders in evaluating the firm if measures are communicated externally.

The main drawbacks of the balanced scorecard are:

- Does not result in a single measure of control. The popularity of measures such as ROI has been because they conveniently summarise the business performance in one measure.
- No clear relation between the BSC and shareholder value – just because an item is measured on the scorecard it does not mean that it will benefit the owners in terms of increasing their return.
- Measures may give conflicting signals. For example, if customer satisfaction is falling but the financial indicators are improving, do management sacrifice one or the other?

- The introduction of the balanced scorecard must permeate through the organisation and its ideas embedded in the culture of the organisation. This may not be easy to achieve, particularly in the short term.

- The business needs to be viewed as a set of processes rather than departments.

15.3.3 Performance Prism

Researchers from Cranfield University developed an alternative model to the Balanced Scorecard, reflecting five key facets of performance, which must remain priorities even when economic conditions suffer a downturn (Adams and Neely, 2002). The Performance Prism identifies five key elements grounded in key stakeholders and the businesses value chain (see Figure 15.4).

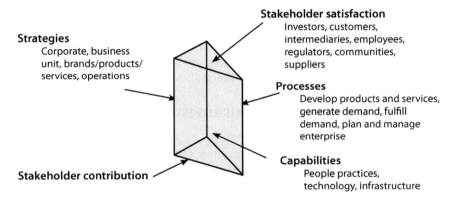

Figure 15.4: Performance Prism Model, adapted from Neely et al. (2002)

This model claims to reflect all stakeholders including shareholders, customers, suppliers, regulators, employees and communities considering not only the stakeholders' needs, but also what the company needs from its stakeholders highlighting stakeholder satisfaction and contribution. This emphasis on stakeholders is what differentiates this framework from others, with a clear acceptance that to achieve shareholder value it is necessary to create broader stakeholder value. The other facets that are central to this model include strategies, business processes and competences and capabilities. The prism model requires careful mapping of the answers to key questions when establishing key performance measures (see Table 15.3).

This model has advantages over the scorecard because it takes a broader view of stakeholders and focuses both on what they want from the business and what they can contribute to the business; this stakeholder perspective provides a more holistic perspective. However, one criticism of this model can be that it tends to generate a large number of performance measures (over 200) what is critical in other frameworks is the process of prioritisation and selection of a limited number of measures.

15

Table 15.3: Questions when defining performance measures, adapted from Neely and Kennerley, 2002 and Adams and Neely, 2002.

Stakeholder satisfaction	Who are our key stakeholders and what do they want and need?
Strategies	What strategies do we have to put in place to satisfy the wants and needs of our stakeholders?
Processes	What critical processes do we need to put in place to execute our strategies
Capabilities	What capabilities do we need to operate and enhance our processes
Stakeholder contribution	What contributions do we require from our stakeholders if we are to maintain and develop these capabilities?

15.4 Performance measurement in hospitality, tourism and events industries

This next three subsections attempt to bring this theory to life by providing some mini hypothetical case studies of how variety of performance measurement frameworks can be implemented in various industrial settings.

15.4.1 Performance measurement in a hotel setting

Hotel companies have embraced the scorecard approach, as they have been monitoring non-financial performance for many years. Implementation of the scorecard has helped many hotel companies review the key drivers of brand value, their business model and their operational effectiveness, for example Hilton and Marriott both utilise a scorecard throughout their organisations. Huckestein and Duboff (1999) reported on the success of scorecard implementation at Hilton in the USA. This is an example where theory and practice are aligned, a typical hotel group scorecard could include the details shown in Table 15.4.

Table 15.4: Hotel Scorecard

Dimension	Key objectives	Areas to be monitored
Financial	Hotel profitability Sales	GOPPar; ROCE RevPAR, occupancy, ADR
Customer	Customer satisfaction Loyalty scheme	Customer satisfaction survey No of loyalty scheme members
Internal business	Sales development Brand standards	No of staff completed customer care training Mystery guest scores
Innovation and learning	Sustainable business Hotel development	Energy usage and recycling statistics No of new operating contracts

15.4.2 Performance measurement in an airline setting

The key to establishing a balanced scorecard is to focus on strategic objectives and then map through the four dimensions to achieve this. Figure 15.5 is an illustrative example of an airline scorecard showing the linkages between different dimensions, here the priority was to improve customer service.

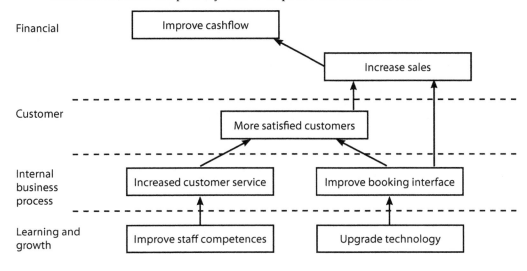

Figure 15.5: Airline Scorecard

15.4.3 Performance measurement in an events setting

Event companies need to focus on gaining sufficient sponsorship and multiple sources of income so a stakeholder approach to performance measurement would be appropriate. Applying the Performance Prism to an event such as a music festival could help manage performance through the identification of key measures, see examples in Table 15.5.

Table 15.5: Events Performance Prism

Prism facet	Example of objectives	Performance measure
Stakeholder satisfaction	Charity engagement	Number of charity partners
Strategies	Increase image and awareness of event	Amount of media coverage, increase in ticket sales
Processes	Project management and logistics	Customer satisfaction survey covering operational aspects
Capabilities	People – make event attractive to volunteers and employees	Application to recruitment ratio
Stakeholder contribution	Artists – maximise impact and satisfy fan base	Customer satisfaction, positive media reviews

The next section considers the use of benchmarks as performance measurement tools which can also be used in a performance management system.

15

15.5 Benchmarking performance

When reviewing performance it is important that a comparison is made. For example; the fact a manager achieved a £10,000 departmental operating profit is difficult to evaluate as an isolated piece of information. It is only when considering this against something else, a benchmark that it becomes a meaningful piece of information for analysis purposes.

A number of benchmarks exist (Figure 15.6), some internal and some external but the key benchmarks are discussed here.

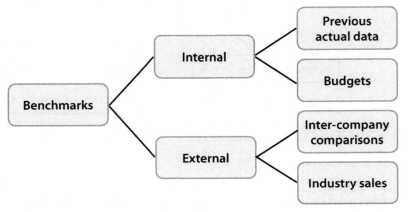

Figure 15.6: Internal and external benchmarks

15.5.1 Internal previous actual data

This can relate to comparing the most recent data with previous data; a previous event to the current one; last month's food sales to this month; or last year's tour revenue to this year. An example of this would be the ratio analysis by year in the earlier financial analysis in Chapter 11. The advantages of such a comparison is: it is your own data, so calculated and presented in a consistent manner; relates to the same specific location/unit/department. However in making such a comparison it assumes last year's data is 'normal' and there is no major changes year-to-year. Examples might be:

- Year 1 Easter falls in April and the next year March, thus skewing monthly data as Easter is more popular for leisure trade
- A flood closed the business for a month last year, thus reducing annual sales.
- A one-off major sporting event took place locally last year which produced a peak in trade; or
- A major development project has taken place, doubling capacity so sales were anticipated to grow significantly between the two years.

Where such differences exist between years this has to be recognised when using such a benchmark, if not, managers will reach the wrong conclusions from the data and this can then impact on decisions.

Using the earlier example of a £10,000 departmental profit, it may be compared to a previous month at £9,000 and be reviewed in a positive light using this benchmark.

15.5.2 Internal budgeted data

A budget overcomes a number of the disadvantages associated with previous data, as it is written specifically for the time period being reviewed, so such abnormalities should already have been taken into account when the budget was written. If the budget required a department profit of £12,000, the achieved £10,000 is now viewed negatively. It may be an extension was built, so the comparison to last year is not realistic and the manager has not achieved the upturn anticipated following the increase in capacity. There is however an assumption that the budget is realistic, and therefore, relevant.

Despite overcoming some of the limitations of benchmarking to previous data, a budget is still only an internal view. It could be that your staffing costs have always been 25%. They are constant year on year and to the budget, so are not considered an issue. However both of these are internal benchmarks – what if the sector norm is only 22%? The limitation of internal benchmarks is just as their name suggests, they are internal and ignore the marketplace the business is competing in.

15.5.3 Intercompany comparisons

Where competitor data is available, comparison to competitors and like organisations provides an external benchmark. In some circumstances it is possible to use non-competing companies in different sectors. For example, in a tourist resort a scuba diving centre may not directly compete with a beachside cafe, but comparing customer numbers and other key statistics you can identify if it is generally tourist trade that is down, or just your specific company with reduced customers. Within chain hotels, unit to unit comparisons can be used almost like an external comparison.

The danger with such comparisons is the issue of comparing 'like-with-like', as discussed in Chapter 2 when reviewing USALI. The issues include: using different accounting practices, establishments of a different size, or different locations. Whilst having an external comparison has many benefits, care has to be taken that the comparison is actually meaningful.

15.5.4 Industry studies and reports

As discussed in Chapter 2, the hotel industry has a long established history of benchmarking performance, both externally and internally with chain operations. This has been facilitated by the adoption of a standard chart of accounts

15

across the industry, namely the Uniform System of Accounting for the Lodging Industry (USALI). This facilitated the provision of industry statistics by firms such as Pannell Kerr Foster (PKF), who have been producing industry trends and statistics reports since 1937 (De Franco, 2006). Now there are several firms providing a range of data to the industry, including Smith Travel Research (STR), who produce amongst other reports a common-sized income statement and HVS who produce hotel valuation reports. The common-sized statement reports from STR are particularly useful as they allow individual hotel general managers to compare their hotel with industry averages constructed from data of similar hotels. Thus there is widespread sophisticated competitor and industry benchmarking carried out across the hotel industry and this is an important performance management tool.

STR equally provides many benchmarking services for the tourism sector. Key economic industry level reports are produced by industry, private and government sources and can aid benchmarking across hospitality, tourism and events. The key to using such data is how to relate it to a specific company or specific situation. The issue of size, location, industry niche all play a part in being able to use data to make valid comparisons.

This chapter has explained the history and development of performance measure-

- ■ To recognised that performance measurement systems are designed to link operations to strategy

- ■ That a range of financial and non-financial measures should to be combined in any scorecard

- ■ Benchmarking is a very powerful management tool

- ■ When comparing figures it is important to compare like with like.

References

Adams, C. and Neely, A. (2002) 'Prism reform', *Financial Management*, May, 28–31.

Atkinson, H. (2006) 'Performance measurement in the international hospitality industry', in P. Harris and M. Mongiello (eds), *Accounting and Financial Management: Developments in the International Hospitality Industry*, Oxford:

Butterworth-Heinemann, pp. 46–70.

DeFranco, A.L. (2006) 'Benchmarking: measuring financial success in the hotel industry', in P. Harris and M. Mongiello (eds), *Accounting and Financial Management: Developments in the International Hospitality Industry*, Oxford: Butterworth-Heinemann, pp. 87–104.

Eccles, R. (1991) 'The performance measurement manifesto', *Harvard Business Review*, January–February, 131–137.

Fitzgerald, L., Johnston, R., Brignall, S., Silvestro, R. and Voss, C. (1991) *Performance Measurement in Service Businesses*, London: CIMA.

Fitzgerald, L., Moon, P. (1996), *Performance Measurement in Service Industries: Making it Work*, London: CIMA.

Huckestein, D. and Duboff, R. (1999) 'Hilton hotels: a comprehensive approach to delivering value for all stakehol ders', *Cornell Hotel and Restaurant Administration Quarterly*, August, 28–38.

Kaplan, R. S., & Norton, D. P. (1992). 'The balanced scorecard - measures that drive performance'. *Harvard Business Review*, **70**(1), 71-79.

Kaplan, R.S. and Norton, D.P. (1996) 'Using the balanced scorecard as a strategic management system', *Harvard Business Review*, January–February, 75–85.

Neely, A. (1999) 'The performance measurement revolution: why now and what next?', *International Journal of Operations and Production Management*, **19** (2), 205–228.

Neely, A., Adams, C. and Kennerley, M. (2002) *The Performance Prism: The Scorecard for Measuring and Managing Business Success*, Harlow: Pearson Education.

Further reading

Grando, A., Tapiero, C. and Belvedere, V. (2007) 'Operational performance in manufacturing and service industries: conceptual framework and research agenda', *International Journal of Business Performance Management*, **9** (2), 110–126.

15

This article makes a good comparison between different sectors and how this may impact on the orientation of operational performance.

Neely, N. (ed.) (2002) *Business Performance Measurement: Theory and Practice*, Cambridge: Cambridge University Press.

This is an edited collection of chapters from leading academics in the field. It covers the functional antecedents of performance measurements, theoretical foundations, key frameworks and applications. This is a theoretical book for more advanced readers and is well referenced, so can support dissertation reading at undergraduate and postgraduate levels.

Self-check student questions

1 What are the main weaknesses of traditional financial performance measures?

2 What do the terms 'lead' and 'lag' mean in the context of performance measures and why is this important?

3 What are the antecedents of the results and determinants model?

4 Explain the four dimensions of the Balanced Scorecard.

5 What is the major emphasis of the Performance Prism that differentiates it from the BSC?

6 Name two companies that provide benchmarking data to hotels.

7 Which performance management system is recognised as one of the most useful for hotels and how can it be used?

8 Why is it important to use both internal and external benchmarking data?

Further questions and problems

1 Identify the key priorities for a small events company which specialises in wedding planning and arrangement for each of the four dimensions of the Balanced Scorecard, identify suitable measures for each quadrant.

2 Your manager wants you to write a report detailing the internal and external benchmarks available and explaining why he should be using them in reviewing performance.

16 Strategic Management Accounting

16.1 Introduction and objectives

Traditionally management accounting has been characterised as providing information to aid managers internally in a firm and as such the focus of the management accounting systems has also tended to be internally orientated. During the 1980s and 1990s a growing number of academics (Johnson and Kaplan, 1987; Bromwich and Bhimani, 1989, 1996) began to recognise that management accounting was not adapting to changes in the modern business environment and as such was not fulfilling its function to aid managers.

In a bid to improve the quality of management accounting information for managers it was necessary to focus more widely on the external environment of the firm and thus the concept of strategic management accounting evolved. Now (strategic) management accounting involves the provision of information, which is externally orientated, market-driven and customer-focused and provides managers with a range of techniques and tools to facilitate strategically-orientated decision making.

After studying this chapter you should be able to:

- Discuss the development and key elements of strategic management accounting

- Understand the difference between traditional and strategic management accounting

- Evaluate key analytical tools which link management accounting with strategy.

16.2 Why strategic management accounting? Definitions and evolution

In order to fully appreciate the development of strategic management accounting it is necessary to evaluate the changes to the external environment of organisations over the last 30 years.

The first main change has been in relation to the competitive environment of organisations. They have seen significant change from the opening of barriers to trade allowing for global competition which in turn has been possible because of advances in technology.

The increase of competition has had the effect of shortening the lifecycle of products. This means that organisations have to work harder to develop new products and services and have less opportunity to recoup costs and generate profit before the decline of the product or service.

The improvement in technology has given more information to the customer allowing the customer to make better informed decisions about which products and services they wish to buy and also to allow the customer to be more proactive in selecting products and services which are tailored specifically for them. In particular the empowerment of customers has resulted in three key challenges for businesses:

- Prices are being forced down because customers are able to find a much wider source of alternatives.
- Quality is being forced up as businesses compete to attract the customer
- Greater variety in the product/service offering is necessary to attract the customer.

Additionally a number of new management techniques have been adopted by firms in light of the above concerns, such as total quality management, just in time and other methods to rationalise the cost of production and consumption.

The above developments have forced organisations to consider their position in their markets, their prices and their costs in a different way than they had done in the past.

Definitions of strategic management accounting began to spring up the earliest pioneer of which was Simmonds (1981) whose definition has subsequently been subsumed into the CIMA definition which is:

> *A form of management accounting in which emphasis is placed on information which relates to factors external to the firm, as well as non-financial information and internally generated information.*

CIMA official terminology, 2005, p. 54

A number of definitions have appeared over the years but no definitive definition of what it is, or what techniques it contains, have been consolidated over the last 30 years.

In their most recent work Roslender and Hart (2010) review much of the literature and contend that three distinct conceptions of strategic management accounting have appeared:

■ The attempt to incorporate strategic ideas into management accounting by taking generic strategy tools and looking at what management accounting information can be used to support strategy.

■ That it is designed to align management accounting with marketing management for strategic positioning. This view looks at the marketing tools used by businesses and uses management accounting within those tools.

■ That it is just a name to group together many of the contemporary approaches in management accounting that have developed which have a strategic implication. There are a number of contemporary approaches to management accounting which have been marked as strategic management accounting techniques because of their external and market orientated content.

16.3 Linking strategy and accounting (strategic versus traditional accounting)

Management accounting systems have three primary purposes:

■ To allow for the allocation of costs between cost of goods sold and inventory for internal and external profit reporting

■ To provide relevant information to aid management decisions

■ To provide information to aid in planning, control and the evaluation of performance.

Whilst these are indeed important and critical requirements of accounting systems, the traditional viewpoint has been to use internal information to achieve them and this is where the failings of traditional management accounting can be seen to be apparent.

The first purpose is in line with financial reporting requirements and a failing of traditional management accounting has been that the techniques used have been orientated to satisfying financial reporting requirements rather than on providing information to help managers make better decisions which is the second purpose. The first purpose is also achieved by using absorption costing methods to achieve the cost used and we have previously commented on the failings of such a system particularly in service industries. Additionally much of the information provided for the second and third purposes has come from internal sources and historical data which have proved to also be inflexible and have failed to consider external factors such as customers or competitors.

To make management accounting more strategic it is necessary to provide information which has an external as well as internal focus and which is orientated towards the future rather than the past. Table 16.1 summarises the key points.

16

Table 16.1: A comparison of the traditional and strategic approaches to management accounting

Traditional approach	Strategic approach
Financial focus	Value focus
Absorption costing for cost allocation	Marginal costing, target costing
Cost control orientation	Customer value orientation
Internally focused	Externally orientation
Performance measurement financial	Multidimensional performance measurement and benchmarking
Fragmented systems	Integrated systems
Accounting and operational information separate	ERP and accounting systems integration
Profit motives short-term	Profit motive longer-term
Pricing short-term cost orientated	Pricing market driven and strategic

The next section will explore some of the key elements of business strategy which have helped to shape strategic management accounting.

16.4 Boston Matrix, risk return and cash

This strategic model derived by the Boston Consulting Group is designed to allow a business to analyse its products and services or business units in terms of their relative market share and the growth of the market (Figure 16.1). By considering the position of the products or services a business can evaluate the balance of its portfolio identify products and services requiring additional investment and those requiring divestment.

The matrix also enables the business to choose the correct tools for evaluating performance based on where the products appear in the matrix.

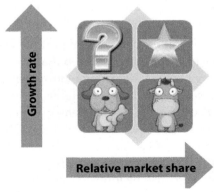

Figure 16.1: The Boston Matrix

Products appearing in the top right box have a high relative market share and the market has high growth potential. These are termed stars and are the products which require investment and which will draw in good cash return for an organisation.

If the organisation is able to keep its relative market share high after the market growth has slowed down the product moves into the bottom right-hand box and these products are termed Cash Cows. These are highly successful products for a business as they no longer require significant investment and as a result will generate cash surpluses for the organisation.

The two left-hand boxes are more problematical for the organisation. The top left box defines products as Question Marks products here require a high level of investment in order to compete in the market but as the organisation does not have a high relative market share it is not able to generate the required cash inflows to compensate for the investment. Strategies here will either be to grow the relative market share and push the question marks into the star box or stop new investment and take what cash is available or finally divest before the question mark becomes a dog.

The final bottom left-hand box represents the products which hold a weak relative position in a market which has low growth potential. A company should not have many products in this category and these products are called Dogs. The strategies here will be to take the cash available as long as the market allows but to restrict investment and to divest if the market weakens.

This model links strategy to management accounting by understanding the level of investment and cash generating abilities of products in relation to the strategic position of the products. Of course there are some weaknesses to the use of this model as market share is not the only criterion that results in a successful product offering and neither is market growth the only factor that makes a market attractive but it does allow product offerings to be strategically evaluated in relation to investment and cash generation which in turn allows for better information for decision making.

16.5 Value generation and value drivers

A firm possesses a competitive advantage over its rivals when it is able to sustain profits which are greater than the average for its industry. A key goal in business strategy is how to sustain a competitive advantage.

Michael Porter (1985) identified two main types of competitive advantage:

Cost advantage	Achieved by provision of a product or service at a lower cost than your rivals
Differentiation advantage	Achieved by provision of a product or service which can be distinguished from the competitors and potentially allows a premium price to be charged

Porter also identifies a third dimension: 'focus', when combining with the scope of operations within a single segment it is important to focus attention more closely. A competitive advantage allows the firm to generate better value to the customer and better profit for itself.

This model links to management accounting by allowing the accounting function to focus on the resources and capabilities of the organisation in a way that will provide information to help further the generic strategy and enhance value.

Porter (1985) developed a further strategic tool to aid in this process called the value chain. This tool allows analysis of the business by looking at its business activities and the linkages between them. The model (see Figure 16.2), indicates that there are primary activities which are the key focus of attention and secondary activities which are there to support the primary activities.

A low-cost strategy will involve looking at the activities in order to increase efficiency and reduce cost. A differentiation strategy will involve evaluating which activities are the ones which add additional value for the customer and ensuring that the additional value can be maintained. Consider the generic strategy of a fast food outlet with that of a Michelin star restaurant, will they be pursuing the same goals and require the same management accounting information?

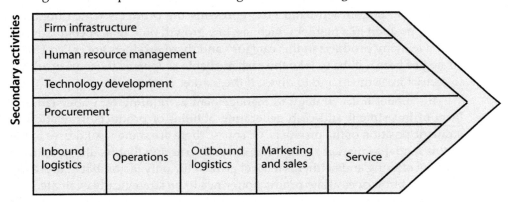

Figure 16.2: The value chain (adapted from Porter 1985).

Table 16.2 is a comparison of fast food outlet with fine dining restaurant supply change elements.

Table 16.2: (a) Primary activities

	Fast food	**Fine dining**
Inbound logistics	Probably outsources, focus on cost and consistency	Typified by local supply, focus on quality and provenance
Operations	Automation, standard processes	Bespoke service, artisan values
Outbound logistics	Automation, customer processing systematic	Customisation, service environment critical, ethos central to delivery
Marketing and sales	Price-based marketing	Reputation and value-based marketing
Service	Counter service, standardised	Silver service, customised

Table 16.2: (b) Secondary activities

	Fast food	Fine dining
Infrastructure	Centralised organisational structures, compliance culture, technical control systems	Entrepreneurial, small businesses, entrepreneurial culture, cultural control systems
Human resources	Low skill levels, standard operating practices, workforce commoditisation, high turnover	High skill levels, HR competences strategically critical, highly valued key staff head hunted
Technological development	Technology important, information systems highly sophisticated automated ordering, standard recipes	Technology less important, based on quality equipment, contemporary high quality fixtures and fittings
Procurement	Probably outsourced, focus on cost and consistency	Typified by local supply, focus on quality and provenance

Strategic management accounting has also been shaped by marketing management. One tool in particular has been particularly useful in aligning management accounting with marketing and that is the product lifecycle.

16.6 Product lifecycle, profit, cash and investment

The product lifecycle shows us that products and services go through a number of stages (Figure 16.3). First, they are introduced then they grow, reach maturity and then decline. By understanding these stages management accountants can provide data to show expected costs and revenues at each stage. An accounting technique called lifecycle costing has developed from this. Within this technique the costs of the product or service are ascertained over its projected life. The aim is to maximise total return over the life of the product. It is possible to look at both the lifecycle of the product and the customer in this way.

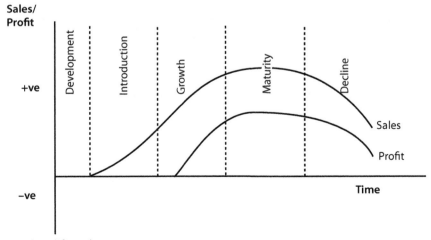

Figure 16.3: Product lifecycle

The product lifecycle can be mapped alongside cash requirements to show the implications for the investment demands associated with different stages of the lifecycle (Figure 16.4).

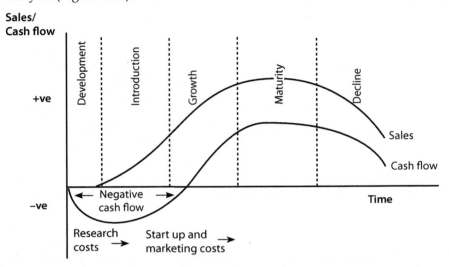

Figure 16.4

16.6.1 Product/service

Figures 16.3 and 16.4 illustrate how the lifecycle of the product appears. The entire lifecycle could be anything from a few months to several hundred years. It is important to know where a product is in its lifecycle, as this will affect the returns expected and the appropriate management information required and action to be taken. In particular at each stage of the lifecycle the cash flow will be different as will the amount of operating expenditure and profitability.

There are several ways to maximise the return that a product/service gives:

- **Maximise the length of the lifecycle** – the longer the cycle, the better the chance to recoup all the cash outlay associated with it. If it is possible to extend the lifecycle in a cost-effective way this too should be investigated.

- **Identify the design costs of the product/service** – the design costs are not considered in traditional management accounting which focuses on the costs of production/service delivery but these costs are affected by the design. The simpler the design the cheaper the costs of production becomes, a simpler service operation, or a less complex menu dish to produce are related to product/service design.

- **Minimise the time to market** – In order to turn the negative cash flow of research and development into positive cash flow the product or service must be able to beat the competitors into the market and therefore the time spent before the introduction must be kept to a minimum.

- **Manage the project's cash flow** – the importance of cash management has been discussed previously but it is worth repeating here as the non-operative cash flows must also be considered.

16.6.2 Customers

Customers also have lifecycles and an organisation may want to maximise the return from a customer. The aim is to extend the lifecycle of a particular customer by encouraging customer loyalty. Existing customers are more profitable than new ones and should be retained where possible. Customers therefore, become more profitable over their lifecycle.

Detailed analysis of the customer or customer segments may enable the organisation to identify customers who are worth keeping and the importance of their retention, this was further developed in Chapter 8. In service businesses maintaining customer engagement is even more important where the service is discontinuous, non-essential and intangible. These factors make it more difficult to keep customers loyal and retention becomes a significant strategic priority. This is evident when you look at hotel company loyalty schemes; major hotel companies offer incentives to encourage customer loyalty (see Table 16.3). Their purpose is to attract new customers and encourage existing customers to buy more, by either increasing the frequency or encouraging them to spend more when they buy, through up-selling.

Table 16.3: Hotel company loyalty schemes

Hilton	Hilton Honors	Blue – all you need to do is enrol online Silver – 4 stays or 10 nights during any calendar year Gold – 16 stays, 36 nights or 60,000 base points earned Diamond – 28 stays, 60 nights or 100,000 base points earned during any calendar year
Hyatt	Hyatt Gold Passport	Gold Passport – entry level membership Platinum – after 5 eligible stays or 15 eligible nights Diamond – after 25 eligible stays or 50 eligible nights
Carlson	Club Carlson	Silver Status – 15 nights/10 stays per year Gold Status – 35 nights/20 stays per year Concierge Status – 75 nights/30 stays per year
Starwood	Starwood Preferred Guest	Preferred Gold – 10 stays or 25 nights in a calendar year. Platinum – 25 stays or 50 nights in a calendar year

The final section will consider some of the contemporary management accounting techniques which have developed under the umbrella of strategic management accounting.

16

16.7 The Balanced Scorecard (BSC)

The Balanced Scorecard was considered in detail in the previous chapter as it has become a well-recognised and well-used tool in performance management. It is often considered to be a strategic management accounting tool as it utilises the criteria that have already been considered:

■ It adds external focus

■ It is used at corporate level to link short-term actions with strategy.

Kaplan (1996) discusses four management processes which allow short-term actions to be linked with strategy, see Figure 16.5.

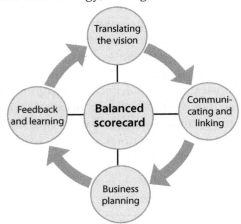

Figure 16.5: Managing Strategy four processes (adapted from Kaplan, 1996, p. 77)

First, the organisation has to consider how the statements of vision and mission can be translated into objectives and measures which can be achieved. Second, those objectives are communicated and appropriate incentives are used to aid achievement whilst also ensuring that all objectives across the organisation are congruent. The third process allows for the business and financial plans to be set in a way which will achieve the long-term strategy. Finally, the fourth process allows the results of the short-term actions to be evaluated against the parameters of the scorecard and enables feedback and corrective action to be made quickly to strategy.

The use of this cycle of processes in the organisation makes the balanced score-card more than just a performance measurement tool by allowing management to focus on critical processes and link them with long-term goals and strategy.

16.8 Activity-based management (ABM)

Chapter 8 introduced activity-based costing and its extension into activity-based management (ABM). The strand of activity based management considered in

Chapter 8 related to the operational side of ABM and performing activities more efficiently. ABM also has a strategic side and is the reason it is often thought to be a strategic management accounting tool.

From a strategic perspective it aims to allow the managers in the organisation to consider which activities it should perform. Altering demand for activities can increase profitability. Key areas where it can be used are in product design and development. In a restaurant the more simply a dish can be prepared the lower the demands on resources. A strong link can be made between ABM and the value chain as each key aspect of the chain can be evaluated in terms of activities.

16.9 Other management accounting tools considered to be strategic

16.9.1 Attribute costing

Attribute costing attempts to control the cost of a product on the basis that it is a series of attributes which the customer values. Attributes can include the specific design features, quality and after sales service offered. It is included as a strategic management accounting technique because of its marketing orientation.

16.9.2 Competitor analysis

There are a number of methods of evaluating competitors, the main ones include benchmarking costs (competitor cost assessment); evaluating the position of the firm relative to its competitors in relation to market share, sales and unit costs (competitive position monitoring); and benchmarking based on financial statements (competitor appraisal based on published financial statements). In earlier chapters these techniques in relation to hospitality, tourism and events were considered through the use of industry provided data.

16.9.3 Brand valuation

This technique combines management accounting data relating to brand earnings and links it with strategic data linked to the brand such as the brand's position, and the nature of the market. It is suggested that this can result in cost-effective brand improvements and customer loyalty.

16.9.4 Target costing

This technique has been considered in detail in Chapter 6 with other pricing techniques, it is included as a strategic tool again because it looks to the market as a starting point.

16

16.9.5 Strategic costing

The technique of strategic costing is attributed to Shank and Govindarajan. They believed that costs must be measured in terms of strategic relevance. They also (1992) developed a costing approach based on Porter's value chain model aimed at demonstrating that the traditional view of costing does not allow for consideration of linkages between activities in the value chain.

Summary of key points

The area of strategic management accounting is one of evolution, the definition of which and context of which will continue to change over time as the business environment changes and the strategies of businesses change. It is clear, however, that there are a number of useful strategy and marketing tools which can influence the management accounting approaches used in organisations.

- Strategic management accounting addresses weaknesses in traditional management accounting.

- The modern marketplace requires a strategic focus to be applied to management accounting information and decision making.

- A number of strategic management accounting tools have been established to meet the needs of strategic management accounting information.

References

Bromwich, M. and Bhimani, A. (1989) *Management Accounting: Evolution not Revolution*, London: CIMA.

Bromwich, M. and Bhimani, A. (1996) *Management Accounting Pathways to Progress*, London: CIMA Publishing.

CIMA Official Terminology 2005 Edition, CIMA

Johnson, H. and Kaplan, R. (1987) *Relevance Lost: the Rise and Fall of Management Accounting*, Harvard Business Press.

Kaplan, R. (1996) 'Using the balanced scorecard as a strategic management system', *Harvard Business Review*, January–February, 75–85.

Kaplan, R.S. and Norton, D.P. (1992) 'The balanced scorecard: measures that drive performance', *Harvard Business Review*, January–February, 71–79.

Kaplan, R.S. and Norton, D.P. (1996) *Translating Strategy into Action: the Balanced Scorecard*, Harvard Business School Press.

Porter, M. (1985) *Competitive Advantage*, New York: Free Press.

Roslender, R. and Hart, S. (2010) 'Strategic management accounting: lots in a name', discussion paper available from http://www.sml.hw.ac.uk/documents/dp2010-aef05.pdf

Shank, J. K. and V. Govindarajan. 1992. 'Strategic cost management: The value chain perspective'. *Journal of Management Accounting Research,* (4): 179-197.

Simmonds, K. (1981) 'Strategic management accounting', *Management Accounting (UK),* **59** (4), 26–29.

Further reading

For a detailed review of the use of strategic management accounting in the hotel sector see Collier, P. and Gregory, A. (1995) 'Strategic management accounting: a UK hotel sector case study', *International Journal of Contemporary Hospitality Management,* **7** (1), 16–21.

For an international comparison of SMA practices see Guildings, C., Cravens, K.S. and Tayles, M. (2000) 'An international comparison of strategic management accounting practices', *Management Accounting Review,* **11**, 113–135.

Self-check student questions

1 Define strategic management accounting.

2 What are the key changes faced by businesses which have helped to shape strategic management accounting?

3 What is are the key elements of the BCG matrix?

4 How can the lifecycle approach be used to maximise return from a product?

5 What are Porter's generic strategies?

6 What is the link between the balanced scorecard and strategy?

7 What is the principal focus of activity-based management?

8 How big a role does competitor analysis have in the hotel industry?

16

Further questions and problems

1 Compare the vision and mission of two hotel chains and evaluate the degree to which their strategies are likely to be similar.

2 Choose an events company and produce a Boston Matrix of its product offerings.

17 Critical Success Factors and Management Information Needs

17.1 Introduction and objectives

Management accounting exists to support managers in their roles and responsibilities. Whether planning, controlling, decision making, organising information is the key to making informed choices. Previous chapters have highlighted how management accounting tools can assist managers. Chapter 16 focused on strategic management accounting, Critical success factors (CSFs) can be used in a variety of ways both at an operational level and strategically, but most research has focused at the strategic level.

After studying this chapter you will be able to:

- Understand management information needs

- Explain the principles of CSFs

- Know how to conduct CSF identification and practical uses; and

- Appreciate industry research into CSFs and industry-wide CSFs.

17.2 Management information needs

To function effectively managers need to have facts (information) to make informed decisions. In modern businesses there is ample raw data – every bill, invoice, e-mail, and letter provides raw data, but the important factor is how this is turned into information that is of use to managers.

- **Raw data** = raw, isolated, unordered facts

- **Management information** = data that has been processed into a form that is meaningful or relevant to the receiver and aids management decision making.

The important elements in this definition are that data has to be processed appropriately and it is not information unless it is understood by the manager and aids the specific decision they need to make as part of their roles and responsibilities. Any data can be processed, but it can only be considered management information if it meets these further requirements.

Good quality information also has to meet certain criteria:

■ *Appropriate volume* – it has to pass the 'Goldilocks test', not too long, not too short, but just right. Too much information can be as much of a problem as too little information. Simple decisions need basic information, but when looking at a multimillion pound investment to make a strategic decision far more detail is required.

■ *Relevant to the decision being made* – it is not management information if it is not relevant to the specific decision being made.

■ *Understood by the user* – the definition of information mentions 'meaningful to the receiver', if they cannot understand it, it is not useful to them, whatever the intention.

■ *Arrive on time* – information after the decision has been taken is useless.

■ *Be accurate* – if the information comes from an internal source it is easier to control its accuracy, when using external data you need to be confident of its reliability and validity.

■ *Be complete* – partial information gives a partial picture which will not fully inform a decision, however some decisions need a quick response, so in those situations speed may outweigh waiting for more information.

■ *Frequency to meet needs* – routine decisions could be made hourly, daily, weekly, monthly, quarterly, or annually. The information flow needs to match the timing of the decision process. An operational manager may be making daily decisions and need key daily statistics, but head office is interested in an overview of key statistics on a weekly or monthly basis.

It must also be understood that information is not free, time in generating it and using it costs money – whilst a manager is spending 15 minutes reading a report it is 15 minutes not spent on other roles and responsibilities. A cost–benefit analysis has to be undertaken as it is important that the cost of the information doesn't outweigh its benefits, both financially and in the quality of decision making.

17

17.2.1 Event decision-making example

A number of outdoor venues are heavily weather dependent; an example of this is the problem of frozen ground at sporting venues. For some football clubs this has been resolved by under-soil heating systems, this is now common in premiership teams in the UK and used by some teams in the US National Football League (NFL). For others a more temporary measure is employed of covering the surface with matting to protect the surface from freezing prior to the event. How does this relate to decision making? Making the wrong call on the weather can be extremely expensive, so having timely and accurate weather information is critical to making this decision.

The decision is finely balanced, take the example of a horseracing track, the time and money involved in deploying over three miles of matting on the course runs into tens of thousands of pounds, so it is not a decision to take 'just in case' given the additional costs involved. However, why bother in the first place? Not deploying the matting and the ground being frozen could mean cancelling the event; this could lose several hundred thousand pounds in revenue.

Another example is that of a rugby stadium with a similar problem, whilst this is a smaller area to cover there are additional costs compared to a horseracing track to mat. They hire the matting and part of the hire conditions is 24-hour security. The costs incurred are therefore, mat rental, security costs and deployment costs. So the accuracy of the information is critical in this decision and making the wrong decision can have substantial financial consequences.

17.2.2 Designing management information systems (MIS)

The problem with designing a management information system (MIS) is where to start and who makes the decisions on its design and functionality. Alternatives to who leads the process are:

- *Accountants* – as a lot of the data goes through this function it is often a starting point, particularly if a management accountant is employed. The danger with this is the system could end up being very accounting focused and as it has been established when considering strategic management accounting, the information needs to reach beyond internal financial reporting to including non-financial information and an external focus.

- *Computing system* – a number of property management systems (PMS), which manage bookings amongst other functions, have built-in management reports. Whilst this is an easy starting point (what the current IT system is capable of), this is not focused around the specific organisation and could be restrictive. System restrictions should only ever be considered as a short-term issue, it can be amended in the medium term.

- *Head office management* – An alternative is that head office leads the process and determines what they believe to be the requirements of the system. This can lead to a system that serves their needs, what they need to know about operations, but not the detail required by other managers further down the organisation.

- *Operational managers* – It would be possible to go direct to operational managers to ask what information they want, but even this is flawed. There is a difference between what they 'want' and what they actually 'need' to aid them in making specific decisions. Likewise they may focus on what they already receive and be blind to new ideas or things they have never heard of.

The best alternative is generally considered to be focusing on what is needed for a specific management role, but to adapt this to suit the needs of the individual undertaking the role. Levels of experience, time in current post and qualifications can impact on an individual's reliance on management information. An experienced manager who has worked at the same venue (conference facility, bar, restaurant, museum, swimming pool or nightclub) for a number of years can walk into the venue and from past experience with purely visual observation know how busy the venue is and estimate customer numbers. A less experienced manager may rely more on written reports to give customer numbers, due to lack of previous observation at the venue.

There is a saying that is quite apt in this situation: 'You don't know what you don't know'. So asking individuals directly what information they need can be unreliable; they stick to what they know and list current information as a need, even if they do not use it currently. There may be things that are wants not needs and do not directly relate to their job; and things are listed 'just in case' they may need it in the future. So such exercises are not a reliable way of determining information needs. An alternative is to find a way of identifying information needs in a structured way that ensures the information system matches with individual manager's roles and responsibilities. Using critical success factors (CSFs) is such an approach that has a number of uses within an organisation.

17.3 Defining critical success factors (CSFs)

Today in many strategy books there will be discussion of organisations' CSFs. They were first developed back in the 1970s, with work undertaken by Bullen and Rockart (1981) over a number of years; they built on earlier work on success factors back in the 1960s. Half a century on, these are common terms in the strategy world and a number of the ideas fit well with strategic management accounting. Bullen and Rockart's initial work related to the information technology sector in the USA, subsequently there has been research and use of CSFs in various sectors around the world, including hospitality.

Whilst the balanced scorecard was a later technique there are some similarities between the two in that they both identify objectives and how to measure them. Within the CSFs approach an organisation's strategy, goals, critical success factors and measures are determined. There are a number of uses of this, which are discussed later in this chapter. The next section will define the elements and process of CSFs in more detail.

17

17.4 The relationship between goals, CSFs and measures

Before looking at these elements a definition and an overview of CSFs is required.

■ **CSFs** = The few key areas where things 'must go right' in order to meet goals

The argument is that within an organisation, time should be devoted to managing and controlling the things that 'must go right' in order to achieve business success, the CSFs. If an organisation identifies and then concentrates on their CSFs they will develop a stronger business.

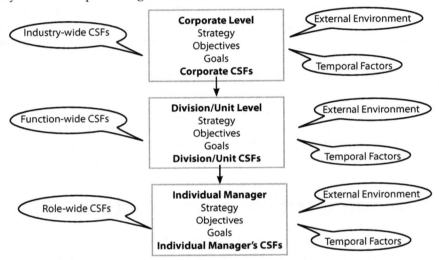

Figure 17.1: Corporate CSFs Framework . (Adapted from Bullen and Rockart 1981)

The corporate CSFs framework (Figure 17.1) gives an overview of CSFs. Starting at the corporate level of an organisation strategy, objectives and goals are formed. The goals are the measureable targets to be met in a specific time frame, so they operationalise the strategy. For each goal it is then determined what is 'critical', what do we have to get right in order to meet the set goals – these are the CSFs, if we fail on these the objectives are not met.

There are also external influences on an organisation, so the external environment, competition, economy, and legislation will influence the organisation. Temporal factors could be internal to a business and have a major impact on the organisation now, thus its current CSFs, but once resolved are no longer CSFs – almost 'emergency CSFs' to deal with a particular crisis that needs resolving.

To the left of the diagram, at corporate level, it shows 'Industry-wide CSFs', there is an argument that some areas critical to success will be shared by all organisations in a specific industry, for example hospitality. Likewise, further down the diagram it shows function-wide CSFs, this could be all hotel restaurants, or all conference facilities, or room divisions, due to the specific function they have.

When considering an individual manager, some of their CSFs may be personal and unique to them as an individual, but as shown on the diagram there will be some CSFs that are common across all managers performing the same role, for example events coordinator, restaurant manager or reservations manager.

Working further down the diagram in Figure 17.1 it shows that the corporate level impacts down the organisation. When looking at the individual manager, their goals, therefore CSFs, are influenced by corporate strategy, the division or unit they work in and their role in the organisation. External factors and any specific current temporal factors also influence the individual's CSFs, as well as all these influences, there will also be the managers' own personal influence based on their personal goals, experience and career aspirations.

To identify CSFs, first goals are identified and then for each goal a number of CSFs are identified and from these the measures needed to monitor the CSFs (see Figure 17.2).

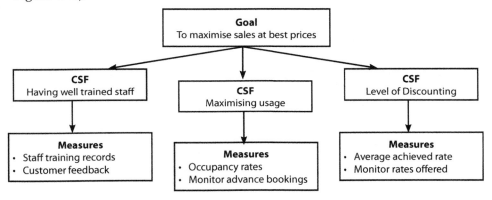

Figure 17.2: From goals to CSFs to measures.

This illustration of CSF terms uses an airline company as an example of how they relate to each other (adapted from Rockart and Bullen 1981).

Table 17.1: CSF terms as used in an airline company

Term	Definition	Example
Strategy	What business are we in?	Regional airline transportation
Objectives	General statement of direction	General profitable air route structure Change to a more efficient air fleet
Goals	Specific targets for a period of time	Withdraw from all routes with less than n% seat usage By year end replace 'X' plane stock with new 'Y' planes Achieve an annual ROCE of 8%
CSFs	Areas where things must go right in order to achieve stated objectives and goals	Receive/maintain approval for higher density routes Receive bank support for capital investment in new plane stock
Measures	A quantifiable target that aids monitoring progress towards CSFs, performance against target	Average % seat capacity usage % of loan funding secured from bank

17

What this means to an organisation, the uses of CSFs and its relation to management information for decision making is covered in specific detail in the next section.

17.5 The use of CSFs in an organisation

There are three potential uses of CSFs:

- A tool for identifying management information needs
- For organisational planning purposes, both operational and strategic; and
- To aid the planning of an organisation management information system.

17.5.1 CSFs for identifying management information needs

At the beginning of this chapter the issue of how to identify management information needs was raised, with the CSFs approach identified as a possible solution. This has been the subject of research in a number of industries in different countries over the decades. The initial focus on CSFs work related to identifying management information needs of key corporate level staff, such as chief executive officers (CEOs), but has been used through an organisation's hierarchy. The work by Jones (1995) considered this within a hotel chain at unit level, and is still the largest project of its kind in this subject area.

Jones' study took an international hotel chain that had been amalgamated through a buyout with a UK national chain. The two parties had very different operational processes and the project took place soon after the merger so it was possible to observe the issues at an operational and strategic level. The study involved interviewing 94 managers within 15 hotels from the two merging parties, this involved general managers, deputy managers and various heads of departments such as: financial controllers; front office managers; room division managers; food and beverage managers; conference and banqueting managers; and restaurant managers. The project was fully supported by head office by the senior vice-president for corporate finance and the UK operational accountant.

Within the study those interviewed identified their goals and developed the needed CSFs and measures to achieve them. This information was also compared to the existing information system.

One major finding was that many goals were often implicit and not explicit, so internalised and known to the individual but not written down or shared across the organisation. Such a situation could be an issue when considering goal congruence and meeting strategic goals. This was clearly illustrated in a large 5* London hotel that had two restaurant managers of equal rank that listed a very different set of goals to each other – how can this meet organisational goals or ensure the department is run effectively? Such a situation could lead to staff confusion and no clear direction. So a clear benefit of identifying individual manager's goals and CSFs is that they can become explicit within the organisation and reviewed routinely in a structured manner, whilst also ensuring the management information system provides the managers with sufficient information to monitor achievement of the identified CSFs.

It is important to note that a number of financial orientated goals led to non-financial critical success factors; this is likely to be the case in other service sectors such as events and tourism. The most frequently cited goal of hotel general managers was to achieve company set profit targets. When CSFs associated with this goal were identified the one most frequently cited was 'having a good management team', followed by 'having the right staff'. The role of heads of departments in delivering financial targets and frontline staff's role in successful service delivery were seen as more important than aspects such as cost controls in delivering profits.

The process aids managers in clearly identifying their information needs and where they need to focus their attention to meet their objectives.

17.5.2 CSFs for organisational planning

At a strategic plan level, CSFs can aid developing a strategic direction and ensure corporate resources are directed towards the few key CSFs that are critical to meeting strategic goals. One element of this can be the use of industry-wide CSFs. Having an in-depth understanding of the CSFs in the sector gives an external strategic view and identifies what the organisation needs to excel at to compete with competitors. Early work in the USA in the 1980s and more recently the work of Brotherton (2004a, 2004b) focused on identifying industry-wide CSFs in the hotel sector. Brotherton (2004b) focused on corporate hotels, whilst his 2004a worked looked specifically at the UK budget hotel sector. As this work covered many companies in the sector it was able to identify CSFs important in the future for the sector, such as: geographic coverage of hotels; value for money; responding to customer demands; having repeat business; positive customer feedback; and high quality standards. If you were in this sector then focusing on these at a strategic level could lead to competitive advantage. Having management information that focuses around these CSFs is going to ensure the organisation is focusing on the right things.

Lower down in the organisation to ensure company goal are met, CSFs can be used to focus resources and achieve a more targeted resource allocation model across the organisation.

17.5.3 CSFs in developing a management information system

As has been established in the last chapter, strategic management accounting is a holistic view of management information needs, combining financial and non-financial information to support management decision making. A number of authors researching into CSFs, including Jones (1995) and Rockart and Bullen

17

(1981), have compared the information needed to report on CSFs measures with an organisation's existing information systems. What has been clear in all these studies is that any financial data required for reporting on CSFs already exists in the organisation and the gaps in the routine information reported by the management information system (MIS) relates to human resources and marketing/market. It is the 'soft' information from customer surveys, market sampling, staff satisfaction, and staff training that is not emphasised enough. This links well to the SMA literature and the work on BSC that also identifies the traditional over emphasis on financial reporting. The key identification a number of people have made, particularly in the service sector, is the critical role staff play in meeting financial goals. This shows the importance of the CSFs process. It doesn't assume financial information is the best way to measure achievement of financial goals and has a strategic and operational role to play in hospitality, tourism and events organisations.

CSFs aid knowing what data needs to be input into the information database. This data can then be drawn out into various targeted reports that meet an individual manager's management information needs. CSFs also ensure the MIS is targeted at focusing managers' attention to the right things to maximise the potential of meeting corporate goals.

Summary of key points

Having a sound management information system is key to managers having the best information to make informed decisions. Critical success factors (CSFs) can aid the development of such a MIS, but equally have other strategic uses. The key points in this chapter are:

- Management need good quality information to make fully informed decisions.

- Designing MISs can be fraught with issues and needs careful planning.

- CSFs can aid an organisation in a number of ways.

- CSFs are the few key areas where things 'must go right to meet organisational objectives'.

- CSFs can change with time and by management role or function.

References

Brotherton, B. (2004a) 'Critical success factors in UK budget hotel operations', *International Journal of Operations and Production Management*, **24** (9), 944–969.

Brotherton, B. (2004b) 'Critical success factors in UK corporate hotels', *Service Industries Journal*, **24** (3), 19–42.

Jones, T. (1995) 'Identifying managers' information needs in hotel companies', in P. Harris (ed.), *Accounting and Finance for the International Hospitality Industry*, Butterworth-Heinemann, Chapter 9.

Rockart, C. and Bullen, J. (1981) *A primer on critical success factors*, Massachusetts Institute of Technology (can be downloaded as pdf)

Further reading

The works provided in the reference section provide the main further reading for this chapter. However, further papers by Brotherton and research applied to hospitality by Geller from the 1980s in the USA are fully referenced in the publications given in the reference section for those wishing to go deeper into this subject.

Self-check student questions

1   Explain the difference between data and information.

2   What are the characteristics of quality information?

3   Define the key CSF terms: 'goals', 'CSFs', and 'measures'.

4   What are the three main uses of CSFs in an organisation?

5   How can CSFs aid corporate level decision making?

6   One of the key features of CSF use is making the implicit into explicit, explain what this means in an operational context.

Further questions and problems

1   For an industry sector with which you are familiar (events, tourism or hospitality) consider what you feel would be operational goals. From these consider what are likely to be the CSFs and measures related to these goals.

2   Your manager is considering using CSFs but is confused about why individual managers will have individual goals, beyond those of the organisation. Explain this concept for your manager.

17

18 Sustainability and Environmental Management Accounting

18.1 Introduction and objectives

Environmental impacts have become a key concern for many businesses as they lead to increased cost. This movement towards greater environmental concern has been spurred on by increasing public scrutiny and governmental legislation. The hospitality, tourism and events sectors may be considers to be potential high impact sectors, therefore have been at the forefront of some of the key developments and changes towards sustainable business. This has led to organisations reporting externally on their environmental efforts through environmental accounting reports. Environmental management accounting (EMA) is an extension of this reporting for internal management use. The relationship is the same as between financial and management accounting more generally.

After studying this chapter you should be able to:

- Identify the key features of environmental management accounting
- Understand how businesses achieve sustainability
- Discuss the key benefits of EMA
- Understand the different methods for EMA reporting.

18.2 The triple bottom line (people, planet and profits)

The triple bottom line or 3BL as it has been termed is founded on the belief that a business's overall success cannot be attributed only to its financial position but also to its ability to address its ethical and environmental performance. Ultimately a sustainable organisation is one which creates value for the shareholders whilst having concern for the environment and the interests of society in general. Businesses have long been required to report on their financial performance through their income statement and statement of financial position; advocates of the triple bottom line believe that the organisation should give the same attention to reporting on its environmental and social position and impact.

In line with the balanced scorecard in Chapter 15, objectives and measures for achieving them are laid out in three key areas economic (profit), environmental (planet) and social (people) (Figure 18.1).

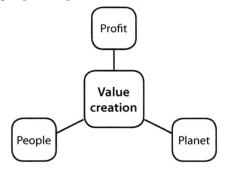

Figure 18.1: The Triple Bottom Line

The profit objectives and measures are no different to those encountered previously and will include return on investment (ROI), sales and profit growth, control of liquidity and gearing.

With regards to the planet the measures for success will include the efficient and effective use of the resources utilised in the organisation's operations and the by-products of the operations.

The people measures will include those which relate to customer satisfaction, employee relations and the impact on the wider community.

The 3BL has a number of benefits for organisations which choose to implement its philosophy:

- The ability to focus on costs which the organisation may have previously felt were out of its control and be able to achieve cost savings in them, is a big advantage, this can be closely linked to ABC drivers.

- The provision of this style of external environmental reporting will provide useful information to customers and suppliers as well as shareholders and

18

the public at large which can make the organisation more appealing. It can be used as part of an organisation's commitments to corporate social responsibility (CSR).

However, the 3BL has not been as widely adopted as the BSC, this may be due to the fact that the social and environmental goals are difficult to measure and control and are likely to be unique to individual organisations or industries. Additionally in industries where there is little legislation or a spotlight on environmental issues it can be considered an unnecessary expense.

18.3 Managing a sustainable business

The ability to create and manage a sustainable business rest on a number of key elements:

- *Stakeholder engagement:* Communication with all the key stakeholders is an important feature, not only providing them with information but receiving information and views from customers, supplier and consumers. This has been a key element in the development of sustainable tourism, resulting in the luxury end of the market becoming more environmentally conscious in line with consumer wishes.

- *Environmental reporting systems:* If the organisation is to set objectives and measures it needs systems in place to ensure that it can provide and analyse data in pursuing its targets. The organisation should make use of generic or industry-specific standards to ensure it is reporting in the right way on the right items. The sustainable business will embed environmental efficiency into its culture and infrastructure.

- *Lifecycle analysis:* In order to promote greater sustainability, an organisation can use the lifecycle model to analyse the environmental and social impacts of its products and this will also enable the organisation to be more responsive to changes in these areas.

Managing a sustainable hospitality, tourism or events organisation could involve consideration of the following specific elements.

- The use of natural resources and energy-saving materials in the fitting of premises and in the construction of a new facility (hotels, conference centre, tourist attraction).

- Landscaping of grounds using native plants and those requiring low impact irrigation. Where natural habitat is removed consideration must be given to replanting.

- Utilising resources (materials and staffing for example) from the immediate community and developing sufficient resources in the immediate community.

- Efficient utilisation of energy through lighting and consideration of alternative sources of power such as solar or wind.

- The use of low-impact products in cleaning and laundry and the reduction in laundry through guest education.

- Development of education and training programmes within the local community.

Having a sustainability policy would be concerned with establishing a strategic, organisation level, policy covering the elements needed for the achievement of the triple bottom line. Published annual environmental accounting reports quantify sustainability achievements into numerical, quantifiable information. EMA provides a more detailed reporting structure for internal management use to be able to monitor progress against targets during the financial year.

18.4 EMA reporting

Following the identification of the need for the organisation to consider its triple bottom line and provide and report on environmental measures and targets it is necessary to examine the mechanisms within the organisation for gathering collating and summarising the data to be used in the reporting.

EMA's specific benefits and uses are sometimes linked to three key areas (IFAC, 2005):

- *Compliance* – This relates to where there are specific legal requirements, or 'self-imposed' environmental policies. EMA aids in meeting the requirements in a cost-effective manner.

- *Eco-efficiency* – Focuses on cost reductions through the more efficient use of resources, such as, electricity, gas, water and raw materials, this reduces costs, but also has an environmental impact by using less resources.

- *Strategic positioning* – This focuses on the organisation's long-term strategy and competitiveness through its use of environmentally-sensitive strategic policies and commitments.

Environmental management accounting provides an extension on the traditional purpose of management accounting to provide useful information for management decision making.

Specifically EMA uses two types of information to aid management decision making:

- *Monetary* – This area looks specifically at the financial impacts of its environmental policy, costs and revenues, investments and liabilities created in an environmental context; and

- *Physical* – This area looks at physical measurement of elements such as CO_2 emissions, energy consumption or material waste from operations.

(Monetary and physical EMA are discussed in more detail later in this chapter.)

18

It is the costs that provide the greater challenge as many environmental costs become hidden in an organisation's general overheads and have to be found and accounted for in order for the organisation to understand the nature and amount of its environmental expenditure.

There are a number of generic categories of environmental cost and ways in which costs can be grouped together, one well recognised way which is useful for internal purposes is to categorise environmental costs in much the same way as total quality management costs can be treated (Figure 18.2).

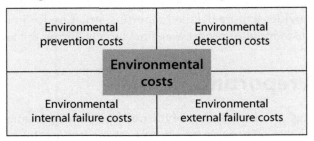

Figure 18.2

- *Environmental prevention costs* – These are the costs incurred in order to safeguard the environment and will include designing and monitoring processes to reduce waste, ensuring appropriate staff training, meeting required standards.
- *Environmental detection costs* – These are the costs incurred in ensuring the organisation complies with legislation, regulations and voluntary standards and will include testing and inspection of processes and waste.
- *Environmental internal failure costs* – These are costs incurred following the production of waste or contaminants which have not been released into the environment and will include recycling scrap and disposing of toxic chemicals.
- *Environmental external failure costs* – These are costs incurred following the production of waste or contaminants which have been released into the environment and will include cleaning up contaminated areas and compensation payments.

If costs are reported in this way, they can be compared with previous periods to show trends and used to benchmark within the organisation and across the industry. Attention can be directed to those areas where the cost has the biggest impact.

18.4.1 Example related to hotel towel usage

One environmental cost recognised across hotels is the daily laundry of guest towels. This uses energy, chemicals in cleaning agents and water resources. Reducing customer towel usage is one environmental element that can have a favourable environmental impact, whilst reducing costs. Instead of automatically providing freshly laundered towels every day, environmental statements are placed in the room explaining the environmental implications of this. A typical instruction to customers is :

"If you wish the housekeeping staff to provide fresh towels in your room please leave them in the bath, towels on the towel rail will not be replaced."

As an example, EMA monitoring of this could look like Figure 18.3.

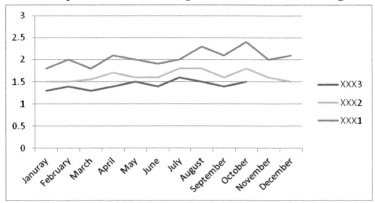

Figure 18.3: Example of EMA monitoring, average towel use per customer per day

In this example in the first year, XXX1, no policy existed. Year XXX2 shows the impact when the policy came in and further reductions were achieved (so far) in year XXX3. This monthly data allows the policy to be monitored – if towel usage starts going up rooms can be checked to see if the policy statement is prominently displayed in all rooms, or it may be a housekeeping staff training issue.

Figure 18.3 highlights the volume of towels used, but this can also be tracked in terms of water usage for example (Figure 18.4). Reducing water usage has a positive environmental impact, as well as a cost saving if water is charged on volume usage. Water usage can be shown in litres for environmental purposes or in monetary value for financial purposes.

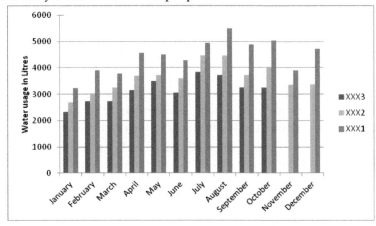

Figure 18.4: Example of EMA monitoring, water usage in laundering towels

Knowing the average water usage per towel and multiplying this by the number of towels used in a month gives the monthly water usage statistics for EMA reporting purposes.

18.4.2 Categories for environmental costs

A business will need to recognise that it must spend money on prevention and detection in order to reduce expenditure on internal and external failure costs. United Nations (2001) split environmental management accounting into various subsections (Figure 18.5).

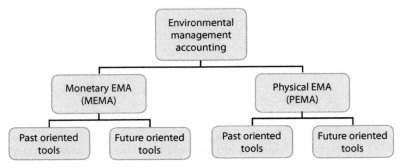

Figure 18.5: United Nations EMA Classifications

- *MEMA – past orientated* examples include reporting environmental spending and external disclosure of environmental related items in monetary value.

- *MEMA – future orientated* examples include the budgeting for environmental expenditure, longer-term capital investment appraisal (CIA), calculating the costs or financial savings of environmental projects.

- *PEMA – past orientated* examples could include records of past material, energy and water usage in physical quantities, benchmarking and evaluating environmental performance against environmental budgets and benchmark data. Such data may also be reported: externally; directly to stakeholders; or perhaps government agencies if required.

- *PEMA – future orientated* examples include budgeting and investment appraisal, but in physical, not monetary terms as in MEMA. The setting of physical quantity targets of resource usage, or CO2 emission targets for example. This could be amending internal processes and procedures of production and service to ones that are more environmentally friendly; this could include environmental requirements stipulated to suppliers to the organisation.

A number of specific management accounting techniques have sprung up in an attempt to aid the identification and management of environmental costs.

18.4.3 Input/output analysis

This method attempts to balance the inflows of materials with the outflows so that if 1000kg of materials are input and only 950kg are evident in the output the other 50kg must be accounted for and costed. This ensures emphasis is placed on the waste from a process which can then be controlled and reduced. Within food and beverage 'plate waste' would be a good example of this, this is where food is returned to the kitchen and becomes scrap, so is wasted. It may be portion sizes should be smaller, or there are particular dishes that need adapting if they produce more plate waste than other dishes.

18.4.4 Flow cost accounting

This method monitors the flow of material and energy through a business over a fixed period and attaches a cost to the flow (Figure 18.6). The aim here is to reduce the quantity and increase efficiency.

In a hotel, water quantity will be monitored in terms of fresh water consumed and waste water expelled. Accor hotel group use this flow concept in their report *Earth Guest Research: The Accor Group's Environmental Footprint* (Accor, 2011), which also includes the use of environmental lifecycle costing.

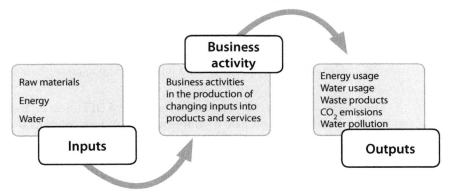

Figure 18.6: Flow of materials, energy and water

18.4.5 Environmental activity-based costing

This method is an extension of the technique discussed in Chapter 8 and links environmental costs with their drives so that the costs can be more transparent and again easier to control. It allows a distinction between those costs which are environmentally driven such as the cost of waste disposal and those which are environment related and are charged to cost centres such as the cost of a water filtration plant. As in the standard critique of ABC there is a difficulty in allocating costs correctly and adequately identifying the drivers for them.

18.4.6 Lifecycle costing

This methodology has been visited in Chapter 16; this time the emphasis is not just consideration of the general costs and revenues incurred over the life of a product or service but also the environmental impacts and costs that follow the life of the product. An example would be clearing a forest to build a hotel and returning the environment back in to a suitable state at the end of its life.

An events example of this is festivals held on farm sites. Camping in fields at such events is commonplace; however this can cause environmental issues and the fields need to be returned to their 'pre-festival' state as quickly as possible. If the site isn't cleared effectively afterwards it could be that when the field is next ploughed remaining bottles, cans and tent pegs damage farm equipment; or if the field is to be grazed by animals they may be injured by glass bottles, or eat a tent peg. At Glastonbury they have made use of large powerful magnets attached to tractors that collect all metal objects rapidly from the fields prior to animals being returned. Collected metal could then be recycled. Other inventions have been the 'biodegradable tent peg' for use at festivals to avoid the problems of metal tent pegs being left in the ground. The use of 'recyclable tents' made 100% from one material (with the tent pegs physically tied to the tent) can be ordered with festival tickets for collection at the event and taken to a recycling point onsite at the end of the event has been another way to aid the rapid return of the field to its agricultural use.

In hospitality, tourism and events many organisations are taking their responsibility to the environment seriously and are producing detailed public environmental statements and producing data which can be used for benchmarking their progress.

Thomas Cook produced a report for its chain of Hi Hotels giving a breakdown of its aims and targets and also a sample accounting report of its use of water and waste production. This provides some detailed monthly EMA information (Hi Hotels International, 2010).

The Accor hotel group as well as publishing its environmental footprint report has designed a calculator which will allow corporate events organisers to track the carbon footprint of conferences, it takes into consideration the number of participants, menu choice and accommodation.

18.5 Environmental management accounting guidelines

The United Nations (UN) produced a report in 2001 which covered recommended procedures and principles of environmental management accounting. These provide detailed information, but would need to be reviewed for use within a specific industry context and country context.

The International Federation of Accountants (IFAC) produced an international guidance document in 2005 which covers the key principles of EMA but also looks at real-life examples of the use of environmental management accounting in a variety of specific situations (IFAC, 2005).

The UK government department, HM Treasury, provides guidance for environmental reporting more generally, not just EMA, but their webpage has links to many reports and guidelines that affect businesses in the UK: www.hm-treasury.gov.uk/frem_sustainability.htm

'The Prince's Accounting for Sustainability Project' (http://www.accounting-forsustainability.org) provides much guidance, research data and examples of environmental reporting within organisations. The approach of these guidelines is to focus on 'integrated reporting', where environmental reporting is combined with financial reporting and not an independent function, or report in organisations. This fits with previous discussions of strategic management accounting, which incorporates non-financial performance with financial performance into one strategic management information system.

An industry specific guideline exists for the events industry. A number of different initiatives were brought together to create a British Standard, BS8901: Sustainable Event Management System, which was published in 2007. The London Olympics 2012 were key partners in developing these standards. Individual events and event organisations can be certified by the British Standards Institute (BSI 2007) as operating events that meet BS8901 standards. Again, this is broader than just EMA, but is a guide to environmental considerations throughout the event management process and it does cover EMA issues.

Summary of key points

Environmental management accounting is becoming a very important topic area across all businesses. The hospitality, tourism and events industries have embraced the environmental ideals more than others. Over time the techniques and theories considered in this chapter will become commonplace in organisations. The initial focus in organisations has been reporting externally; more recent developments in EMA allow an internal management focus for reporting, following established EMA reporting guidelines.

- Triple bottom line (people, planet and profits) is the focus of the need for a sustainability accounting system.
- Managing a sustainable business requires management to manage its resources in a sustainable way; environmental accounting aids this.
- Environmental management accounting (EMA) provides a detailed internal reporting system concerning performance against environmental targets.
- EMA benefits include compliance, eco-efficiency and strategic positioning.
- EMA can be reported in monetary terms and physical terms and can be used to record past events, or in planning for the future.
- Environmental guidelines can be used to aid organisations in developing their own EMA system.

18

References

Accor (2011) *Earth Guest Research: The Accor Group's Environmental Footprint*, Accor (available online from www.accor.com)

BSI (2007) *BS8901: Sustainable Event Management System*, BSI Group

Hi Hotels International (2010) *Environmental Report 2010*, Thomas Cook (available online from http://sustainability2010.thomascookgroup.com)

IFAC (2005) *International Guidance Document: Environmental Management Accounting*, IFAC. (http://www.ifac.org/sites/default/files/publications/files/international-guidance-docu-2.pdf)

UN (2001) *Environmental Management Accounting Procedures and Principles*, United Nations.

Further reading

Abdel-Kader, M. (ed.) (2011) *Review of Management Accounting Research*, Basingstoke: Palgrave Macmillan.

Within the book, which is of general interest to management accounting research there is a chapter by Bennett, Schaltegger, and Zvezdov, that is specific to environmental management accounting research.

Rikhardsson, P.M., Bennett, M., Bouma, J.J. and Schaltegger, S. (eds) (2005) *Implementing Environmental Management Accounting: Status and Challenges*, Springer.

This publication is not industry-specific and is part of a series of books published annually from papers at the EMAN conference. EMAN stands for the Environmental Management Accounting Network.

Whitbread (2010) *Good Together Recommendations and Conclusions Report 2010 – A debate on the future of sustainable hospitality*, Whitbread.

This document produced by Whitbread looks at the future of sustainability in the hospitality industry and is an outcome of a debate with a number of bodies and industry experts. It is broader than EMA, but gives a good industry overview. It can be viewed as a pdf from their website: www.whitbread.co.uk

Self-check student questions

1 What do the 3 Ps refer to in the triple bottom line?

2 Identify the key elements for managing sustainability.

3 What is the difference between monetary and physical EMA?

4 What are the four main tools for conducting EMA?

5 How could EMA be utilised to monitor towel usage in hotel rooms and why is this an environmental issue?

6 Give examples of EMA tools, as per the United Nations EMA classifications.

7 Explain the possible elements of the 'inputs/outputs' of a business from an environmental perspective.

8 What is BS8901? How can it assist event managers?

Further questions and problems

1 Choose two hospitality, tourism or events companies and research their environmental mission statements and objectives in terms of environmental concern. How similar are their aims? How could EMA aid the delivery of their environmental mission?

2 Choose an airline company and identify their reporting on their environmental impact. Are there any additional environmental reporting requirements for airlines?

18

19 Not-for-profit Organisations

19.1 Introduction and objectives

Not-for–profit organisations are often overlooked in management accounting texts but, particularly in events, hospitality and tourism sectors, they are any important part of the economy and it is essential to consider how management accounting can be fully utilised to support such organisations.

After studying this chapter you should be able to:

- Define not-for-profit organisations

- Understand the importance of this sector within hospitality, tourism and events

- Analyse management accounting techniques of particular use within these organisations; and

- Understand how the not-for-profit nature influences accounting orientation and importance.

19.2 Defining a not-for-profit organisation

A not-for-profit organisation is one whose key focus is not on generating profits, also referred to as non-profit organisations. This sector encompasses charitable organisations and governmental bodies of all shapes and sizes. Just like 'for profit' organisations these vary in sizes from a local village-based charity to large international charities which are multimillion pound operations. Governmental bodies again can range from local government, to national government to international bodies. This can include police forces, national health services, and social care facilities. The full range of the community, social and voluntary organisations are endless.

In such organisations the end motive is not to generate profits to return to owners or those that control the organisation. That doesn't mean money and financial control are not critical to survival. In such organisations the terms profit and loss are replaced with surplus and deficit. Such organisations will have a social, environmental, or cultural goal and producing a surplus to reinvest back into this is part of their survival and growth to benefit their assigned 'good cause'.

In essence in the not-for-profit sector, monetary value can be seen as a 'means to an end', aiding the meeting of its goal and purpose, but monetary value is not an end in its own right. A number of estimates exist country by country of the size of the sector. A number of sources estimate over 1.4 million in the USA, a report in Australia (Commonwealth of Australia, 2010) estimated 600,000 in Australia, contributing $43 billion to Gross Domestic Profit (GDP) and accounting for 8% of employment. In terms of their development over the years, such organisations have had to be more cost-efficient and just as is the case with profit-based commercial organisations, productivity is of increasing importance.

Johns Hopkins University, USA, have undertaken much work into the classification of non-profit organisations and their work on the International Classification of Non-Profit Organizations (ICNPO, see Table 19.1) is well recognised (United Nations, 2006). Their classification is the standard used in many countries and recognised by the United Nations. ICNPO breaks down such organisations into 12 activity sections and each of those is further subdivided. The following provides examples of what is included in this classification.

Table 19.1: ICNPO 12 classifications

Classification	Includes
Culture and recreation	Arts, performing arts, sports, zoos, aquariums, sports clubs, recreation and social clubs
Education and research	Schools, further & higher education, universities, adult education, research bodies, medical research, social science research, policy studies
Health	Hospitals, nursing homes, hospices, mental health services, health education services
Social services	Child services, including day care and welfare, youth services, family services, services for the elderly and the disabled, disaster and emergency prevention and control, refugee assistance
Environment	Animal protection and welfare, wildlife preservation and protection, pollution assessment and control, environmental management
Housing and development	Community and housing projects, housing associations, job training projects, community furniture projects
Law, politics and advocacy	Civil rights organisations, ethnic associations, victim support, offender rehabilitation, political parties and associations
Philanthropic intermediaries and voluntarism promotion	Grant-making foundations, fund raising organisations and promotion of volunteering organisations
International	Exchange and cultural programmes, international disaster and relief organisations, international human rights and peace organisations
Religion	Churches, synagogues, mosques, monasteries, religious associations
Business associations, professional bodies and trade unions	Professional organisations, labour/trade unions, business associations that promote or advise businesses
Not classified elsewhere	Cooperative schemes, non-profit manufacturers and retailers

19

19.3 Their significance to the hospitality, tourism and events sectors

The impact of the not-for-profit sector on the hospitality, tourism and events sector can be separated into two key groups: not-for-profit organisations working in providing hospitality, tourism and event based services; and not-for-profit organisations that use hospitality, tourism and events organisations, particularly in relation to fund-raising opportunities.

19.3.1 Example – British Heart Foundation

Their mission relates to having a leading role in fighting disease related to the heart and blood circulation system and to reduce its impact and reduce death rates (British Heart Foundation). Their total income in 2011 is reported as £233,398,000. This comes from: return on investments; profits from retail activities (mainly shops); legacies; and fundraising. Fundraising makes up 30% of this total income. One key way they encourage fundraising is through the running of events – viewing their website (www.bhf.org.uk) it is possible to see the range of events that take place – walks, hikes, jogs, runs, skydives, swims, international challenges, school and youth group events, to name a few.

So whilst this is a charity with a mission that is not financial it is a multimillion pound operation and has to raise funds in order to achieve its mission. It has to have tight financial controls, both to record and manage the income coming in and to ensure administrative costs are kept to a minimum so maximum financial resources are available to meet their charitable mission. The employment of a finance team, event managers, fundraising managers, and grant funding staff (monitoring research grants) all ensure things run smoothly.

Events managers in this environment need to maximise participation and fundraising by individuals, whilst ensuring the event costs are kept to a minimum in order to maximise the surplus available for achieving the set mission. Food and beverage facilities required at such events show the hospitality aspect of such events. International charity challenges can be arranged directly by such charities or outsourced to tourism and travel companies and tend to be fully inclusive 'holiday' style packages.

19.3.2 Hospitality and the not-for-profit sector

When considering the ICNPO it can be seen a number of organisations are involved in the provision of hospitality services. These include catering in hospitals, prisons, children's homes, schools, universities, museums, 'meals-on-wheels' and staff catering facilities. In addition to these not-for-profit operations, commercial hospitality venues can be involved in running charity events. Such activity may be viewed as part of their corporate social responsibility (CSR) and seen as a way of giving back to the local community and to society more generally. Celebrity charity balls can be high profile events relying on high profile catering and 5* hotels in key locations.

19.3.3 Tourism and the not-for-profit sector

Challenge-based events, whether national or international are big business and many commercial tourism companies work alongside charities to arrange these overnight charity challenges, often including flights, accommodation, local guides, and food. Other charities are specifically set up to provide holiday and adventure opportunities for disadvantaged children and families or those with disability, so are charity sector tourism providers.

19.3.4 Events and the not-for-profit sector

The charity sector is of major importance to the events industry and a major employer. Events are a major part of most charities' fundraising efforts – these can include sporting events, music events, balls, social events. Such events can range from the very small local school social or sporting event to multimillion pound international events.

A classic example is that of Band Aid (www.bandaid.org.uk), were registered as a charity in 1985 – in 6 months it had raised $6 million, but the live aid concert of July 1985 was an international music event held in many venues around the world concurrently – this event raised $80 million for the charity. The charity has continued since that date with further live music events.

Whilst Band Aid Live is an example of a major large scale international charity event the more recent 'Oxjam' events in aid of the charity Oxfam are on a different scale (www.oxfam.ord.uk/oxjam). Oxjam has the strapline 'local music, global impact' these events are small scale and run by volunteers around the country, so multiple small-scale events.

Given the size of the not-for-profit sector and its particular relationship to hospitality, tourism and events it is of strategic importance and the specific needs of management accounting in this sector need to be considered.

19.4 The implications for management accounting approaches

As discussed in earlier chapters, traditional management accounting techniques were designed for use in manufacturing back in the 1800s. Whilst newer techniques and those more suited to service industries have been developed, alongside strategic management accounting much of the focus has been on commercial organisations, with financial orientated goals. In this section the issues specific to not for profit organisations and how management accounting techniques can be utilised by them are discussed.

19

19.4.1 Issues of accountability

Whereas commercial operations are accountable to shareholders and lenders, not-for-profit organisations can often be held far more publicly accountable, so under far more scrutiny financially and in their decision-making processes. Donors will want to see their money going to the good cause in hand and not being 'wasted' on administration. Providers of grants may set strict guidelines and set reporting requirements and conditions. Publically funded organisations, such as local authorities, police forces, and education providers will be held accountable to users of the services, society as a whole and government for what they achieve for the money provided for the service. Charities will be held accountable morally if they accept funds from inappropriate sources – such as a cancer-related charity accepting sponsorship from a tobacco company.

Given the number of stakeholders to consider and the public accountability, decision making can be a long process. The attitude to risk is usually far more conservative than commercial operations due to the level of accountability and potential negative publicity if things go wrong.

19.4.2 Cost control and budgeting

It has been mentioned a number of times that keeping costs to a minimum and within budget are critical in such organisations. Within local government budgets are allocated for a year at a time, often being further broken down into monthly budgets. Such control can be very strict, with no possibility of going beyond the budgeted cost figures – this can lead to rigid budgetary control. This can lead to inflexibility when trying to responding to changes in the short-term, in comparison commercial operations which are relatively free to adjust and amend budgets and respond more rapidly to changes in the external environment.

Cost control and budgeting, particularly cash budgeting, are important management accounting tools that are utilised in not-for-profit situations. Often this is in a very traditional cost accounting sense with little flexibility within a financial year – this then leads to a need for a separate mechanism to deal with the exceptions and emergencies that may arise.

19.4.3 Decision making

Decision making in this sector can be seen as conservative and not risk taking in nature. Decisions are well considered, often made by committees and look beyond the financial implications of the decision. Having such a bureaucratic decision-making process does eliminate unnecessary risk, but can lead to problems when responding to crisis situations where decisions need to be made quickly. To overcome this in a number of situations emergency decision-making processes also need to be in place.

An example of this emergency decision making is for emergency response procedures in local government. In 2007 the county of Gloucestershire, UK, had major flooding and actions needed to be taken quickly to respond to this. In this situation a 'joint emergency response' protocol comes into operation and decision making goes into the hands of 'Gold Control'. Gold Control brings together strategic decisions makers from local authorities, emergency services and in this case water companies and electricity companies to coordinate decision making without the normal long-term full committees having to meet.

An example of these procedures in charities is emergency appeals to international emergencies, such as tsunami relief efforts, famine, flooding, earthquakes, etc. In such situations a set protocol is set up to raise specific funding and set emergency relief procedures come in to play.

Long-term decision making can use investment appraisal techniques the same as commercial operations (PBP, ARR, NPV or IRR). However, these processes judge the value of a financial investment in relation to their financial return and this may not strategically be most important in a not-for-profit organisation. Whilst financial aspects of projects need to be considered, other outputs may be better indicators in making such decisions. Therefore a cost–benefit analysis, which is broader in nature, can be more useful.

An example of a cost–benefit analysis might be expenditure on a new road (Figure 19.1). The judgement on the investment would not be looking at financial return, but may look at fewer accidents on a known accident black spot, or eliminating traffic jams that are costing local business staff time, etc.

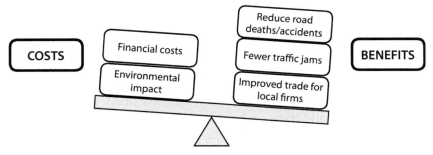

Figure 19.1: Expenditure on a new road, the balance of costs and benefits.

A local authority developing a museum may have more emphasis on providing a facility for the local community, social benefits and tourism development than the financial returns of the specific project.

In considering long-term investments match to strategic direction and impact on the charities' goals, which are often non-financial, will take priority over pure financial gain.

19.4.4 Pricing

There is an assumption sometimes that in not-for-profit organisations you are not selling as such, so 'normal' pricing considerations do not apply. There are a number of areas to pricing in charities. First, a number of charities will have a retail

19

'profit' making arm in order to raise additional funds for their good cause. These can be charity shops, selling new items, online occasion cards and gift sales. These need to make sure they cover costs and return a substantial surplus to the good cause, in addition a fair price, or premium may have been paid to the producers of Fair Trade products for resale. Second, when organising fundraising events it is usual to have an entry or registration fee – the purpose of this fee is to contribute to the costs associated with the event, so any fund raising by individuals taking part goes straight to the charitable cause and is not reduced by administrative costs. Third, there is the concept of 'social inclusion pricing'.

In running charity events the costs can be kept to a minimum by the use of volunteers and having commercial sponsors. For example, budgeting administration costs, such as sending entry details, administering websites, hire of venues, and printing sponsorship forms, and entry numbers must be estimated far enough in advance so that an entry or registration fee can be set at a level that covers costs and is at a level that participation ('customers') will be encouraged. This is similar to pricing in commercial 'for profit' organisations, but the opportunity for 'loss leaders' is not appropriate. Risk is also an issue here, as they will be risk adverse. A worst-case scenario would be to run an event to raise funds for a charity and for it to not cover its own costs, so not only does it not aid fundraising but it takes away from existing funds of the charity.

The use of social inclusion pricing is common in state run/local authority run facilities such as museums and leisure centres. Such facilities are run for the nation or local society, so part of their remit could be to maximise local participation. Consider the example of a local-authority-run leisure centre. Why is it being run? If you look up the mission of such a venue it will normally relate to providing a facility for the local community, to get people active, provide a facility for local schools and sports groups to use. In order to do this its pricing policy has to encourage all sectors of society, so reduced prices for children, the elderly, the unemployed and those on low wages is important in meeting the stated mission. Working with the health service to get people active, so focusing on lifestyle change is encouraged through the pricing strategy, it is not about maximising financial returns as the key priority – this is an interesting comparison to a commercially operated facility where the motivation for running a gym is purely for commercial financial returns reasons.

19.4.5 Performance analysis

As has been discussed in previous chapters, the traditional form of performance analysis is purely financially based. Given the level of public accountability in the not-for-profit sector financial reporting is key to these organisations, however the difference is the purpose of such reporting. As discussed earlier in this chapter, the percentage of money that is available for the 'good cause' relies on keeping running costs (administration costs) to a minimum – thus a key financial performance indicator is the percentage of these costs to income. This can be used as a measure of whether certain events are a success and worth repeating, or to withdraw from certain activities if the return provides a to lower percentage return.

However, as already stated, in this environment, money is only a means to an end so meeting the organisation's goals is likely to involve looking at non-financial performance measures as well.

Table 19.2: Performance measurement examples

Example organisation	Suitable measure
A cancer-based charity	Success will be measured in research developments that impact on survival rates, so a reduction in deaths for particular cancers would be a performance indicator. Some research could take many years, so this is looking at the medium to long term, not short-term 'returns'. Awareness campaigns can be measured by the number of people asking for information, or having initial cancer screenings.
A human aid charity	These will be measuring how many people have been aided. For example numbers supplied with fresh drinking water, anti-malaria treatments given, reduction in infant deaths.
Local authority/ government	The key here is quality of the service provided, so measures related to service delivery is key. Rating of local schools, roads, waste services, libraries, etc. all providing key information, as does usage statistics.
A telephone advice line	Such a service can be measured relating to the number of calls taken/people assisted in a given period.

19.4.6 Strategic management accounting

Referring back to technique and tools identified in the SMA chapter it is clear a number of these can be adopted or adapted for use in the not-for-profit sector. SMA, by its nature, looks beyond just the internal financial perspective in analysing performance and this fits well with the focus of not-for-profit organisations where financial returns are a means to an end, not the ultimate goal themselves.

The balanced scorecard (BSC) and critical success factors (CSFs) are particularly useful in that they are driven by organisational goals and objectives in a way that allows measures and management reports to be focused around the specific needs in these organisations.

19.4.7 Environmental management accounting

There are two imperatives here:

- First, where there is grant, public or charitable funding involved the 'wasting' of resources will be under scrutiny, whether it is recycling, minimising fuel usage, or running a 'paperless' office to aid the environment; and

- Second, the charity or government organisation may have a specific remit related to people and/or the planet. When this is the case they have a moral duty to run their own organisation by means of 'best practice'.

19

Referring back to the previous chapter where EMA was discussed in detail, all the tools and reporting frameworks are viable in the not-for-profit sector. EMA has been developed from an environmental, not a profit base imperative, with United Nations (UN) recommending practice. Due to this, EMA can be very useful and applicable in the not-for-profit sector.

Summary of key points

The not-for-profit sector is not widely covered in detail within management accounting literature, however within hospitality, tourism and events there are many not-for-profit organisations, or commercial operations that work alongside such organisations. Key aspects of this chapter have been:

- Not-for-profit organisations are a major sector of the economy that need to use management accounting tools to maximise returns and control costs.

- Public accountability can led to 'conservative', low-risk-taking decision making, that often takes a long time through a committee process.

- ICNPO identifies the range of not-for-profit sectors that exist, many are in, or work with hospitality, tourism and events organisations.

- Management accounting in NFP organisations needs to reflect the fact profits are not their ultimate goal; money is a means to an end, not the final output in many cases.

- Strategic management accounting techniques can be important as they integrate non-financial information and goals.

References

Band Aid (2012) *www.bandaid.org.uk*

British Heart Foundation (2012) *www.bhf.org.uk*

Commonwealth of Australia (2010) *Contribution of the not-for-product sector: Productivity Commission Research Report*, Australian Government.

Oxfam (2012) *www.oxfam.ord.uk/oxjam*

United Nations (2006) ISIC Annex ICNPO, Meeting of the Technical Subgroup of the Expert Group on International Economic and Social Classifications, New York, 19–23 June 2006 (available as pdf from UN).

Further reading

Papaspyropoulos, K.G., Blioumis, V., Christodoulou, A.S., Birtsas, P.K. and Skordas, K.E. (2012) 'Challenges in implementing environmental management accounting tools: the case of a nonprofit forestry organisation', *Journal of Cleaner Production*, 29–30, 132–143.

Although in a different industry sector this provides a real-life working example of EMA in a not-for-profit environment.

Mango (www.mango.org.uk) is a registered charity which aids and advises charities on financial reporting (internal and external). The website provides downloadable guides and information related to budgeting, internal control and reporting.

National Council for Voluntary Organisations provides advice on making management accounting effective in the voluntary sector (www.ncvo-vol.org.uk/advice-support/funding-finance/making-management-accounts-effective-tools).

Self-check student questions

1 Define 'not-for-profit' sector, with examples of organisations.

2 What roles can hospitality, tourism and events play in the NFP sector?

3 Explain the specific considerations that need to be made when using management accounting in NFP organisations.

4 List the key management accounting tools that can be used in NFP organisations.

5 Explain how the BSC and CSFs can be utilised fully within the NFP sector.

6 Environmental management accounting can be important in NFP organisations – what type of organisations specifically?

Further questions and problems

1 Research the information for two leisure centres: one a commercial operation; and one run by a local authority or by a charity. Conducted a comparative analysis between the two, paying particular interest to their stated mission statement, pricing policies and local community initiatives.

2 You are the national events manager for a leading charity. When organising a fundraising 'charity fun run' how can management accounting tools ensure it is the most cost effective and maximises fundraising opportunities?

19

20 Current Issues in Strategic Managerial Accounting

20.2 Management accounting change over time

The development of management accounting tools and techniques has been documented throughout this textbook. The start of the discipline as 'cost accounting' in the 1800s, through to 'management accounting', and more recently 'strategic management accounting' has been referred to in a number of chapters. Here this is reviewed and the future considered (see Figure 20.1).

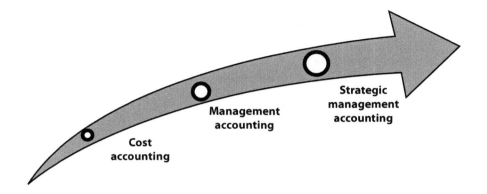

Figure 20.1: The development of management accounting

The development and issues over time in the generic field of management accounting are well documented in the work by Johnson and Kaplan (1987), Bromwich and Bhimani, (1989, 1994), and discussed in Chapter 16. Within this textbook the use of management accounting has been specifically focused around the needs and uses of management accounting, from a strategic managerial perspective and applied to hospitality, tourism and event contexts.

20.3 Use of management accounting in hospitality, tourism and events

Strategic management accounting's development from cost accounting's manufacturing industry roots, becomes a common theme when exploring the 'usefulness', or 'validity' of some techniques for use in a service sector. Some techniques, such as total absorption costing and full cost pricing, are sometimes inappropriate within these specific service industries, though they work in manufacturing environments. Figure 20.2 identifies some of the management accounting tools and techniques that are useful in hospitality, tourism and events, all of which (amongst others) have been explored within this textbook.

As shown throughout this textbook and summarised in Figure 20.2, there are many generic management accounting techniques that do have value in hospitality, tourism and events.

More traditional management accounting techniques identified in Figure 20.2 are of use in aspects of hospitality, tourism and events. The key within this textbook has been not only demonstrating these techniques but detailing their application within these specific sectors. Generic coverage of these techniques and tools is often with manufacturing examples, so makes it difficult to translate this knowledge into a service sector environment, as has been achieved here.

20

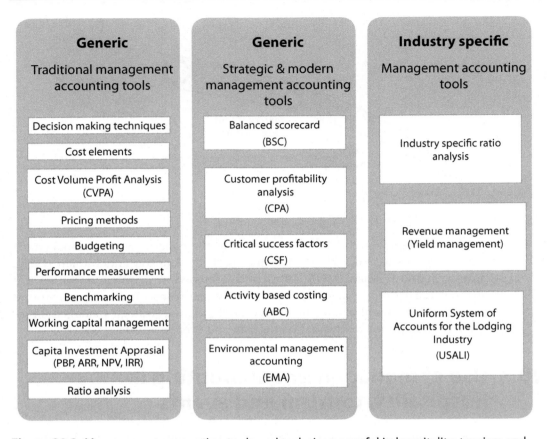

Figure 20.2: Management accounting tools and techniques useful in hospitality, tourism and events

Generic modern and strategic management accounting (SMA) techniques highlighted in Figure 20.2 demonstrate strategic management accounting firmly has a part to play across hospitality, tourism and events sectors. Given the wider focus of SMA, to encompass non-financial data and its external focus it fits well with service industries.

Adoption and adaption are important phrases, whilst some approaches can be utilised unchanged, others can be adapted to meet specific industry needs, for example the use industry specific ratios alongside generic ratios for financial analysis purposes.

There is discussion of techniques in this textbook that have been developed within hospitality, tourism or events, i.e. do not originate from the generic management accounting literature. An example would be the development of yield management that started within airlines. This has spread more broadly to sophisticated revenue management systems within hospitality and other closely linked environments. The Uniform System of Accounts for the Lodging Industry (USALI) in use since the 1920s is also an example of a specific development.

USALI does use the principles of responsibility accounting which is generic, but to generate an industry-specific tool. This has also allowed the development of benchmarking beyond that available in many other industries.

Within the strategic management accounting literature, as discussed in Chapter 16, changes in the external environment such as: globalisation, increased competition, faster pace of change, and environmental concerns have all had an impact. In financial accounting this has led to the need for international financial reporting standards (IFRS) that permeate over national boundaries. IFRS terminology is therefore becoming more widely utilised within management accounting, to reflect the changes in financial accounting. This is evident in the accounting terminology used within this text.

Corporate social responsibility (CSR), where firms demonstrate their 'corporate conscience' has also led to the use of concepts, such as 'triple bottom line' reporting (profit, planet and people) – this was also discussed in Chapter 18. Within the management accounting arena the key outcome of this has been the development of environmental management accounting (EMA), as discussed in Chapter 18. The focus beyond profits (or instead of profits), the 'planet' and 'people' elements is also strong in the not-for-profit sector, as explored in Chapter 19. The not-for-profit sector utilises a number of management accounting tools, but the focus, on a 'good cause' in such charity organisations impacts on their management accounting practices.

This evidence further supports the case that management accounting has a vital role to play across hospitality, tourism and events organisations.

20.4 The role of the management accountant

In the generic management accounting field it is viewed that the role of the management accountant has changed over time (Burns and Baldvinsdottir, 2005; Hopper et al., 2001). This is also mirrored within hospitality applied research by authors such as Burgess (2006). Burgess has conducted a number of studies, including longitudinal studies of the role of financial controllers within hotels. The outcomes of this research have developed over the years.

Research shows that in the later part of the 20th century the traditional role of a 'bean counter', working in isolation from unit management was changing. Financial controllers were taking a more active role at unit level hotel management, being viewed as part of the management team and working alongside managers and working with them to aid their decision-making process. However, into the 21st century, as many organisations considered how to cut costs in order to progress in a competitive environment, like many other industries centralising 'support functions', and outsourcing became more popular. By 2006, Burgess was concerned if there was actually a future for financial controllers at the unit (hotel) level. Evidence suggested a number of chain hotels were moving financial control-

20

lers into regional or national 'hubs' to support a group of individual hotels. There has also been some evidence of outsourcing the accounting function altogether.

This is not just the case in hospitality, in the events sector, a number of horseracing courses in the UK have moved away from venue-based management accountants to a more centralised base needing less staffing. One of the issues this raises is the need for 'non-financial' managers to have sufficient accounting skills at unit level. This stresses the point that managers across hospitality, tourism and events need to develop a sound working knowledge of management accounting in order to be effective.

Most research has related to larger organisations, where such a function as management accounting exists. As discussed in Chapter 13, a number of businesses in these sectors fall into the category of SMEs, or micro-business, so it is the owner/manager, or manager that is performing the management accounting function (preparing management accounting reports), both from an accounting and a managerial perspective.

20.5 Contemporary applied research

Scapens is a famous researcher in the generic field of management accounting, in his 2006 paper, 'Understanding management accounting practices: a personal journey' (Scapens, 2006) he reflects personally on how he believes 'practice based' (industry based) management accounting research has developed over his time as a researcher. He views this as going through four particular phases, as shown in Figure 20.3.

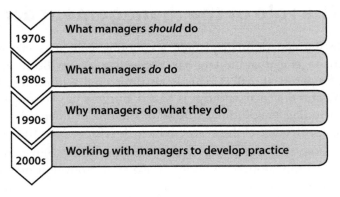

Figure 20.3: Changes in management accounting practice research

A simplification of his reflections in this paper are that back in the 1970s academic researchers believed all the management accounting tools needed for organisations to use, existed; it was just a case of getting managers to use them. By the 1980s, researchers focused more on field research in organisation that discovered what management accounting tools were being used (mainly surveys of practice). This developed in the 1990s to then asking 'why?' this became critical when considering the perceived 'gap' between theory and practice. An example of this would be the use of flexible budgeting. Theoretically it is seen has having many benefits, yet surveys of practice over time have shown only around 20% of companies actually use it. Research in the 1990s then focused in such cases to understand why academic theory was not being used in practice. By finding out why certain management accounting tools were, or were not, utilised gave a deeper understanding to researchers. Within the 21st century, Scapens (2006) sees the role of researchers in management accounting to be working alongside managers in industry to aid them in developing practice.

Applied research into a specific industry, such as hospitality, mirrors the development pattern outlined in the generic area of management accounting over this period. However academic management accounting research applied specifically to tourism is limited in volume and almost non-existent within the events sector. This is evident within this textbook where reference to applied journal articles has had to focus around that which exists, namely hospitality applied management accounting research.

Even within hospitality applied research it has been recognised that the vast majority of management accounting research is applied specifically to hotels (estimated over 90%), with only a few studies applied to restaurants (Atkinson and Jones, 2008, 2011). Atkinson and Jones' 2011 review of management accounting research across hospitality and tourism found only a few studies related to accounting, with single figures of papers majoring on a management accounting topic applied to tourism.

There are a number of academic journals dedicated to hospitality, tourism or events, alongside those more generally applied to the service sector. A number of authors have surveyed these over the years to review the percentage of articles from each 'discipline' area. Baloglu and Assante (1999) identified under 8% of articles in the 'top 5' hospitality applied academic journals were in the area of accounting and finance, of which management accounting is included alongside financial management and financial accounting. This is reflected in Atkinson and Jones' 2011 paper which identified just over 100 hospitality and tourism applied management accounting journal articles in a period covering 11 years, averaging less than 10 papers a year.

The references and areas for further reading at the end of chapters do include links to applied research papers; the above mentioned applied reviews (Atkinson and Jones, 2008, 2011) include detailed reference lists of the majority of research output available in the field for those readers wishing to explore research in this subject area more deeply. For an historical perspective, see Harris and Brander-Brown (1998) who reviewed hospitality applied finance and accounting research that had taken place from the 1970s, through to 1998.

The 'state of the art' of hospitality applied research can be summarised as having a history of over 40 years and has developed, both in subject areas and methodological approaches during that period of time. Despite this, the volume

20

of research is still lower than that of hospitality applied to other areas, such as operations management, marketing or human resource management (HRM). This still provides a rich research ground with many opportunities to add to knowledge through more research in the future.

The current state of research into management accounting within tourism and events can be described, at best, as minimal. This provides many opportunities for new research in this field. The tourism and events applied discussion of management accounting topics within this textbook identifies that some fantastic opportunities exist for research in these area. Such research development can assist in improving the use of management accounting by managers within tourism and events sectors, whilst also adding to academic knowledge in the discipline.

20.6 Managerial accounting and the reader

Students of management study many disciplines, including operations management, marketing and HRM, some are easier to access and understand than others, accounting is often seen as the most difficult. Yet accounting, and in particular managerial accounting, provides vital knowledge and tools for managers to support their day-to-day decision making. In addition as managers, you will be held accountable for the resources you are utilising and the decisions you make; managerial accounting (as we have shown in this book) has a fundamental role to play in provision of information for decision making and reporting on performance. Thus managerial accounting is both critical to general management students and is not a subject that should be left to the accountants.

The authors of this textbook are all active researchers in this applied field of research and have many years' experience in teaching management accounting to 'non-accounting' students. Therefore they all have a genuine interest and enthusiasm for the subject. However they also recognise some managers in industry and students alike do not share this, some view anything numerical as 'something to leave the accountant to do' it is hoped this textbook has aided the reader in understanding the importance of management accounting information as an integral part of management decision making, both at an operational and strategic level in the organisation – thus it should be understood that the use of management accounting information is of importance to managers across the organisation. Some students and managers understand management accounting information is something with which they need to engage yet still view it as a 'necessary evil'. It is hoped the industry-focused examples and the managerial focus of this textbook takes such readers beyond this view to a deeper understanding of the subject.

There is a genuine need for the use of management accounting for decision making, planning and control purposes across hospitality, tourism and events organisations, whether it be at an operational or strategic level there are specific management accounting tools that provide a useful aid to managers.

The authors genuinely hope this textbook will inspire managers to further understand and use management accounting tools in the workplace, but also encourage students to research further into applied management accounting to add to the body of current knowledge for the future development of these sectors.

Summary of key points

This chapter has drawn together what has been covered within this textbook and discussed it in respect to its importance to managers within hospitality, tourism and events. As part of this it has: drawn comparisons between generic and industry applied considerations; how management accounting has changed over time; the role of the management accountant; industry applied management accounting research; and more general observations to readers of the importance of this subject area across hospitality, tourism and events. The key points are:

- Management accounting has developed from manufacturing cost accounting into strategic management accounting over the last century.

- A vast variety of management accounting tools and techniques exist that are valid and useful for hospitality, tourism and events organisations.

- The management accounting function is changing, making it critical that managers in organisations have their own sound financial skills; and

- There is a history of applied management accounting research in hospitality, with opportunities for further research across hospitality, tourism and events.

References

Atkinson, H. and Jones, T. (2008) 'Financial management in the hospitality industry: themes and issues', in B. Brotherton and R. Woods (eds), *The SAGE Handbook of Hospitality Management*, London: SAGE, pp. 228–256.

Atkinson, H. and Jones, T. (2011) *Hospitality and Tourism Management Accounting*, Contemporary Tourism Series, Oxford: Goodfellow Publishing.

Baloglu, S. and Assante, L.M. (1999) 'A content analysis of subject areas and research methods used in five hospitality management journals', *Journal of Hospitality and Tourism Research*, **23** (1), 53–70.

Bromwich, M. and Bhimani, A. (1989) *Management Accounting: Evolution not Revolution*, London: CIMA.

Bromwich, M. and Bhimani, A. (1996) *Management Accounting Pathways to Progress*, London: CIMA Publishing.

20

Burgess, C. (2006) 'Hotel unit financial management: does it have a future?', in P. Harris and M. Mongiello (eds), *Accounting and Financial Management: Developments in the International Hospitality Industry*, Oxford: Butterworth-Heinemann.

Burns, J. and Baldvinsdottir, G. (2005) 'An institutional perspective of accountants' new roles – the interplay of contradictions and praxis', *European Accounting Review*, **14** (4), 725–757.

Harris, P. and Brander Brown, J. (1998) 'Research and development in hospitality accounting and financial management', *International Journal of Hospitality Management*, **17** (2), 161–182.

Hopper, T., Otley, D. and Scapens, B. (2001) 'British management accounting research: whence and whither: opinions and recollections', *British Accounting Review*, **33**, 263–291.

Johnson, H. and Kaplan, R. (1987) *Relevance Lost: the Rise and Fall of Management Accounting*, Harvard Business Press.

Scapens, R.W. (2006) 'Understanding management accounting practices: a personal journey', *British Accounting Review*, **38** (1), 1–30.

Further reading

The reference list in this chapter covers many key research articles in this subject area for those wanting to gain a deeper understanding of the development of research in the field of management accounting. The 'review articles' referenced have extensive reference lists to over 100 applied research papers so can be used as a 'gateway' to applied research into management accounting.

Answers to self-check questions

Chapter 1

1   What are the key differences between financial management, financial accounting and management accounting?

Section 1.2

2   How might aspects of hospitality, tourism and events overlap or work together?

Section 1.3

3   What are the key characteristics associated with businesses within these sectors?

Section 1.4

4   What is the manager's role in relation to strategic managerial accounting?

Section 1.5

Chapter 2

1   What is the difference between cash and profits?

Section 2.3

2   How can external annual financial accounting statements be used by managers within an organisation?

Section 2.4

3   What are the benefits of having international financial report standards?

Section 2.4

4   Explain the main purpose of the income statement, cash flow statement and the statement of financial position.

Section 2.4

5   As a manager what could be the benefits of using the USALI?

Sections 2.5 and 2.6

6   What industry advantages are there if using the USALI?

Section 2.6

Chapter 3

1   Explain what you understand by the 'elements of cost'.

Section 3.2

2   Distinguish between 'direct' and 'indirect' costs and give examples of each.

Section 3.2.2

3   Define 'fixed' and 'variable' costs, what is the main difference between them?

Section 3.3

4   What is a semi-variable cost?

Section 3.3.3

5   A banqueting suite is trying to ascertain the cost structure for a single menu:

Standard menu 'D'	Cost per head (fixed and variable)
100 customers (covers)	£25.30
150 covers	£20.90
200 covers	£19.75

Portion size and quality of the food and service were the same in all cases. Calculate the fixed and variable portions of the total cost (note: same process as for semi-variable separation). Estimate the cost if 175 covers were sold.

Using Hi/Low method 100 covers = £2,530, 200 covers = £3,950 difference = £1420/100 units = £14.20 variable cost per unit, therefore fixed costs = £1,110.

175 covers = F.C. £1,110 + (£14.20 * 175) = £3,595

6   From the data and your answers from question 5, sketch two graphs showing the following against level of activity:

(i) variable cost; and

Section 3.3.1

(ii) fixed cost.

Section 3.3.2

Clearly label each line on your graphs.

7   How can you identify semi-variable costs and separate them into the fixed and variable elements?

Section 3.4.2 and subsections

8   What does the term 'operational gearing' refer to and why is this important.

Section 3.4.5

Chapter 4

1   Define these key CVP terms: breakeven point, contribution margin, margin of safety.

Section 4.2

2 How can CVP analysis aid business planning?

Section 4.2

3 White Weddings has to decide whether to accept a contract to run a wedding. They want to make £2,000 profit and the fixed costs are £4,000. The contribution per guest (sale) after variable costs is £25. How many guests would there need to be in order for them to achieve their required profit from the event?

£4,000 + £2,000 = £6,000/£25 = 240 wedding guests needed to generate the profit required.

4 Explain the importance of the margin of safety in decision making.

Section 4.3.2

5 What are the lines drawn on a breakeven chart?

Section 4.3.3

6 Explain what a profit–volume chart shows you.

Section 4.3.3 and Figure 4.4

7 What are the underlying assumptions of CVP analysis?

Section 4.3.5

8 Describe the phases in the design of a computer spreadsheet.

Section 4.5 and sub-sections

Chapter 5

1 Discuss why only relevant costs need to be considered in a short-term decision.

Section 5.2

2 List and describe the main categories of short-term decisions.

Section 5.5 and sub-section

3 Why do short-term decisions have long-term implications for an organisation?

Section 5.6

4 How might a manager mitigate against the impact of scarce resources?

Section 5.7

5 Take a specific sector with which you are familiar (events, hospitality, or tourism) and consider what opportunities exist for outsourcing and what the implications of this might be.

Section 5.9

6 Using the data from the Peace Yoga Retreats example in this chapter, explain how relevant costing impacts on the decision-making process.

Section 5.5.2

A

Chapter 6

Explain the different cost bases available when using cost-plus pricing.

1   Explain the difference between 'mark-up' and 'gross profit margin' when pricing.

Section 6.2.1.3

2   What is contribution margin pricing?

Section 6.2.1.5

3   What is meant by 'price discretion'?

Section 6.2.1.5 and Figure 6.2

4   How can target costing aid pricing?

Section 6.2.1.7

5   The market will bear a price of £120/day delegate rate for conferences. The company wish to generate a 60% contribution towards fixed costs and profit. Use target costing to calculate the target costs per person.

£120 * 60% = £72 contribution, therefore £120 – £72 = £48

6   Explain the economists' view of pricing.

Section 6.2.2

7   Discuss the alternative market-based approached to pricing and how they may be utilised.

Section 6.2.3

Chapter 7

1   Define what is meant by the terms 'yield management' and 'revenue management'.

Section 7.1.1

2   On a specific flight there are 240 seats available, at a maximum price of £200 per seat. However only 180 seats are sold, with an average achieved ticket price of £110. Calculate the yield management % from this data.

240 * £200 = Maximum revenue = £48,000

180 * £110 = Actual revenue = £19,800

$$\frac{£19,800 * 100}{£48,000} = 41.25\%$$

3   Describe the characteristics required for revenue management to be of significant value.

Section 7.3

4 Two customers stay in identical budget hotel rooms in the same hotel, on the same night; one has paid £29, whilst the other has paid £59. Using revenue management, explain this situation.

Sections 7.3 and 7.4

5 Why might revenue management not be appropriate in retail product sales with a long 'shelf-life'?

Sections 7.3 and 7.4

6 Define the two strategic drivers of revenue management.

Section 7.4

7 Explain revenue management drivers in relation to Kimes and Chase's four quadrants model.

Section 7.4

8 Why does revenue maximisation not always lead to profit maximisation?

Section 7.5

Chapter 8

1 How can marketing and finance departments working together improve profitability?

Section 8.3

2 Explain the difference between total absorption costing and activity-based costing.

Section 8.4

3 What are the key elements of ABC?

Section 8.4.2

4 How does activity based management (ABB) build on ABC?

Section 8.5

5 Explain the difference between a traditional hotel accounting approach and that used in CPA.

Section 8.6

6 Describe the term 'cost driver' in relation to ABC. Give an example of a cost driver in events, hospitality and tourism.

Section 8.4.2.1

7 How can CPA aid management decision making?

Section 8.6.3

8 Explain the principles of profit sensitivity analysis and how it can aid managers.

Section 8.7

A

Chapter 9

1   Budgets have many uses; discuss the roles budgets can have in an organisation.

Section 9.2

2   There are a number of limiting factors identify these and discuss them using illustrative examples related to hospitality, tourism or events.

Section 9.3.1

3   Detail the components of the master budget and the individual budgets that will need to be prepared before the master budget can be completed.

Section 9.3.2

4   Why is it important to have a detailed monthly cash budget? What financial issues might an organisation face without a cash budget?

Section 9.3.3

5   Explain how a flexed budget could be used within a hospitality, tourism or events business with which you are familiar.

Section 9.4.2

6   Explain what the advantages of responsibility accounting are and explain the various 'responsibility centres' that exist.

Section 9.5.1

7   Explain the terms 'beyond budgeting' and 'better budget', how do these two concepts differ?

Section 9.6

8   A music festival is offering a 'Ticket-Plus' package for £250. It includes a ticket, car parking, programme, and a souvenir tee shirt. Using the full prices below, how much revenue should be allocated to each element in the package?

Festival 'Ticket-Plus'	Individual price	@ 89%
Festival ticket	£230	£205
Car parking for weekend	£20	£18
Festival programme	£10	£9
Souvenir tee shirt	£20	£18
Total at full price	£280	£250

£250/£280 = 89%

Chapter 10

1   What makes an event unique in relation to the use of management accounting?

Section 10.2

2   What is the purpose of having a detailed event budget?

Section10.3.4

3   Past experience shows for every event ticket sold, £24 is spent at the bar. If ticket sales are estimated at 6,000, what is the budgeted bar sales revenue?

Budgeted bar sales = £24 * 6,000 = £144,000

4 Why is it important to monitor actual versus forecast data in the run up to an event?

Section 10.3.5

5 Explain the relationship between health and safety guidance and event management accounting decisions.

Covered in many sections throughout the chapter, but particularly related to planning (pricing) and during the event, the key being health and safety may come at a financial cost, but needs to be prioritised.

6 What management accounting considerations should be made by managers whilst an event is taking place?

Section 10.4 and all its subsections cover this.

7 How can management accounting assist in the review of financial performance after an event?

Section 10.5 and its subsections

8 How can past event information be utilised in planning future events?

Section 10.5.6

Chapter 11

1 What are the four main techniques for analysing financial information?

Section 11.2

2 When calculating index numbers, what is the 'base year' and why is its selection important?

Section 11.3

3 What are the main benefits of common-sized statements and ratios?

Section 11.4

4 Trade payables and trade receivables are also referred to as what?

Example 11.4

5 Which two key ratios contribute to the return on capital employed (ROCE)? For each explain what they reveal.

Section 11.17.1 and Figure 11.1

6 If asset utilisation was getting worse, which ratios would you calculate to try and explain the reasons.

7 What is the cash operating cycle and how is it calculated?

Section 11.7.1

8 Which operational ratios are most commonly used in the hotel industry for external benchmarking?

Section 11.9.3

A

Chapter 12

1 What are the key elements of working capital?

Section 12.2

2 Name the three working capital policies a business can follow.

Section 12.3

3 How can overtrading be spotted?

Section 12.6.3

4 What are the main items of stock of a hotel?

Section 12.5

5 Calculate the economic order quantity given the following data:

Annual demand	7000 units
Ordering cost	£1.20 per order
Annual holding cost	£1.68 per unit

$$Q = \sqrt{\frac{2 \times C_0 \times D}{C_h}}$$

= 100 units

6 What are the main factors to consider before giving credit to a customer?

Section 12.7, 12.7.2, 12.7.4

7 What is the purpose of a cash flow forecast?

Section 12.9.2

Chapter 13

1 What are the advantages of using equity capital?

Section 13.3.1

2 What are the main types of equity capital?

Section 13.3 (including subsections)

3 How do preference shares differ from ordinary shares?

Section 13.3.3

4 What are the advantages of using debt finance?

Section 13.3.4

5 Describe the features of bonds.

Section 13.3.6

6 What method of financing are now most commonly used in hotels?

Section 13.6

7 How can the size of operation impact on sources of finance available?

Section 13.5 and 13.6.3

8 What does FDI stand for?

Section 13.6

Chapter 14

1 Why is capital investment appraisal strategically important to an organisation?

Section 14.2

2 Name four CIA methods that can be utilised.

Section 14.2

3 What are the disadvantages of using a profit-based approach?

Section 14.4

4 Explain how discounted cash flow (DCF) aids capital investment appraisal.

Section 14.6

5 Which and how many methods would you recommend using prior to committing to a £1m development project?

A number of sections, including 14.12, the key is it is a larger sum of money, so a number of methods, including DCF methods are vital.

6 The hotel has a maximum of £800,000 available for capital investment

	Project A	Project B	Project C	Project D	NPV table @ 5%	
Cash flows	£000s	£000s	£000s	£000s		
Year					Year	5%
0	−400,000	−400,000	−200,000	−200,000	0	1
1	200,000	4,000	106,000	5,000	1	0.9524
2	200,000	4,000	106,000	5,000	2	0.9070
3	10,000	320,000	6,000	105,000	3	0.8638
4	10,000	320,000	4,000	105,000	4	0.8227

Note: these figures are cash flows; depreciation is straight-line over 4 years.

Calculate the payback period, accounting rate of return and the net present value for each of these proposals (18 marks)

From a financial perspective, recommend which project(s) the hotel should fund, with supporting justification for your answer, including method based discussion. (7 marks)

(BAHA, Question 2, Strategic Management Accounting Paper January 2012)

A

		A	B	C	D
ARR average investment		2.5%	31.0%	5.5%	5.0%
ARR initial investment		5.0%	62.0%	11.0%	10.0%
Payback period		2 years	3 yrs, 3 mths	1 yr, 11 mths	3 yrs, 10 mths
NPV					
Cash Flows/year	5%	A	B	C	D
0	1	−400000	−400000	−200000	−200000
1	0.9524	190480	3809.6	100954.4	4762
2	0.907	181400	3628	96142	4535
3	0.8638	8638	276416	5182.8	90699
4	0.8227	8227	263264	3290.8	86383.5
		−11255	147117.6	5570	−13620.5
		Reject			Reject

For formula and discussion see sections 14.3–14.8. Note projects A and D would be rejected using NPV, this is not 'ranked' 3rd and 4th, but should not invest.

7   Using the data from question 6, calculate the IRR. How does this impact on your decision making?

See section 14.9 for calculations, the exact figure/answer will vary with discount percentage used in the calculation and the amount of rounding. Usually those rejected in NPV would not even been calculated using IRR. However you should find B the highest.

Chapter 15

1   What are the main weaknesses of traditional financial performance measures?

Section 15.2

2   What do the terms 'lead' and 'lag' mean in the context of performance measures and why is this important?

Section 15.2

3   What are the antecedents of the results and determinants model?

Section 15.3.1

4   Explain the four dimensions of the Balanced Scorecard.

Section 15.3.2

5   What is the major emphasis of the Performance Prism that differentiates it from the BSC?

Section 15.5

6   Name two companies that provide benchmarking data to hotels.

Section 15.5.4

7 Which performance management system is recognised as one of the most useful for hotels and how can it be used?

Section 15.5

8 Why is it important to use both internal and external benchmarking data?

Section 15.5, including subsections

Chapter 16

1 Define strategic management accounting.

Section 16.2

2 What are the key changes faced by businesses which have helped to shape strategic management accounting?

Section 16.3

3 What are the key elements of the BCG matrix?

Section 16.4

4 How can the lifecycle approach be used to maximise return from a product?

Section 16.6

5 What are Porter's generic strategies?

Section 16.5

6 What is the link between the balanced scorecard and strategy?

Section 16.7

7 What is the principle focus of activity-based management?

Section 16.8

8 How big a role does competitor analysis have in the hotel industry?

Section 16.9.2

Chapter 17

1 Explain the difference between data and information.

Section 17.2

2 What are the characteristics of quality information?

Section 17.2

3 Define the key CSF terms: 'goals', 'CSFs', and 'measures'.

Table 17.1

4 What are the three main uses of CSFs in an organisation?

Section 17.5

5 How can CSFs aid corporate-level decision making?

Section 17.5.2

6 One of the key features of CSF use is making the implicit into explicit, explain what this means in an operational context.

Section 17.5, including subsections

A

Chapter 18

1   What to the three Ps refer to in the triple bottom line?

Section 18.2

2   Identify the key elements for managing sustainability

Section 18.3

3   What is the difference between monetary and physical EMA?

Section 18.4

4   What are the four main tools for conducting EMA?

Section 18.4 and Figure 18.2

5   How could EMA be utilised to monitor towel usage in hotel rooms and why is this an environmental issue?

Section 18.4.1

6   Give examples of EMA tools, as per the United Nations EMA classifications.

Section 18.4.2

7   Explain the possible elements of the 'inputs/outputs' of a business from an environmental perspective.

Section 18.4.4

8   What is BS8901? How can it assist event managers?

Section 18.5

Chapter 19

1   Define the 'not-for-profit' sector, with examples of organisations.

Section 19.2 and Table 19.1

2   What roles can hospitality, tourism and events play in the NFP sector?

Section 19.3, including subsections

3   Explain the specific considerations that need to be made when using management accounting in NFP organisations.

Section 19.4, including subsections

4   List the key management accounting tools that can be used in NFP organisations.

Section 19.4, including subsections

5   Explain how the BSC and CSFs can be utilised fully within the NFP sector.

Section 19.4.6

6   Environmental management accounting can be important in NFP organisations – what type of organisations specifically?

Section 19.4.7

Index